OPEN BUDGETS

OPEN BUDGETS

The Political Economy of Transparency, Participation, and Accountability

Sanjeev Khagram
Archon Fung
Paolo de Renzio

Editors

Brookings Institution Press
Washington, D.C.

Copyright © 2013

THE BROOKINGS INSTITUTION

1775 Massachusetts Avenue, N.W., Washington, D.C. 20036
www.brookings.edu

Library of Congress Cataloging-in-Publication data

Open budgets : the political economy of transparency, participation, and accountability / Sanjeev Khagram, Archon Fung, and Paolo de Renzio, editors.
    pages   cm
  Includes bibliographical references and index.
  ISBN 978-0-8157-2337-0 (pbk. : alk. paper)
  1. Finance, Public. 2. Budget. 3. Transparency in government. 4. Government accountability. I. Khagram, Sanjeev. II. Fung, Archon, 1968– III. De Renzio, Paolo.
  HJ141.O64 2013
  352.4—dc23   2013004914

9 8 7 6 5 4 3 2 1

Printed on acid-free paper

Typeset in Adobe Garamond

Composition by R. Lynn Rivenbark
Macon, Georgia

Printed by R. R. Donnelley
Harrisonburg, Virginia

Contents

1

Overview and Synthesis: The Political Economy of Fiscal Transparency, Participation, and Accountability around the World

SANJEEV KHAGRAM, PAOLO DE RENZIO, AND ARCHON FUNG

Raising, allocating, and spending public resources are among the primary functions and policy instruments of any government. Government budgets, as well as off-budget fiscal instruments such as state-owned enterprises and sovereign wealth funds, profoundly affect economies, societies, and ecosystems. Decisionmaking around government revenues and expenditures has historically been shrouded in secrecy—the purview of heads of state, finance ministers, and central bankers, along with a few select officials in executive agencies. Often, other ministries, government branches (including parliaments), the business community, civil society organizations, and the broader citizenry have had little or no access to information on public financial management. The quantity and quality of engagement and the inclusion of these nonexecutive actors in fiscal decisionmaking and oversight processes have been severely limited.

In recent years, however, interest and action with respect to transparency, participation, and accountability in fiscal decisionmaking have surged around the world. Indeed, over the past two decades, several broad trends have brought fiscal transparency, participation, and accountability into sharp focus:[1]

We thank the International Budget Partnership, the Ash Institute for Democratic Governance and Innovation at Harvard University, and the John Parke Young Endowment in Global Political Economy at Occidental College for financial and administrative support for this project.

1. The International Monetary Fund defines fiscal transparency as "the clarity, reliability, frequency, timeliness, and relevance of public fiscal reporting and the openness to the public of the government's fiscal policymaking process" (IMF 2012, p. 4). Participation in fiscal matters is defined as the existence and effectiveness of opportunities for ministries other than treasury or finance, government branches such as legislatures, civil society groups, and citizens to engage with and influence the formulation and implementation of

1

—The proliferation of good governance norms and standards that emphasize greater transparency, participation, and accountability in all government matters,

—Numerous transitions from closed, authoritarian political regimes to ones characterized by policy contestation, separation of powers, political party competition, an organized civil society, an engaged citizenry, and an active media,

—The introduction of modern public finance management systems and good practices in countries around the world,

—Greater decentralization and devolution of powers to subnational levels of government, including the power to raise, allocate, and spend public resources,

—The growth in the number and operational capacity of independent civil society organizations (CSOs) seeking to be informed about and actively participate in government decisionmaking, and

—The dramatic growth, spread, and use of information and communication technologies around the world.

The global financial and economic crises that began in 2008 further revealed that the disclosure of government fiscal risks and positions was inadequate. This lack of transparency contributed to government fiscal crises in many countries (epitomized by Greece), which created additional perverse incentives for governments to cloud rather than open their fiscal data.[2] Ordinary citizens began calling for greater accountability in the use of public resources—from the streets of Athens and the Arab spring to the tea party and Occupy Wall Street movements in the United States.

Given the fundamental importance of—and increased focus on—these issues and trends in the global economy, it is surprising to find that rigorous analysis of the causes and consequences of fiscal transparency, participation, and accountability is thin at best. This volume seeks to fill this gap in existing knowledge, deploying multiple research methodologies and examining a range of quantitative and qualitative evidence.[3]

We focus on three broad sets of questions. First, *how and why do improvements in fiscal transparency and participation come about, and how are such changes sus-*

---

fiscal policies. Accountability is defined as the degree to which public officials are held responsible for the way in which they conduct fiscal policy. The term "fiscal" is often deemed to be more comprehensive than "budget," as it covers activities and operations that may not fall within regular budget processes and institutions. Examples may include extra-budgetary funds such as pension funds, oil funds, and the like, state-owned enterprises, and quasi-fiscal activities. In this volume, however, the terms "fiscal" and "budget" are used interchangeably.

2. See IMF (2012).

3. Initial drafts of the statistical and comparative papers synthesized later in this chapter were discussed at a workshop held in Washington, D.C., in April 2010. A draft comparative paper on civil society influence was discussed at a workshop in Washington, D.C., in September 2012. Authors of in-depth

tained over time? That is, what are the key factors and causal mechanisms that contribute to improvements or regressions in these aspects of fiscal decisionmaking? Second, *under what conditions and through what type of mechanisms do (or might) increased fiscal transparency and participation lead to more government responsiveness and improved accountability, including outcomes such as better fiscal management, reduced corruption, shifts in budget allocations, and improved public services?* Running across these two broad questions is a third set of queries regarding the complex interrelationships among transparency, participation, and accountability in fiscal matters. In particular, *does greater transparency contribute to greater participation?*

In this chapter, we begin by summarizing the relevant—and limited—theoretical and empirical literature on fiscal transparency, participation, and accountability. We then examine broad cross-country evidence through a set of statistical and comparative studies, looking for conditions (variables) that are associated with higher levels of budget transparency, a major subset of fiscal transparency. The summaries of country case studies that follow (chapters 2 through 9 of this volume) provide a much richer and more nuanced understanding of the causal mechanisms and trajectories that different countries followed as their fiscal systems opened up and became more inclusive (or sometimes regressed).

Overall, our findings suggest that four main causal triggers stand out as contributing to fiscal transparency and participation within countries: (a) *political transitions* that not only bring an end to autocratic rule, but also bring about political contestation and alternation, giving voice to opposition parties and greater powers to oversight bodies such as legislatures; (b) *fiscal and economic crises* that force governments to tighten controls over the public purse and put in place mechanisms and incentives for fiscal discipline and independent scrutiny; (c) widely publicized *cases of corruption* that lead reform-oriented actors to react strongly and compel governments to provide better public access to fiscal information; and (d) *external influences* that promote global norms to empower domestic reformers and civil society actors, rather than undermine domestic reform processes with interventions that bypass local institutions and seek fiscal information to satisfy external demands rather than to inform a domestic public debate. These factors often interact in complex combinations

country case studies presented and received comments on their draft chapters at a workshop held in February 2011 at the Ash Center for Democratic Governance and Innovation of the Harvard Kennedy School. Further research and revisions of the statistical, comparative, and country case studies, as well as additional in-depth case studies, were completed through 2012. Not all of the background papers are included in the current volume; these statistical, comparative, and in-depth case studies can be found at http://internationalbudget.org/.

to shape the trajectories in different countries by fostering or impeding advances in fiscal transparency and participation.

The evidence presented in this volume details tentative responses to the first set of questions that we started with, identifying key factors and mechanisms (particularly combinations and sequences) that are associated with higher levels of fiscal transparency and participation and their improvement over time. However, evidence is more limited of how greater public availability of fiscal information—and related opportunities to engage with the budget process—may affect government accountability, broader public finance management, and quality of service delivery. There are various examples of legislators becoming more demanding vis-à-vis the executive and of civil society campaigns achieving significant but isolated success, but the evidence for the positive impacts of transparency on accountability and responsiveness remains far from systematic or definitive.

We conclude the chapter by looking at some promising trends in the evolving international context, and suggesting strategic lessons and a research agenda.

Fiscal Transparency, Participation, and Accountability: What Would We Have Expected?

At present, there is no holistic or integrated theory on the political economy of fiscal transparency, participation, and accountability. The analytical framework and orienting ideas summarized here are drawn from the broader literature on good governance, transparency, democracy and democratization, participatory politics, and the political economy of reforms, as well as from the emerging empirical literature assessing the impact of development interventions in the areas of transparency, accountability, and governance.[4]

Correlates of Fiscal Transparency

The conditions that are likely to be associated with more open government, specifically in the fiscal realm, can initially be classified into three broad categories: political, economic, and cultural or historical.[5] In addition, the interactions among these conditions need to be analyzed in relation to country contexts, taking into account the actors involved, their potentially conflicting interests, power, and capabilities, the institutions that shape their behavior, and the incentives that such institutions create. This, in turn, will help to explain how and why specific outcomes occurred (or not).

4. See Florini (2007); Fung, Graham, and Weil (2007); as well as McGee and Gaventa (2010) and J-PAL (2011).

5. La Porta and others (1999); Triesman (2000); and You and Khagram (2005).

Political conditions often associated with transparency include elections, political competition, government size, and decentralization.[6] Electoral competition and political rights may create pressures to open up government processes to public scrutiny. In addition, transitions from authoritarian regimes increase the possibilities for political contestation and so open the field to a range of domestic actors—opposing parties, politicians, CSOs, and independent media—who seek information about government fiscal activity to advance their own agendas. However, the presence of electoral democracy may only increase transparency and participation after it has reached a certain threshold or if other conditions, such as higher levels of political competition or a vibrant civil society and media, are present. Decentralization may or may not increase transparency, depending on the interactions with other conditions such as regional inequalities in the distribution of power. Finally, it is unlikely that transparency will be enabled in situations of violent conflict.

In terms of economic correlates, many studies have found the level of development (per capita income) to be strongly related to various measures of transparency.[7] The spread of education and the expansion of middle classes may give rise to pressures for transparency, as better-off citizens come to desire greater quality and efficiency in the provision of public goods and gain the resources to express that interest politically. Some studies have found that trade openness, presumably operating through increased economic competition and economic growth, is associated positively with transparency to a significant degree. Conversely, countries with larger endowments of natural resources seem to be significantly less transparent.[8] Larger natural resource endowments may dampen pressure for transparency, as the government relies less on taxation to raise revenue. Greater levels of inequality can also contribute to lower levels of transparency through material and normative mechanisms.

Cultural and historical accounts of the quality of government institutions focus on the effects of religion, social values, colonial heritage, legal traditions, and ethnolinguistic fractionalization.[9] Such factors create more or less favorable normative resources that condition the extent to which transparency (and participation for that matter) are understood as a component of legitimate government. Egalitarian or individualistic religions such as Protestantism may encourage challenges to nontransparent behavior, whereas hierarchical religions such as Catholicism, Eastern Orthodoxy, and Islam may discourage such challenges. Protestantism's link with economic development and democracy offers two additional

6. Alt and Lassen (2006); Alt, Lassen, and Rose (2006); Lassen (2000); and Bastida and Benito (2007).
7. For example, see Bellver and Kaufmann (2005) and IBP (2013).
8. See de Renzio, Gomez, and Sheppard (2009).
9. La Porta and others (1999).

causal pathways. Some scholars have suggested that ethnolinguistic fractionalization decreases the quality of government institutions. Colonial experience and legal systems are closely linked potential correlates of good governance and transparency. For some, legal systems reflect the relative power of the state vis-à-vis property owners. Whereas the British common law system was developed as a defense against attempts by the sovereign to expropriate property, the civil law system was developed as a sovereign instrument for state building and economic control.

Political Economy Dynamics

Political economy dynamics shape the transparency, participation, and accountability of government decisionmaking beyond the structural conditions identified above.[10] On the one hand, those who would benefit from the lack of transparency and participation by shifting public funds to their political supporters or preferred projects or by skimming profits directly, and those who simply would rather avoid the harsh light of public scrutiny, often hold powerful positions and are well organized to defend their interests. On the other hand, those who would benefit from increased openness and inclusion in fiscal processes and practices are typically numerous and poorly organized: they include government officials who have been excluded from the budget-making process and citizens who use public services such as health, housing, education, and transportation.

Although these political economy mechanisms are powerful and have often prevented change, other dynamics sometimes break through the obstacle of concentrated interests to contribute to greater fiscal openness and inclusiveness. For example, cracks in the iron grid of business-as-usual politics sometimes result from highly publicized scandals involving the (mis)use of public resources. These scandals, and crises more broadly (such as domestic or global economic crises), create opportunities for reform-minded political entrepreneurs to gain support on platforms of transparency and participation.

Similarly, different factions of political elites can be divided against one another. One side or another may view increased transparency as a tool in this competition. Politicians might favor budget transparency as a way to control the discretion of entrenched (and possibly corrupt) bureaucrats. This may be the case particularly when processes of political liberalization create new factions of hard-liners and soft-liners among the ruling elite or when, during subsequent periods of greater political democratization, avenues such as elections open up for competing political actors to promote transparency and participation as part of broader reform campaigns.[11] Sometimes, a faction of political elites will favor transparency reforms

10. See Fung, Graham, and Weil (2007) and Florini (2007).
11. O'Donnell and Schmitter (1986).

because they lose little through such reforms and may gain the support of an important constituency that favors transparency. Such dynamics, however, often require well-organized and vocal domestic CSOs pressing for openness. Similarly, government or independent quasi-government officials (such as civil servants or auditors) may be empowered and motivated to push for change.

International forces can also contribute to greater fiscal transparency and participation. International donors and powerful states press for formal fiscal transparency as part of the package of good governance measures—and often conditionalities—linked to foreign aid. Transnational advocacy coalitions and networks, which link foreign and international organizations with domestic civil society groups, pressure governments to become more open and inclusive.[12] Potent, but more difficult to discern, international norms and the perception that openness and inclusiveness are modern and appropriate practices can press political actors to change their laws, policies, and operating procedures.[13]

The political economy of fiscal transparency and participation is likely to occur in a multilevel way; the factors and mechanisms just described operate interactively. Opposing political parties, for example, can use scandals and crises as windows of opportunity to form alliances with reform-minded political elites and civil servants. Civil society organizations can form partnerships with organizations operating at the local grassroots level, with international organizations, and with advocacy groups based in other countries to pressure for more change.

Moreover, the emergence and evolution of the political economy of fiscal transparency and participation will likely be a complex process. The conditions, factors, and mechanisms that trigger initial improvements may be quite different from those that contribute to their deepening and broadening over time. Indeed, a seemingly stable and robust set of institutions at a particular point in time may quickly become outdated if it does not adapt to new demands and circumstances. Countries may get stuck or even regress, as when powerful actors use even more sophisticated means to obscure fiscal positions and practices. The political economy of fiscal transparency, participation, and accountability is not likely to be a linear or teleological process. And the conditions, factors, and mechanisms that contribute to increased transparency are likely to be somewhat different from those that contribute to greater participation or accountability.

Accountability, Government Responsiveness, and Impacts

Supporters of government openness are often quick to claim that transparency and participation in public policies and processes inevitably bring about a host of

---

12. Khagram, Riker, and Sikkink (2002).
13. Meyer and others (1997).

important benefits, including long-term development outcomes. Unfortunately, such claims are hard to prove, although evidence of impact is slowly accumulating. Statistical research, for example, has found evidence that governments with more transparent public finances are characterized by better fiscal performance, lower sovereign borrowing costs, and lower levels of corruption.[14]

The story of the education sector in Uganda has come to epitomize the benefits of fiscal transparency and community monitoring of public services. After a survey found that almost 80 percent of grants to local governments for primary school materials did not reach their intended beneficiaries, the government started publishing information on such transfers in newspapers and posting it on school bulletin boards. A follow-up survey found that, as a result of this campaign, leakage had been reduced to 20 percent of total grants.[15]

Another study found that public dissemination of audit findings in selected Brazilian municipalities led to increased accountability of politicians seeking reelection. The higher the level of corruption in local finances reported by the audits, the less likely were incumbent politicians to win the election. And the impact on government accountability was higher in municipalities where radio stations reported on the audit findings.[16] Various researchers have also documented how participatory budgeting processes contribute to extending service provision and redirecting public resources toward poor neighborhoods, while also reducing clientelism and spurring the creation of new civic associations.[17]

However, these examples may indicate only isolated impact. Even with more robust fiscal transparency and participation systems in place, there is no guarantee that these will produce such downstream, substantive effects. Fiscal information is often difficult to understand, and few potential users have strong reasons to act on that information when the main benefits are public goods and when openness and inclusiveness are not automatically transformed into citizen influence on policy decisions. In fact, the history of transparency-enhancing initiatives is replete with great efforts to create disclosure regimes that subsequently are used only slightly or yield little benefit. So why do more transparency and participation sometimes play a critical role in particular outcomes, such as improving the quality or quantity of public services?

It may be that all steps in an "action cycle" of accountability must be in place for fiscal transparency and participation to yield substantive outcomes and

---

14. See Alt and Lassen (2006); Benito and Bastida (2009); Glennerster and Shin (2008); and Hameed (2005).

15. Reinikka and Svensson (2004).

16. Ferraz and Finan (2008).

17. Abers (2000); Santos (1998); Baiocchi (2005); Baiocchi, Heller, and Silva (2011); and Wampler and Avritzer (2004).

impacts. Simply placing information in the public domain or opening up spaces for public participation does not ensure that these will be used or used wisely. Peoples' responses to information are inseparable from their interests, desires, resources, cognitive capacities, and social contexts. Three fundamental questions therefore need to be kept in mind when assessing the effectiveness and impact of fiscal transparency and participation initiatives: Who uses the information and engagement opportunities being made available? For what purpose do they use them? What broader benefit accrues to a specific group of "users" or to society as a whole? Moreover, it is important to assess whether users consider the kind of information and engagement to be important for realizing their agendas and whether the information is accessible and understandable to them.[18]

As this summary of existing knowledge shows, coming to a better understanding of how improvements in fiscal transparency and participation come about and the extent to which they bring about an increase in government accountability and other types of impact is no easy feat. Unpacking complex causal mechanisms and dynamics, considering a large number of actors, taking into account context-specific political economy considerations, and overcoming methodological limitations are only some of the challenges posed. In this volume, we take on these challenges by examining a wide array of evidence, from cross-country statistical and comparative studies investigating specific factors affecting fiscal transparency to a series of in-depth country case studies selected to reflect a variety of contexts, conditions, and trajectories. The results of these analyses are presented in the following sections.

Statistical and Comparative Studies on Fiscal Transparency

Rigorous analysis of the conditions and consequences associated with fiscal transparency remains surprisingly scarce.[19] This section synthesizes the results of statistical cross-country research, focusing on five recent papers that look into some of the possible correlates of fiscal transparency.[20] These studies were carried out using Open Budget Index (OBI) data from the 2008 survey as a measure of

18. This framework grows out of the transparency "action cycle" developed by Fung, Graham, and Weil (2007).

19. Alt, Lassen, and Rose (2006), in one of the very few studies of this kind focusing on the evolution of transparent budget procedures across U.S. states, found that these are affected by both political dynamics and past fiscal conditions.

20. Only some of the most important results are reported here. Readers interested in more detail should refer to the studies themselves, which can be found at http://internationalbudget.org/. These papers were commissioned by the International Budget Partnership in 2009 and were aimed at addressing some of the gaps in the literature and at verifying the usefulness of the Open Budget Index as a quantitative measure of budget transparency.

budget (and fiscal) transparency, although most of the results were confirmed using more recent data.

The Open Budget Index, launched by the International Budget Partnership (IBP) in 2006, is an independent, comprehensive, biannual effort to assess budget transparency across countries. It is based on a detailed questionnaire assessing the public availability and comprehensiveness of eight key budget documents (see box 1-1) and drawing on international guidelines promoted by the Organization for Economic Cooperation and Development (OECD) and the International Monetary Fund (IMF).[21] Countries' OBI scores can range from zero to 100, and data are subjected to an extensive peer review process to ensure their accuracy and objectivity.

Two main features make OBI data particularly suited to statistical cross-country analysis and preferable to other available sources. First, OBI assessments are carried out by independent researchers and are based on objective, factual information about the availability and content of government budgets. Second, data are collected simultaneously across countries, providing a comparative cross-national snapshot of the state of fiscal transparency at a particular point in time. Moreover, the fact that the survey is carried out at regular two-year intervals means that subsequent rounds should provide a firmer basis for time-series analysis to test and refine these initial findings.[22]

Elections and Political Competition

Wehner and de Renzio (2013) investigate a simple correlation that exists between competitive political systems and fiscal transparency by looking at two key sources of demand for fiscal information: citizens and legislators. Citizens as voters can, where governing power is derived from free and fair elections, use the ballot box to punish executives who govern badly. When such a threat exists, as Rosendorff and Vreeland (2006) argue, executives have an incentive to provide more credible and detailed information on economic management to the public in order to minimize the risk of being unfairly dismissed. In other words, electoral accountability breeds transparency. Moreover, this posited effect might depend on the maturity of democratic systems, as voters "learn" how to demand and use fiscal information to hold their governments accountable over time. In this sense, it

21. The OECD, in its "Best Practices for Budget Transparency" (OECD 2002), recommends publishing seven types of budgetary reports and details the kind of information they should include. The IMF first published its *Code of Good Practices on Fiscal Transparency* in 1998 in the wake of the Mexican and Asian crises (Petrie 2003) and then updated it in 2001 and 2007 (IMF 2007a). Together with its accompanying manual (IMF 2007b), the code provides a detailed assessment framework, used as the basis for so-called Reports on the Observance of Standards and Codes. However, the IMF does not produce a composite indicator that promotes cross-national comparison.

22. More details on the Open Budget Index are available at http://internationalbudget.org/. See also de Renzio and Masud (2011).

Box 1-1. Eight Key Budget Documents

A *pre-budget statement* presents the assumptions used in developing the budget, expected revenue, expenditure, and debt levels, and the broad allocations among sectors.

The *executive's budget proposal* presents the government's detailed declaration of the policies and priorities it intends to pursue in the upcoming budget year, including specific allocations to each ministry and agency.

The *enacted budget* is the legal document that authorizes the executive to implement the policy measures the budget contains.

Governments should publish three review documents during the course of budget execution. First, the executive should issue monthly or quarterly *in-year reports* on revenues collected, expenditures made, and debt incurred. Second, the executive should publish a *midyear review* to discuss any changes in economic assumptions that affect approved budget policies. Third, the executive should issue a *year-end report* summarizing the financial situation at the end of the fiscal year; this report should include an update on progress made in achieving the policy goals of the enacted budget.

Best practice requires that a body independent from the executive issue an annual *audit report* covering all activities undertaken by the executive.

Budget documents are usually lengthy and contain technical information. Thus governments should also publish a *citizens budget*—a simplified summary of each of the seven budget documents discussed here issued in languages and through media that are widely accessible to the public.

---

may take some time after the onset of democracy for electoral accountability to result in enhanced fiscal transparency.

Using 2008 OBI scores as a measure of the dependent variable and different measures of democracy and democratic age, Wehner and de Renzio (2013) find that the holding of free and fair elections is positively, significantly, and strongly correlated with budget transparency. In fact, a switch from autocracy to democracy (defined by free and fair elections) improves a country's OBI score by almost twenty points, after controlling for several other variables (see table 1-1). How long a country has been holding free and fair elections does not seem to be that important; coefficients are much smaller and in some cases not significant at standard levels. This reflects an encouraging finding: rapid improvements in transparency (though not necessarily participation or accountability) can be achieved during windows of democratization without having to wait for slow processes of learning and adaptation.

Besides electoral processes, legislatures provide a second arena in which demand for fiscal information and disclosure may arise. Past research has highlighted the way in which political competition might affect the level of fiscal transparency.[23] On the one hand, single-party majority governments will most

---

23. Alt and Lassen (2006) and Alt, Lassen, and Rose (2006).

Table 1-1. *Democracy, Democratic Age, and Fiscal Transparency*[a]

Variable	(1)	(2)	(3)
Democracy	18.76		18.20
	(4.64)***		(4.71)***
Age		21.38	1.59
		(8.53)**	(8.50)
Ethnolinguistic fractionalization	16.00	13.13	16.12
	(9.80)	(10.62)	(9.88)
Civil law	–13.81	–12.16	–13.70
	(4.87)***	(5.69)**	(5.04)***
GDP per capita	7.61	6.52	7.47
	(1.62)***	(2.29)***	(2.03)***
Latitude	45.63	44.69	45.71
	(11.07)***	(12.72)***	(11.19)***
Constant	–36.91	–22.93	–36.06
	(12.93)***	(15.92)	(14.36)**
Observations	85	85	85
Adjusted R^2	0.56	0.49	0.55

Source: Further details in Wehner and de Renzio (2013).
*** Significant at the 1 percent level.
** Significant at the 5 percent level.
a. Ordinary least squares regressions. Robust standard errors are in parentheses. The dependent variable is the 2008 OBI.

likely face weak demand by the legislature for information on actions taken by the executive. On the other hand, the higher the level of political party competition and therefore the probability of losing power in the next election, the more a government will have an incentive to promote transparency and reduce discretion, in order to tie the hands of its competitors in the case of electoral defeat.

Table 1-2 shows the results of statistical tests of this hypothesis using a Herfindahl-based measure of partisan fragmentation. Again, coefficients are positive, significant, and large. An increase from two to three parties with equal shares of seats in the legislature is predicted to add about seven points to the OBI score, controlling for other factors. Given that political competition may not lead to increased demand for fiscal disclosure in countries where legislative representation is not based on free and fair elections, Wehner and de Renzio (2013) also test the model for a restricted sample of democratic countries, obtaining very similar results.

The Contradictory Effects of Oil Wealth

Research on the "resource curse" has provided ample evidence that the presence of large quantities of natural resources has perverse effects on countries' political

Table 1-2. *Political Competition and Fiscal Transparency*[a]

Variable	(1)	(2)
Partisan fragmentation	41.79	71.53
	(11.86)***	(17.12)***
Ethnolinguistic fractionalization	3.35	4.09
	(8.97)	(10.55)
Civil law	−18.08	−18.00
	(4.49)***	(4.09)***
GDP per capita	7.92	8.88
	(1.55)***	(1.71)***
Latitude	36.71	32.27
	(11.20)***	(11.87)***
Constant	−42.12	−65.21
	(13.00)***	(18.50)***
Sample	Full	Democratic
Observations	83	53
Adjusted R^2	0.52	0.64

Source: Further details in Wehner and de Renzio (2013).
*** Significant at the 1 percent level.
a. Ordinary least squares regressions. Robust standard errors are in parentheses. The dependent variable is the 2008 OBI.

and economic development, leading to slower and more volatile economic growth, less democracy, more frequent civil wars, heightened corruption, and an overall decline in the quality and effectiveness of government institutions.[24] Results from the 2008 OBI report show a negative correlation between dependence on oil and gas revenues and budget transparency.

Ross (2011) examines in more detail this preliminary finding of a correlation between depending on oil and gas revenues and low budget transparency. Using "oil income" per capita as a measure of resource wealth, Ross's first important finding is that oil wealth has a negative effect on budget transparency only among autocracies. As table 1-3 shows, there are no significant differences in OBI scores between oil-producing and non-oil-producing countries when considering the overall sample. But differences become large and significant when considering subsamples of countries defined by their type of regime.

This pattern is shown more clearly in figure 1-1: among democracies, oil wealth is associated with more transparent public finances, while among authoritarian states more oil wealth is clearly correlated with lower OBI scores.

Even more interesting, as shown by the regression results in table 1-4, among democracies the link between oil wealth and transparency is spurious and simply

24. See Ross (1999); Stevens and Dietsche (2008); Frankel (2010); and Karl (1997).

Table 1-3. *Average 2008 OBI Scores of Oil-Producing and Non-Oil-Producing States*[a]

Indicator	Number	Oil producers	Non-oil-producers
All countries	85	39.9	39.6
Income			
Low income (below $2,000)	22	22	24.2
Middle income ($2,000 to $15,000)	49	38.2	42.7
High income (above $15,000)	14	53.6	71.8
Type of regime			
Autocracy	34	18.9**	33.4**
Democracy	51	56.5*	43.3*

Source: Ross (2011).
** Significant at the 5 percent level.
* Significant at the 10 percent level.
a. States are categorized as "oil producers" if they produced at least $100 in oil and gas per capita in 2006 (in 2000 dollars).

reflects the fact that oil-rich countries have higher incomes; these higher incomes are significantly correlated with higher OBI scores (columns one and two). In autocratic regimes, in contrast, the negative effect of oil wealth remains significant even after controlling for countries' level of income. Oil wealth seems to exacerbate an autocratic government's lack of transparency (columns four, five, and six).

What are some of the possible reasons for the negative effect that oil wealth has on budget transparency? Ross (2011) tests various possible explanations, but the only one that is at least partly backed by the statistical analysis is that oil wealth hinders transparency because it helps autocrats to maintain political control. This finding supports similar arguments made by other researchers who suggest that oil wealth increases the value of remaining in power and therefore causes dictators to reduce transparency, hiding their government's corruption and inefficiency.[25]

Aid Dependency and Donor Behavior

Prior evidence also suggests that countries characterized by low levels of budget transparency tend to depend heavily on donor assistance to finance public spending. The average score in the 2008 OBI for the thirty countries that received more than 5 percent of their gross national income in foreign aid is twenty-four, compared with a score of sixty-two for countries that did not receive any foreign aid over the same period. This association might be spurious, as aid-dependent countries tend to have low incomes and low-income countries

25. For example, Egorov, Guriev, and Sonin (2009).

Figure 1-1. *Oil Wealth and Budget Transparency in Democracies and Autocracies*

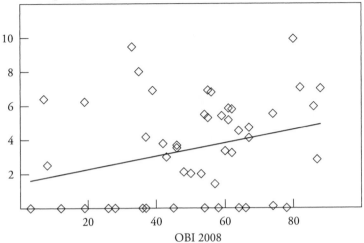

a. Democracies

Oil income per capita (log) 2006

OBI 2008

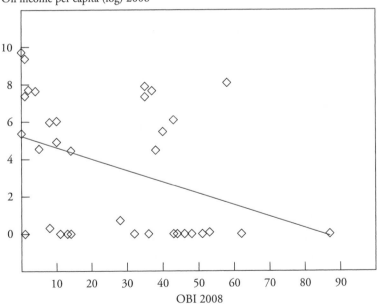

b. Autocracies

Oil income per capita (log) 2006

OBI 2008

Source: Ross (2011).

Table 1-4. *Correlates of Open Budget Index 2008*[a]

Variable	(1)	(2)	(3)	(4)	(5)	(6)
Oil income	2.67	0.27	–2.42	–4.06	–2.52	–5.48
(log)	(2.23)**	(0.27)	(2.30)**	(3.87)***	(2.06)**	(5.01)***
Income	13.24	12.02	8.31	16.19		
(log)	(6.61)***	(3.11)***	(2.26)**	(3.96)***		
Polity					1.71	
					(2.36)**	
Human rights						–4.81
						(2.32)**
Sample	Democracy	Democracy	Autocracy	Autocracy	Autocracy	Autocracy
Observations	51	51	34	34	32	34
Adjusted R^2	0.11	0.47	0.15	0.36	0.44	0.44

Source: Ross (2011).
*** Significant at the 1 percent level.
** Significant at the 5 percent level.
a. Ordinary least squares regressions. Robust standard errors are in parentheses. The dependent variable is the 2008 OBI.

tend to be less transparent. Also, rather than low budget transparency being the consequence of high aid dependency, the direction of causality could go the other way.

The notion that aid dependency may have a negative effect on recipient-country institutions is not new. Research has shown that prolonged aid dependency may undermine long-term institutional development by weakening incentives for reform and providing governments with a "permanent soft budget constraint."[26] Donor support, which is focused almost exclusively on the executive, can also undermine domestic institutions and skew political accountability, in what has been called the "aid-institutions paradox."[27] Finally, aid dependency can weaken state capacity by attracting qualified staff away from government jobs, fragmenting government planning and budgeting systems, and providing inadequate technical assistance.[28]

Existing research, however, has not focused specifically on the linkages between aid dependency and transparency. In an analysis of a subsample of sixteen highly aid-dependent countries, de Renzio and Angemi (2012) find preliminary evidence that aid dependency per se may not negatively affect fiscal transparency. As the panels in figure 1-2 show, the correlation between OBI scores (for 2008) and levels of aid dependency in aid-dependent countries is close to zero.

26. Brautigam (2000).
27. Moss, Pattersson, and van de Walle (2006).
28. Brautigam and Knack (2004).

Figure 1-2. *Budget Transparency, Aid Dependency, and Donor Engagement*

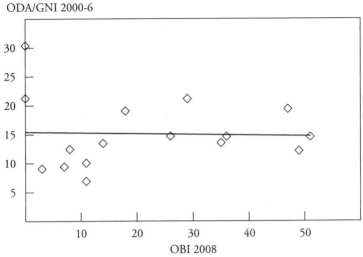

a. OBI and aid dependency

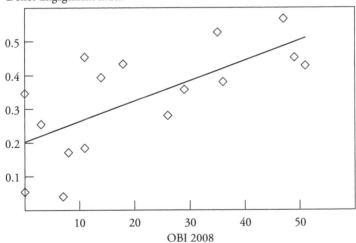

b. OBI and donor engagement

Source: The Donor Engagement Index is calculated based on indicators 5a, 5b, and 9 of the Paris Declaration Monitoring Survey (OECD, Development Assistance Committee 2009) on the use of country systems and program-based aid, and on donor-funded technical assistance for public financial management
provided to each country. Further details in de Renzio and Angemi (2012).

Rather, aid modalities and donor interventions seem to play a larger role. In particular, donor efforts to channel more of their aid through partner-country budget systems and to strengthen partner-country public financial management systems (for example, through technical assistance) are associated with higher standards of budget transparency. Evidence from comparative case studies shows that, over the past decade, many countries carried out reforms partly aimed at enhancing budget transparency, with substantial technical and financial support provided by donor agencies.

However, reforms often had only limited success, partly because they were not well adapted to the local context and partly because donors put limited emphasis on improving public access to budget information. Moreover, donor efforts to promote reforms that could strengthen budget transparency were often offset by other characteristics of donor interventions—namely, their fragmentation, lack of transparency, and limited use of program aid modalities such as budget support and pooled sector funding.

Accountability and Impact

Evidence of how the increased availability of fiscal information and opportunities for engaging in the budget process led to enhanced accountability and other significant impacts is much more scarce. Two additional statistical papers commissioned as part of this research provide preliminary evidence that fiscal transparency is correlated with some positive outcomes.

Hameed (2011) tests the claim that fiscal transparency is an important factor in improving the ability of financial markets to assess a government's fiscal position and thus its ability and willingness to service its debt obligations. In this sense, better access to financial markets, through higher sovereign credit ratings and lower risk premiums, is a major benefit of an increase in fiscal transparency. Using OBI data and building on previous literature that used other indicators of fiscal transparency to examine the impact of various forms of transparency on financial markets, Hameed finds that fiscal transparency does indeed lead to higher sovereign credit ratings and lower sovereign spreads—the risk premium calculated above the interest on government bonds considered "safe," such as U.S. treasury bills—even after taking other factors into account.[29]

Fukuda-Parr and others (2011) look at a more complex question, investigating the possible links between fiscal transparency and human development outcomes. They build on the findings of previous researchers, such as Bellver and Kaufmann (2005) and Islam (2006), who have found positive relationships between indica-

---

29. Hameed (2005) and Glennerster and Shin (2008).

tors of transparency and a variety of human development indicators such as literacy and longevity.

The basic argument is that transparent budgets matter for development for two primary reasons. First, they provide citizens with the information that allows them to hold their government accountable for the use of public resources and to steer public policy priorities toward sectors that are key to human development outcomes. Second, they help to focus attention on development results and to limit wasteful spending and corruption.[30]

In fact, Fukuda-Parr, Guyer, and Lawson-Remer (2011) find that the Open Budget Index is positively correlated with a large number of human development indicators and with public spending on key human development sectors such as health and education. Once these correlations are tested using multivariate analysis and including control variables such as income levels and regional dummies, however, the budget transparency coefficient loses statistical significance in most analyses, highlighting the difficulties in carrying out this kind of research.

Caveats

The statistical and comparative analyses summarized above provide some interesting findings on the conditions and consequences associated with fiscal transparency as measured by the Open Budget Index. Nevertheless, these results need to be interpreted carefully, as they suffer from a series of limitations. First, the average effects shown in regression analyses inevitably hide important exceptions that may provide insights on some of the key conditions leading to improved fiscal transparency. For example, Mexico and Colombia are much more transparent than the average among oil-producing countries, while Uganda and Ghana perform much better than other aid-dependent countries.

Second, while the Open Budget Index is a solid and comparable measure of budget transparency based on the publication of key reports across various phases of the budget cycle, it does not cover all the elements that concern a government's fiscal position, which often do not appear in its budget. This may involve revenues from natural resource extraction and foreign aid, but also other extra-budgetary operations, such as spending through state-owned enterprises or quasi-fiscal activities. Third, the cross-sectional nature of the OBI data inevitably precludes a deeper investigation of what may have brought about changes in budget transparency over time and the actual direction of causal relations; also the analysis does not consider additional factors that might be associated with and

30. See, for example, Goetz and Jenkins (2001); Rajkumar and Swaroop (2008); and Reinikka and Svensson (2004).

contribute to improved transparency in fiscal matters and cannot be captured in statistical studies, such as the potential influence of civil society, political scandals, or emerging international norms. Finally, given the lack of a comparable data set on participation in budget processes, statistical analysis cannot cover additional aspects of our key research questions.

Country Case Studies of Fiscal Transparency, Participation, and Accountability

In-depth, historical country case studies in this volume allow a much richer investigation of the political economy of fiscal transparency, participation, and accountability and address some of the limitations of statistical analysis identified above. This volume includes case studies of fiscal transparency in eight countries: Brazil, Mexico, and Guatemala in Latin America; Senegal, South Africa, and Tanzania in Africa; and South Korea and Vietnam in Asia.[31] This wide set of case studies allows us to probe more deeply some of the structural conditions associated with different levels of fiscal transparency and participation—complementing the comparative statistical studies discussed above—and to assess the extent to which these have resulted in greater accountability and impact on development outcomes.

The country case studies were selected to ensure variation along multiple dimensions, in order to increase our confidence in the robustness of the findings and the conclusions drawn from their analysis, individually and as a set. These dimensions include (a) levels of fiscal transparency and changes over time, (b) structural characteristics of the economy and society, (c) types of political institutions and their change over time, (d) organization and mobilization of domestic CSOs, and (e) historical or colonial legacies, among others. Each case study looks at the historical trajectory of fiscal transparency and participation and examines the complex causal mechanisms that shaped their evolution over time. The country case studies synthesized below are presented for each country in order from the highest to the lowest levels of fiscal transparency as measured through OBI scores.

South Africa: A High-Transparency, Low-Participation Regime

South Africa has consistently ranked at the very top in the OBI rankings since 2006 and was ranked in first place in 2010, with a budget transparency score of ninety-two out of 100, higher than that of countries such as New Zealand and the United States. In chapter 2, Steven Friedman asks how such an unexpected trans-

---

31. We also draw on additional case study material from Peru, Uganda, Kenya, and China.

parency outcome has occurred in a developing country still plagued by inequality, poverty, and social exclusion and what it has meant for participation in government decisionmaking on fiscal matters. What have been the broader political economy dynamics of fiscal accountability in South Africa?

Certainly the big shift in transparency occurred with and as part of the transition led by the African National Congress (ANC) from the apartheid regime to a democratically elected government. Prior to the 1994 elections, by all accounts, little information was accessible to the vast majority of the population. The dramatic change in transparency was not driven solely by a political commitment to citizen empowerment and parliamentary politics. In addition, the National Treasury used fiscal transparency to accomplish two interrelated goals—manage a looming fiscal crisis in 1996 driven by the overspending of provincial and local governments and signal to both the domestic and largely white business elites as well as international financial market actors (rating agencies, foreign investors) that the governing black political leadership could manage public finances efficiently and effectively.

Thus the introduction of significant budget transparency reforms—the 1999 Public Finance Management Act is often cited as a significant milestone and a model for other countries—and their persistence over time were not largely the result of robust demands by Parliament, opposition parties, trade unions, CSOs, or the electorate at-large. Rather, they resulted from the relative insulation of the National Treasury and other government agencies from these pressures. Friedman argues that, ironically, the comparatively high levels of budget transparency in South Africa have been maintained because the ruling party and politicians face little political risk from countervailing pressures. For example, almost two-thirds of parliamentarians represent the ANC and therefore do not question the executive too strongly. This situation is symptomatic of broader conditions such as the relatively weak mechanisms for accountability within the ANC itself and from opposition parties and civil society.

Given these circumstances, budget transparency has not been accompanied by wide use of available fiscal information. The main actors that have used information about the allocation and spending of public resources are organized large-scale business and, to some extent, the trade union federation (Cosatu). Some civil society organizations—specifically the Institute for Democracy in South Africa (Idasa)—have promoted fiscal transparency generally since the transition, and others are increasingly making demands about the allocation of public resources using publicly available budget information.[32] Even the media have

32. These are the Public Service Accountability Monitor, the Centre for Economic Governance and AIDS in Africa, and the Treatment Action Campaign.

been relatively inactive in using budget information to inform the public and hold government accountable.

There are some examples of the impact of civil society work using budget information, including Idasa's work on the Child Support Grant and the Treatment Action Campaign's victorious court case securing the distribution of anti-retroviral treatment in public hospitals, but these are isolated cases that have not led to more systematic shifts or greater accountability in public spending and service delivery. Therefore, despite high levels of budget transparency, there is limited evidence in South Africa of effective or sustained engagement and over-sight of government fiscal management by key actors (Parliament, civil society, the media). As a result, budget reporting mechanisms are strong, but participation and accountability in government fiscal matters are weak.

Brazil: Punctuated Improvements in Fiscal Transparency and Participation

In chapter 3, Jorge Alves and Patrick Heller investigate how Brazil improved budget transparency over the last quarter century. Although not as dramatic as improvements in South Africa (the country ranked nine in the 2010 OBI, with a score of seventy-one out of 100), Brazil's transparency is nevertheless puzzling because the country is known for its high levels of inequality and corruption. However, demands for participation and engagement in fiscal decisionmaking have grown much more in Brazil than in South Africa. Two broad social trans-formations catalyzed the initial improvements in fiscal transparency, participation, and accountability in Brazil. In each of these transformations, civil society formations pushed for structural changes that resulted in still greater engagement and influence for them.

The first social transformation was the process of redemocratization that included the transition from authoritarian rule and passage of the 1988 citizen constitution. A highly mobilized civil society profoundly influenced the content of the constitution, pressing for provisions for citizen involvement in sectoral pol-icy formulation and budgeting processes (which helped to set the context for sub-sequent participatory budgeting at the municipal level across the country). And the emergence of electoral politics with a set of strong political parties led to meaningful competition and alternation in power. The second process is linked to the macroeconomic stabilization that occurred during the 1990s. While the *Real* Plan succeeded in curtailing hyperinflation, it also exposed massive deficits asso-ciated with excessive spending, patronage politics, and overborrowing in subna-tional government budgets. This resulted in a fiscal crisis, which led to the adop-tion of a new Fiscal Responsibility Law in 2000 that included provisions for the publication of budget data and for stronger audit institutions.

Fiscal transparency rules and practices were improved only in 2009, when a set of corruption and political scandals created an additional window of opportunity. A coalition of progressive legislators, the federal Comptroller General's (internal audit) office, academic institutions, and CSOs seized the opening to defeat strong opposition from conservative congressional representatives and mayors as well as public sector unions that did not want salary information published. A congressional Transparency Law was pushed through that expanded the public disclosure aspects of the 2000 Fiscal Responsibility Law and introduced real-time, online publishing of comprehensive budgetary information across all levels of government, a measure that had been stalled in the legislature since 2003.

Fiscal and administrative decentralization linked with redemocratization and the strength of leftist political parties and civil society groups in subnational units also generated opportunities for experimentation in fiscal transparency and participation, especially from the 1990s on. Two fiscal governance innovations have emerged as relatively successful in Brazil: participatory budgeting and community health councils. Participatory budgeting involves direct participation of community representatives in budget making in numerous municipalities across the country, and community health councils deliberate on health care priorities and oversee their implementation, among other responsibilities.

More than any of the other countries examined in this volume, with the possible exception of South Korea, Brazil's transparency reforms have been accompanied by greater popular participation and accountability in fiscal decisionmaking. Sophisticated CSOs possess the capability to incorporate budget information into their agendas.[33] Furthermore, arenas of voice and contestation—not least participatory budgeting programs—enable them to translate this information into policy and public action. The private sector seeks and uses fiscal data, and political parties dig up and expose the fiscal malpractices of their political opponents. Bureaucratic rules and capacities to disclose budget information have been strengthened at all levels of government, and the national media's watchdog role has become more proactive and extensive. And a new transparency "portal" powered by twenty-first-century information and communication technologies has been launched.

Yet serious challenges for fiscal participation and accountability remain. The budget process is still marred by opaque areas and by serious distortions in resource allocation. Moreover, demand for budget information remains very weak outside a small circle of highly capable civil society groups, academics, and the

---

33. This is evident, for example, in the work of the Institute for Socio-Economic Studies and the Brazilian Institute for Socio-Economic Analyses.

business and media sectors, limiting the potential impact of the large amount of fiscal information that is publicly available. Empowered participation is far more likely at the local level than at the federal level.

South Korea: An Upward Spiral of Transparency, Participation, and Accountability

South Korea has reached a comparatively high level of budget transparency— equivalent to that of Brazil but lower than that of South Africa—and is the highest-scoring country in the Asian continent, as measured by the 2010 OBI. In chapter 4, Jong-sung You and Wonhee Lee argue that South Korea has made great progress with respect to fiscal participation and accountability, with some back-sliding in recent years.

During the authoritarian regime, secrecy was the norm. Shielding the budget from public view was deemed necessary for efficient public financial management, and citizen participation in budgetary processes was forbidden. The transition to electoral democracy during the 1980s brought initial openings. The first elected government undertook incremental but key reforms to increase transparency and participation. The highly capacious and largely accountable bureaucracy implemented these reforms, and the National Assembly actively engaged in budget making for the first time. New CSOs were created that focused not only on transparency generally, but also more specifically on fiscal decisionmaking.[34] The reintroduction of full autonomy for local governments created new arenas for engagement.

The Asian financial crisis of 1997 was another important trigger for improvements in South Korea. A combination of external pressure, mostly from the IMF, for improved fiscal management and demands from an increasing number of stronger and more vocal civil society groups led the National Assembly to pass a new bill on fiscal soundness. A newly elected president from the opposition liberal party launched the "IMF-plus" reforms that broadened and deepened fiscal transparency and participation and created a Special Committee on Fiscal Reform in the National Assembly.

The virtuous loops generated by the combination of reformist presidents, vigorous debates among parties in the National Assembly, a highly competent and meritocratic bureaucracy, an ever-broadening and well-organized civil society sector—which even secured an ex officio seat on the National Assembly's Budget Committee—and constructive international influences became stronger through

---

34. Some of the most prominent are the People's Solidarity for Participatory Democracy and the Citizens' Coalition for Economic Justice.

the period from 2000 to 2007. The National Assembly established a Budget Office in 2004 and revised its act in 2005 to require public hearings on all budget bills. After numerous public hearings and conferences, a new National Fiscal Act was passed in 2006 that laid a solid legal foundation for fiscal transparency, participation, and accountability. The National Assembly, CSOs, and the Board of Audit and Inspection are all actively engaged in fiscal decisionmaking. This has led to a significant reprioritization of public spending toward social welfare—a shift long advocated by civil society—a greater focus on the effectiveness and performance of public spending, and a drastic reduction in corruption indicators.

However, since 2008 some backsliding has been evident in the otherwise upward spiral of change in South Korea. The election of a presidential candidate from a more conservative party, along with the impact of the global economic downturn, has resulted in extra public funds being spent to boost the economy through a supplementary budget that was not subject to regular principles and practices of transparency and participation. In addition, the government has pushed through a series of large projects to renovate the four main rivers of the country, exempting them from the usual preliminary feasibility tests. The strength of the engagement and oversight capabilities of the National Assembly, the supreme audit institution, the media, and CSOs is now being tested.

Mexico: Partial and Uneven Improvements in Transparency and Participation

In chapter 5, John Ackerman explores the recent patterns of continuity and change in Mexico's fiscal transparency. Dramatic political shifts set the backdrop, including the emergence of electoral democracy, with the election of opposition candidate Vicente Fox in the 2000 elections, increased competition between political parties, a burgeoning civil society, and enactment of a model Freedom of Information Law in 2002. Based on these contextual changes, Mexico—like South Africa, Brazil, and South Korea—might be expected to exhibit high levels of fiscal transparency and participation.

Yet in 2010 Mexico recorded a middling OBI score of fifty-two out of 100. Budget information is available, but is neither comprehensive nor reliable. Significant amounts of public resources are hidden in hundreds of government "trusts." Oversight by the legislature and supreme audit institution is weak, while civil society participation in budget making is almost nonexistent and often aimed at defending special interests. What explains this relatively slow and modest pace of change?

Before 1997, fiscal transparency was mostly absent in Mexico, as symbolized by the existence of a presidential "secret account." Despite a major financial crisis in 1994–95, which highlighted the need for more fiscal transparency, budget oversight only started to improve in 1997, when the ruling Party of the Institutional Revolution lost control over the lower house of Congress after seventy years of uninterrupted rule. Some key reforms were enacted, including abolition of the president's secret account and creation of an independent supreme audit institution.

After 2000, new alliances and increased political competition in Congress led to a series of major reforms aimed at strengthening budget openness and accountability, including the Law of Superior Oversight, which further empowered the supreme audit institution, and the Federal Budget and Treasury Responsibility Law in 2006, which provided an elaborate legal framework for transparency and oversight of government spending. A further major development was the passage of constitutional reform in February 2007, which included a long list of guarantees on transparency and right to information. These changes gave constitutional backing to Mexico's 2002 Freedom of Information Law and received unanimous support from all political parties.

In practice, however, this increasingly sophisticated institutional framework has not been effective in promoting popular participation and accountability in fiscal matters. Several factors help to account for this paradox. While bureaucratic capacity does exist in Mexico, there remains a strong legacy of civil servants being predominantly concerned with maintaining their discretionary powers and promoting their political careers, achieved by favoring particular (and usually elite) interest groups and political parties. This is facilitated by the low effectiveness and lack of coordination in oversight institutions.

The supreme audit institution, while ostensibly independent on paper, remains highly vulnerable to pressures from the executive branch, its reviews are quite tardy, and its sanctioning power is highly restricted. The importance of oil revenues in Mexico is also an important factor. Easy access to funds from the state oil company, along with executive and bureaucratic dominance of the budget process, has contributed to the persistence of unaccountable discretionary spending, limiting the pressure for implementing fiscal reforms.

The level, breadth, and depth of civil society mobilization and media presence during and subsequent to the democratic transition have been comparatively weaker than that of other countries. And although a handful of highly professionalized CSOs exist, there is no broad-based coalition with nationwide and grassroots links that could have a significant impact on fiscal decisionmaking.

Guatemala: A Continuing Gap between Formal Institutions and Actual Practices

The trajectory and current pattern of fiscal transparency, participation, and accountability in Guatemala are similar to those in Mexico in many ways, although the combination and sequencing of factors and dynamics that contributed to them are somewhat different. Guatemala's OBI score was fifty out of 100 in 2010, almost equal to that of Mexico. In chapter 6, Aaron Schneider and Annabella España-Najera help to solve the puzzle of the divergence, even schizophrenia, between (a) substantial de jure fiscal transparency reforms and occasional windows of opportunity for fiscal participation and accountability and (b) generally poor de facto practices in fiscal decisionmaking in contemporary Guatemala.

The emergence of a relatively robust legal framework in Guatemala was initiated in 1992 with passage of the Law of Government Contracts mandating transparency in public procurement as part of efforts to curb corruption. The next major step forward came in the aftermath of the Peace Agreement in 1997, with enactment of the Organic Budget Law by a freshly elected government that enjoyed popular and legislative support and used it to push through ambitious reforms. Almost simultaneously, the then president pushed through the *sistema integrado de administración financiera* (SIAF), which computerized and put Guatemalan finances online, with technical and financial support from international donor agencies.

Other reforms followed, including passage of the Access to Information Law in 2008 that matched international best practice for the disclosure of budget information and introduction of development councils to promote citizen participation in budget processes at the local level. Under both the Berger government and the current Colom administration, online information increased further, with the Ministry of Finance expanding the amount of budget information readily available to the public.

In most cases, these advances in the legal and regulatory framework for fiscal transparency, participation, and accountability occurred because of temporary and often fortuitous political openings in Guatemalan politics, brought about by elections, peace settlements, and corruption scandals. When such windows appeared, technocrats and international supporters stepped in and pushed through reforms. Increased access to fiscal information allowed civil society groups like Acción Ciudadana and the International Center for Human Rights Investigations to use budget data to analyze public spending patterns and expose malfeasance. But powerful actors have blocked further reform and preserved important areas of privilege, capturing for themselves a significant portion of public resources. The extensive use of trust funds and social funds, for example, clearly demonstrates a pattern in which public resources are regularly shifted off-budget or outside the purview of more transparent formal institutions.

Despite some important advances achieved during key watershed moments, therefore, the general pattern of budgeting in Guatemala includes significant weaknesses in fiscal transparency, participation, and accountability. While formal rules and institutions have advanced and available fiscal information has increased, actual change in behavior has been limited and so has the impact of actors seeking to hold government accountable. Guatemalan economic elites remain powerful and organized, but are fragmented along sectoral, familial, and regional divisions, preferring to exploit informal arrangements and pursue narrow interests and particularistic benefits rather than promote a coherent plan for state reform and a broader social contract. Such fragmentation is mirrored in political life, where the party system is highly volatile and most parties are little more than personalized vehicles for the advancement of individual politicians. This situation is complicated further by a weak civil society sector, unable to extend beyond a narrow urban and middle-class presence.

Tanzania: Entrenched Politics and Accountability

As with many of the other countries covered in this volume, budget openness has progressed since Tanzania's democratic transition in the early 1990s. In 2010 Tanzania received an OBI score of forty-five out of 100, placing it in the lower middle of the pack of nations that the index covers, but among the better-performing African countries. In chapter 7, Barak Hoffman argues that, while domestic forces have exerted some pressure, Tanzania's transparency reforms result mostly from the efforts of a relatively secure ruling party to legitimize itself in the eyes of demanding international donor organizations that finance a considerable share of public spending. This configuration yields a weak version of the pattern observed in South Africa and one more similar to that of Guatemala. There are substantial provisions for budget information, but that information is rarely used by countervailing political agents or CSOs. The entrenched ruling party affords few channels through which outside parties can use budget information to influence public decisions.

To this day, the dominant political force in Tanzania is the party created by Julius Nyerere, the Chama Cha Mapinduzi (CCM), or Party of the Revolution. In the 1960s and 1970s, constitutional and political reforms centralized power under the CCM by creating a one-party state and then subordinating the state to the party. The party remains the only organization capable of exerting control over the whole country in a hierarchical fashion, with village leaders who report upward to party chairs at ward and then district and regional levels and regional chairs who sit on the party's Central Committee. Although its power has been attenuated, the CCM remains the hegemonic political organization even after Tanzania's democratic transition. Because the party, anticipating popular demands, led the nation's shift to multiparty governance, it was able to fashion electoral provisions highly favorable to maintaining its own position.

Despite the entrenched advantages of the CCM, budget transparency has increased steadily, if modestly, in Tanzania over the past two decades. These measures are largely the result of the efforts of international donor agencies to compel the government to stem corruption and financial mismanagement. Soon after the country courted international donor agencies in the 1990s, a series of scandals exposed massive corruption in the privatization of public sector enterprises and other areas. In response, donor agencies catalyzed a series of reforms that created oversight and regulatory agencies such as the Control of Corruption Bureau, the Public Procurement Regulatory Authority, and the National Audit Office. Donor agencies also secured several laws and policies that increase fiscal transparency. The 2001 Public Finance Act requires the government to make budget data publicly available, while the adoption of a modern financial management system was a condition for accessing debt relief.

The partial information provided through these fiscal transparency measures has been used only episodically by political and civil society actors. When rifts emerge within the CCM, factions use information against one another. More systematically, parliamentary debate about proposed budgets has become more robust. Some CSOs have used budget information to criticize government failures to deliver services and to expose corruption and leakage through follow-the-money campaigns. Among the most well known are Haki Elimu's campaigns to improve the quality of primary education. These campaigns and associated accountability initiatives, however, are limited by the restricted political environment and weak capabilities of CSOs as well as the absence of channels for effective redress.

In Tanzania, then, the availability of public budget information has not yet resulted in sustained increases in participation or accountability. Budget information is a necessary but far from sufficient condition for either. Entrenched political powers who benefit from the lack of accountability have blocked further outcomes—such as effective oversight institutions and robust independent political and civic organizations that use information in meaningful arenas of political contest—from developing and taking root.

Vietnam: A Technocratic and Gradual Alternative Pathway to Good Governance?

There was little to no indication of an increase in fiscal transparency in Vietnam until very recently. In the 2010 OBI Vietnam scored a meager fourteen out of 100, the lowest in Southeast Asia, similar to countries with much less impressive records of economic reform and development. Unlike in other countries, in Vietnam gradual political openings, the move to a market economy, and major financial crises did not pave the way for radical fiscal transparency reforms.

Yet in chapter 8, Jonathan Warren and Huong Nguyen argue that some progress has been made in Vietnam. Just one decade ago, the entire budget in

Vietnam was deemed a state secret—the country's OBI score in 2006 was just three out of 100. Nowadays, enacted budgets and execution reports are published on government websites, institutional mechanisms of oversight have been strengthened, and there is greater opportunity for public input. The interesting puzzle therefore resides in these unexpected (though very early-stage) improvements in budget openness in what is otherwise a seemingly unfavorable context.

Since embracing Doi Moi, or Renovation, in the late 1980s, Vietnam has changed from a relatively isolated, centrally planned economy to a state-led mixed economy that is well integrated into global markets. A series of important legislative and policy initiatives were adopted, such as the Public Administrative Reform Master Plan, 2001–2010 (2001), State Audit Law (2003), and Anticorruption Law (2005), to bring the country in line with so-called international good governance "best practices," including with regard to fiscal decisionmaking institutions, processes, and policies. Some moves have been made toward political competition, in that elections are now held for the National Assembly.

Yet with a few exceptions, candidates for government offices must be members of the Communist Party of Vietnam and be vetted by the Fatherland Front, a voluntary government organization anchored in mass participation and popular associations that supervises government activities. The National Assembly has been granted the authority to approve budgets and has become increasingly bold in challenging the government. Deputies call government ministers to testify before the National Assembly, frequently press them to explain the performance of their ministries, and periodically reject government proposals. In addition, other branches of government have been developed and strengthened to varying degrees. The judicial branch has been granted more independence. An independent audit institution, State Audit Vietnam, was created in 1994 and given responsibility for auditing all agencies and organizations using state monies. As of 2005, it reports to the National Assembly rather than the Politburo.

These gradual and minimalist improvements have been driven largely by top-down, technocratic reforms promoted by the national government to demonstrate its adherence to global norms of good governance and to maintain domestic legitimacy vis-à-vis increasing domestic pressure to curb corruption. Vietnamese political leaders are keen to signal their willingness to move toward internationally accepted good practices as part of their ideological commitment to political and economic modernization. They are motivated by a desire to increase foreign aid and private investment and therefore the country's international legitimacy. In turn, donors such as the World Bank have continued to press and support the government to introduce fiscal transparency reforms.

Civil society, measured in terms of volunteer organizations or nongovernmental organizations, remains very weak. And even though press freedoms have expanded, the central government, especially the Politburo, is largely considered beyond reproach. The Fatherland Front, however, has taken a predominant role in bringing popular concerns to the National Assembly. It collects opinions, petitions, and grievances through surveys and consultations with its network of mass organizations. These are reported every year at the opening of the National Assembly and carry political weight; they have included strong calls to address corruption and waste and to strengthen and promote openness and transparency.

The case of Vietnam is interesting, then, because it challenges the centrality of open elections and political party competition as necessary for increases in fiscal transparency. Instead, Vietnam has seen a gradual broadening of political space and oversight in budgetary matters and a modest increase in the amount of fiscal information being put in the public domain, within the parameters of a strong and persistent one-party state and with limited interventions by organized civil society groups and the media.

Senegal: The Perils of Hyper-Presidentialism

Senegal falls in the bottom ranks of all the countries included in the OBI, with a score of only three out of 100 in both 2008 and 2010. Even though Francophone African countries on average score worse than their Anglophone or Lusophone counterparts, Senegal's poor ranking is surprising, as the country is often seen as a regional leader, both in economic performance and in social activism. In chapter 9, Linda Beck, Seydou Nourou Toure, and Aliou Faye take a closer look at Senegal's fiscal transparency, uncovering some shifts toward greater transparency and participation in the national budget process over the past two decades. The OBI measure may fail to register these changes, however, because budget information often diffuses through informal processes and much of the debate about the budget and participation in budget making occurs in the legislature.

Public budgets in Senegal were formulated by a strong executive in a highly centralized way, with little outside consultation or debate for most of its history. Beginning in the late 1990s, however, a series of legal and regulatory reforms opened somewhat the circle of information and participation around budget issues. As with Tanzania, major pressure for these reforms came from donor agencies, but also from regional organizations such as the West African Economic and Monetary Union, whose directives are key to safeguarding the value of the common regional currency. Senegal's Poverty Reduction Strategy Papers—preconditions for debt relief and financing from the World Bank and the IMF—provided civil society forums for dialogue about national policies and government budgets.

Beginning in 1998, President Diouf instituted an annual "budget orientation debate" in which members of Parliament discussed the details of the budget proposed by the Ministry of Finance for fifteen days. New constitutional provisions introduced in 2001 enabled Parliament to review the president's proposed budget for a longer period and to amend it. Nevertheless, the executive still dominates the budget process, given the weak analytical capacity, lack of political autonomy, and anemic opposition of the legislature. Similarly, an Audit Court was created in 1999 with powers to review budget practices and implementation, report to the public, and impose sanctions for mismanagement. Until recently, however, it lagged several years behind in its audits of public spending, rendering them virtually useless in promoting better transparency and accountability in fiscal matters.

Senegal's reforms, while leading to limited improvements in fiscal transparency, participation, and accountability, have been hindered by three main factors. The first is a form of hyper-presidentialism and a dominant party system that limit the separation of powers and contestation critical to a more transparent and participatory budget process. The second is donors' contradictory involvement in budget and policymaking, which contributes to replacing citizens and legislators as key accountability actors in the fiscal decisionmaking process. Finally, neither journalists nor CSOs have been especially active in pressing the government to disclose fiscal information in a more complete and official way, contenting themselves with informal leakages of budget information; they have not engaged the government on budget matters in any significant way.

Mali, another Francophone African country, scored thirty-five out of 100 in the 2010 OBI, much higher than Senegal despite seemingly less favorable contextual conditions. But Mali's political system is characterized by lower levels of presidential dominance—partly due to the fact that the president lacks a legislative majority—and its civil society has been more active on budget issues. These two factors help to explain the differing levels of fiscal transparency in Senegal and Mali.

Overall Findings

What explains differences in the level of fiscal transparency and participation? Bringing together evidence from statistical, cross-national, and in-depth country case studies, we find that four main factors affect fiscal transparency, participation, and accountability across countries. They are related to (a) processes of political regime change and increasing political competition, (b) fiscal and economic crises, (c) corruption scandals and the media, and (d) external (international, global, regional, and transnational) influences.

First, *political transitions* from authoritarianism to political competition through elections and multiparty systems tend to be associated with higher levels of transparency (and to a certain extent engagement). Statistical cross-country evidence in this respect is complemented by strong case study evidence from

South Africa, Brazil, South Korea, and to a lesser extent Mexico, Guatemala, Tanzania, and even Senegal.

The impact of political liberalization and increased political competition, however, is subject to some caveats. The simple fact of holding regular elections, for example, does not guarantee that a transparency dividend will automatically accrue. The nature of the political regime that emerges from the transition process is very important, particularly the degree of competitiveness of party politics—as highlighted in one of the statistical papers and in some case studies—but also the strength of opposition parties and the relative power of legislatures vis-à-vis the executive. In Mexico, alternation in power as a result of elections was not sufficient to overcome vested interests working against transparency or to guarantee adequate oversight. In Guatemala, the extreme volatility of party politics prevented a good legal framework from having an impact on actual transparency and participation practices.

Moreover, as the cases of South Korea and Brazil clearly show, broader and deeper democratization processes only bring about more transformative changes in public access and participation when linked with the presence of reform-minded politicians and technocrats or when based on strong relations between progressive political parties and capable CSOs that see the budget as an important arena for engaging with the government. In South Africa, in contrast, a lack of electoral competition meant that fiscal transparency did not and was not a risk to the ruling ANC's political position or policies.

A second factor affecting fiscal transparency is linked to governments' need to respond to *fiscal and economic crises* and to restore (or at least create the perception of) fiscal discipline. Both South Africa and Brazil, for example, responded to looming fiscal crises in the 1990s by introducing important fiscal transparency reforms aimed at countering the profligacy of subnational governments—which was straining public finances—and keeping their spending in check. Reformers in South Korea also reacted to the 1997 Asian financial crisis by introducing wide-ranging reforms that deepened fiscal transparency, but also increased the legislature's oversight role in controlling public finances. These measures were meant not just to maintain domestic fiscal discipline, but also to signal to international financial markets that the government was serious about keeping its house in order and attracting foreign investors. Fiscal and economic crises, therefore, can open up important windows of opportunity that reformers both within and outside government have used strategically to push through accountability-enhancing measures.

Third, *political and corruption scandals* often trigger reforms. In Brazil and Guatemala, some of the key reforms opening up access to fiscal information and ensuring increased citizen engagement in budget processes were introduced following public outcry over reported cases of corruption. In both of these countries, ad hoc coalitions of like-minded reformers were able to seize the opening produced by the urgent need to respond to pressure exerted by independent media and public opinion. In Kenya, most of the key pieces of legislation were introduced by the Kibaki government after it was swept to power on an anticorruption platform. Even in Vietnam and China, where corruption scandals may not be widely reported and the media lack independence, governments responded to mounting popular concern over increasing levels of corruption by opening up some space for fiscal transparency and participation, though almost exclusively at the local level, where services that affect the large majority of the population are delivered.

Finally, *external influence* by donors and international agencies, along with the emergence of international norms, also plays an important role. In South Africa, South Korea, Mexico, Guatemala, and Vietnam, for example, the norms of behavior and best practices promoted, among others, by the IMF through its *Code of Good Practices on Fiscal Transparency* and related manual, originally published in 1998, certainly constituted a standard that technocrats within governments adopted to signal good governance practices. Such a standard-setting role was complemented, in lower-income countries, by the provision of technical assistance supporting public financial management reform programs and by the use of conditionalities linking financial assistance to increased fiscal transparency and, in some cases, civil society participation in policy and budget processes.

These donor interventions are inherently contradictory and not always effective, as shown in one of the cross-country papers summarized above. In Uganda, for example, a period of positive collaboration around poverty reduction policies between donors and the government, leading to significant improvements in both transparency and participation, was followed by a period of increasing distance and misunderstandings. In Tanzania, heavy dependence on foreign assistance—particularly in the form of direct budget support—brought about better fiscal transparency, but may have undermined domestic accountability mechanisms, given donors' superior capacity and influence. A similar pattern occurred in Senegal, where donors pushed the government to be more transparent, but mostly because of their own need for fiscal information.

Table 1-5 shows the presence and importance of each of these four causal factors in the case study countries. Political transitions, political competition, and fiscal or economic crises were the key factors associated with countries that achieved higher levels of transparency. Corruption scandals were often important catalysts in many countries, but did not have a consistent or sustainable influence. External influence played a more limited role in our case studies, including Guatemala, Tanzania, and Senegal. Perhaps more important, combinations and

Table 1-5. *Factors Affecting Fiscal Transparency in Case Study Countries*[a]

Country	Political transitions, elections, competition	Fiscal and economic crises	Corruption scandals	External influences
South Africa	X	X	x	x
Brazil	X	X	X	x
South Korea	X	X	x	x
Mexico	x	x	X	
Guatemala	x		X	x
Tanzania	x		X	X
Vietnam			X	x
Senegal				x

Source: Authors.

a. X indicates a major role or presence, while x indicates a minor role or presence.

sequences of these factors often contributed to changes in fiscal transparency, participation, and accountability.

Combinations and Sequences

These causal factors clearly worked not in isolation, but in different combinations, configurations, and sequences. Furthermore, increases in fiscal transparency did not automatically bring about greater popular engagement with newly available budget information, much less greater public accountability. In order to understand the constellations and sequences of factors that lead to changes in fiscal transparency, participation, and accountability and some of the challenges and obstacles that may prevent those improvements from taking place, in this section we offer a four-way classification of ideal country types, drawing from the evidence gathered in our study that might apply to a broader set of contexts. We specifically look at countries' dynamic evolution over time and the paths they have followed.

Among the countries included in our set of case studies, South Korea and Brazil have improved the most, especially on the dimensions of engagement with fiscal information and public accountability in addition to transparency. Over time, they have developed institutional mechanisms and capacities that guarantee not only that a large amount of fiscal information is disclosed to the public, but also that opportunities exist for different actors to engage with the budget process at various levels of government. This has brought about several benefits, from a greater focus on social sector spending and a reduction in corruption in South Korea to increased scrutiny of executive action and better prioritization of local public investment in Brazil.

These two countries represent a wider group of *middle- and high-income inno-vators* who reaped the most benefit out of fiscal transparency and participation, thanks to a combination of domestic factors that include democratization (coupled with political pluralism), an active civil society that demands both access to infor-mation and opportunities for participation, and a focus on fiscal discipline. The path followed by these countries partly mirrors that of several countries now among the richest and most transparent, such as Canada, Australia, New Zealand, and the Scandinavian countries, where a similar configuration was reached over a much longer period of time. Countries that are not far from this ideal type include Chile in Latin America, the Philippines in Asia, and some Eastern European coun-tries like Slovenia and Poland. These countries are among the few that attempt to incorporate international good practice effectively and to push its limits.

In countries like South Africa, Mexico, Guatemala, and Kenya, trajectories have been more contradictory and outcomes more limited. While all countries have seen some improvement in their level of fiscal transparency—including South Africa's outstanding performance on the OBI—corresponding increases in active participation and oversight have not fully materialized. Some of the char-acteristics of these countries are shared by a much larger group of *hybrid reform-ers*, where specific characteristics of domestic politics, in the form of limited elec-toral accountability and an entrenched elite, coupled with a general weakness of CSOs and citizen pressure, have prevented deeper and broader changes from tak-ing root. A large number of other (mostly middle-income) countries fall within this ideal type, including several Latin American countries such as Peru and Argentina, but also Russia, India, Malaysia, and Indonesia, for example. In all of these countries, combinations of political transitions, fiscal crises, scandals, and external incentives have played a role, but have not gelled or combined to bring about the kind of virtuous circle of transparency, participation, and accountabil-ity seen in the first category of countries. The breadth—and size—of the coun-tries included in this group calls for understanding the key constraints and iden-tifying interventions that might help to unlock their potential and deliver the full benefits of reform.

Among low-income countries, Uganda and Tanzania belong to a group of *aid-dependent improvers*, which perform reasonably well in the public provision of budget information and where, in a few notable instances, various actors use budget information to hold government accountable, such as the Parliament in Uganda and some civil society groups in Tanzania. In these countries, improve-ments in fiscal transparency and participation came about thanks to a combina-tion of (partial) political transitions, corruption scandals that put pressure on gov-ernment through an active and independent media sector, and heavy donor presence and pressure. Other aid-dependent countries that fall within this ideal type include some African countries such as Ghana, Mali, and Namibia and possibly some Central American countries such as Nicaragua and Honduras (recent political crises notwithstanding). As shown in our cross-country research, donor interventions do not always bring about expected outcomes, despite their focus on promoting good governance. In the countries belonging to this group, however, external assistance may have been more effective thanks to a particular focus on improving domestic accountability and the presence of reformers both inside and outside government that were supported by and allied with donor agencies.

The fourth and final ideal type emerging from our research consists of *stalled authoritarians* like Vietnam and China, where the autocratic nature of the political regime may not allow fiscal transparency and participation to go beyond a low threshold and where improvements, where and when they happen, are slow and gradual. In these countries, governments are intent on maintaining a strong hold on both economic and social processes. They might open up their books in a limited way to conform to international standards or to address questions of their domestic legitimacy, but they are quick to crack down on the first signs of dissent or demands for more accountability. Other countries that might belong to this category are Ethiopia, Yemen, and countries in Central Asia. Improvements in fiscal transparency, participation, and accountability in these countries might only materialize in the medium to long term, given the difficulties that both domestic and external actors face in achieving more government openness and responsiveness.

Figure 1-3 depicts graphically some of the trajectories that countries in each of the four groups or ideal types have followed. These four ideal types represent what we believe is a useful way of categorizing and sorting through the evidence and depicting a range of pathways toward increased fiscal transparency, participation, and accountability. In turn, these point the way toward identifying potentially useful entry points for reformers at both the international and the country levels. Of course, other ideal types are likely to exist. Specifically, conflict and postconflict countries or resource-dependent autocracies, often with specific combinations of factors and challenges, may complement the typology we have developed.

Accountability and Impact

Among the case studies, evidence of the use and impact of available fiscal information is mostly limited to some of the better-performing countries, such as Brazil and South Korea. In most of the other cases, in fact, transparency did not generally lead to broad demands for increased participation or to more robust engagement and oversight. Potential users of information such as journalists, CSOs, ordinary citizens, and even politicians often failed to take advantage of budget data being put in the public domain. Clearly, it may be more difficult to increase the use of information than the extent of its provision. Transparency may

Figure 1-3. *Trajectories over Time, by Country Group or Ideal Type*

Fiscal transparency and participation

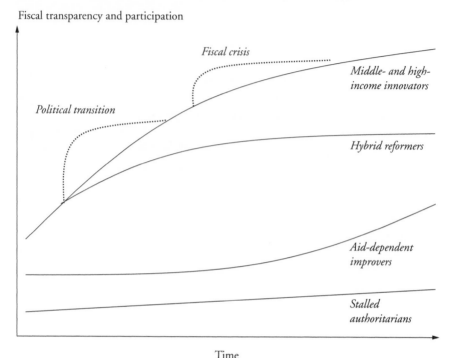

Time

Source: Authors.

produce some of its most powerful benefits in invisible ways. Officials may refrain from behaving badly for fear of exposure when regular fiscal disclosure is required.

These possibilities notwithstanding, the country case studies show that would-be users faced significant obstacles in the use of fiscal information to engage in fiscal decisionmaking. Legislators lacked the expertise and capacity for analysis or lacked real avenues and incentives to translate information into pressure for holding the executive accountable. Media attention to these processes was episodic—primarily during times of fiscal or economic crises or corruption scandals. Civil society organizations did not always see the information as relevant to their agendas, did not know how to incorporate it usefully into their strategies, or operated in an environment in which they could not transform information into influence.

In some cases, civil society groups managed to mount effective campaigns and affect fiscal policies and processes in significant ways. The Treatment Action Campaign's work on antiretrovirals in South Africa, Fundar's campaign on the use of agricultural subsidies in Mexico, and Haki Elimu's basic education activities in

Tanzania are among a growing body of cases of what capable organizations can do when they combine budget analysis with advocacy efforts. Their impact can be significant, but it tends not to be systemic, because wider participation and engagement remain circumscribed in most countries.

Transparency, therefore, is achieved more easily than participation. Both are necessary, but far from sufficient for bringing about more accountability in public finances and other hoped-for outcomes, including improved service delivery, reduced corruption, and sustainable human development more broadly. According to the evidence we gathered, the links between fiscal transparency, participation, and accountability are often weak, interrupted, incomplete, or, in the best of cases, difficult to unearth and explain and dependent on idiosyncratic factors and conditions. This clearly represents a challenge for individuals and organizations interested in promoting the cause of fiscal transparency and participation and in arguing for its expected benefits.

Of the two statistical papers examining the consequences of fiscal transparency, one presents convincing evidence that fiscal transparency lowers governments' cost of accessing international financial markets to service debt, therefore providing an important argument in favor of opening budgets.[35] The second records some preliminary but inconclusive correlations between open budgets and some human development indicators. Throughout the country case studies, evidence that improved access to fiscal information leads citizens and oversight bodies to use such information to engage in budget processes and hold government accountable is more difficult to come by; even more scarce are cases of such pressure resulting in changes in government policies and improvements in service delivery. There are various cases of legislators becoming more demanding vis-à-vis the executive and of civil society campaigns achieving significant but isolated success. Thus far, then, the evidence for the positive impacts of transparency on accountability and development is far from systematic or definitive.

In the early stages of scholarship in this emerging field, many proponents presumed that achieving increases in fiscal and other kinds of governmental transparency would automatically result in greater accountability. As scholars such as Jonathan Fox, John Gaventa, and Rosemary McGee point out, however, this relationship is not that straightforward.[36] As Fox writes, "Truth often fails to lead to justice." The evidence assembled through this project supports that broad thesis.

To understand when the truth about budgets and fiscal realities leads to greater justice and accountability, it is helpful to think of the relationship between transparency, participation, and accountability as a set of increasingly demanding, and

---

35. See Hameed (2011) and Fukuda-Parr and others (2011).
36. Fox (2007) and McGee and Gaventa (2010).

Figure 1-4. *The Transparency, Participation, and Accountability Funnel*

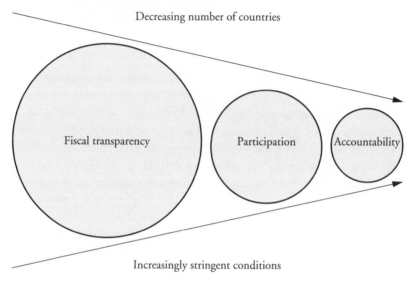

Source: Authors.

so decreasingly common, phenomena. As the case study chapters show in detail, many countries have improved the transparency of their budgets. It is only in a relatively small proportion of these countries, however, that organizations and individuals have proved capable of understanding and using that information to participate—either formally or informally—in the politics of budgeting decisions. Even smaller still is the set of countries and situations in which participation has resulted in increased public accountability. This relationship between transparency, participation, and accountability is depicted in figure 1-4 as a kind of funnel that is wide at one end (the number of cases that achieve transparency) but quite narrow at the other end (the number of cases that achieve accountability).

In many of the countries covered by the Open Budget Index and in most of the country case studies in this volume (especially South Africa, Brazil, and South Korea but also Mexico, Guatemala, and Tanzania), substantial advances have been achieved in fiscal transparency. Many kinds of actors could potentially use budget information to increase government accountability, including civil society organizations, journalists in media organizations, and opposition or reform politicians.

Despite greater availability of information about budgets and the fiscal process, however, our case studies find less participation in the use of budget information than open budget advocates might desire. In some countries, CSOs, independent media, and political opposition are underdeveloped or weak and so lack the capabilities to use budget information effectively. In the countries examined in this volume, South Africa most starkly illustrates this drop-off between high transparency and low participation. In other instances, these organizations may possess capability in principle but lack orientation and experience in using budget information and accountability and so rely on more familiar advocacy and mobilization strategies.

As transparency does not automatically generate participation and use of information, so participation does not assure accountability. Those who seek accountability may lack effective avenues and channels through which to deploy budget information. Or targets of accountability—government and other politically powerful groups—may be so dominant that they can ignore or easily resist information-based campaigns and shaming strategies.

One important task for subsequent research is to improve our understanding of the factors that determine the shape of the funnel from transparency to participation to accountability. Some factors will arise from long historical trajectories that determine the configuration of political forces and the extent of civil society organization and political contestation. Other factors, however, may be more amenable to reform—such as institutional avenues to deploy information-based accountability strategies and the capabilities and orientation of media and reform groups. For those who seek to increase accountability through the use of information, the task is to alter these factors and change the shape of the funnel so that the drop-off is not so steep.

The Evolving International Context

Over the last two to three decades, domestic factors were predominant in determining the levels and changes in fiscal transparency, participation, and accountability, as shown in our country case studies. However, the international context of players, norms, and incentives has dramatically evolved and is increasingly contributing to changing domestic dynamics on the ground. This changed global environment is being shaped by four key factors and trends.

First, international norms and assessments of fiscal transparency have proliferated over the past fifteen years. Principles and guidelines have been issued by the IMF, the OECD, the International Organization of Supreme Audit Institutions, and the International Parliamentary Union, among others, providing direction to governments on how to open their budget processes to public scrutiny and proactively disseminate fiscal information.[37] The IMF—through its Reports on the Observance of Standards and Codes—the Public Expenditure and Financial Accountability (PEFA) program, and the IBP have conducted assessments of

37. See, for example, IMF (2007a) and OECD (2002).

scores of countries. In particular through the Open Budget Index, the IBP created a way to compare levels of budget transparency across countries and, increasingly, over time. The first OBI was launched in 2006, and governments around the world have shown increased interest in the results. The most recent iteration, published in January 2013, includes a new section on participation in budget processes, introducing new standards for what governments can do to involve their citizens in fiscal decisionmaking processes. More generally, a wave of transparency reforms, from anticorruption policies to freedom of information laws, has swept across countries around the world and at the international level.

Second, over the past decade, civil society's interest, capacity, and engagement with fiscal and budget issues have increased dramatically. The transnational network of civil society groups working on budget-related issues and using analysis of budget information as an important tool in their policy advocacy has grown rapidly in the past ten to fifteen years. When the first conference calling together such groups was organized by the U.S.-based Center on Budget Policies and Priorities in 1997, a mere half a dozen organizations showed up. At a global assembly held in Dar es Salaam in November 2011, nearly 100 civil society organizations from fifty-six countries discussed the development of collaborative international advocacy efforts to increase fiscal transparency and enhance civil society participation in fiscal matters. They signed a joint declaration favoring more open budgets across the world.[38]

The work of some civil society organizations is widely recognized both at home and abroad, and they are often seen as leaders and innovators in their field. Many of them have established collaborative relationships with finance ministries, parliamentary budget committees, audit institutions, and media outlets in their countries. They have also built coalitions with a wide range of other civil society actors to enhance the likelihood of their voice being heard and their advocacy objectives being met. This represents an important break from the past, as new actors enter the policy arena and begin to alter existing power structures, information practices, forms of engagement, and policy agendas.

Civil society's capacity to influence fiscal transparency, participation, and accountability is much greater than it was a decade ago, and evidence to back up this claim is increasing. In a broad review of existing evidence, McGee and Gaventa (2010) find that transparency and accountability initiatives driven by civil society can make an important difference. With the usual provisos about drawing universal generalizations, they show how, under some conditions, civil society interventions in favor of transparency and accountability have resulted in (a) increased

---

38. The declaration, and further details about the movement, can be found at www.makebudgets public.org.

state or institutional responsiveness; (b) less corruption; (c) the building of new participatory spaces for citizen engagement; (d) the empowerment of local voices; and (e) better use of the budget and more effective delivery of services.

The International Budget Partnership has also been documenting the impact of civil society work based on budget analysis and advocacy. In a study based on six organizations in six countries, civil society groups were found to have been effective in interpreting and disseminating budget information to enable broader civil society and other actors to engage with the budget process in more meaningful ways.[39] The case studies also provided significant evidence that budget work can have a direct impact on improving budget systems and on pro-poor budget allocations and results. Conversely, however, budget transparency and monitoring are no panacea; many such transparency efforts seem to have little impact on goals such as improved service delivery or public accountability.

More recently, the IBP has started using a more rigorous methodology to document a series of cases of civil society campaigns, some of which are mentioned in this volume (such as the Treatment Action Campaign in South Africa), but many others are happening in very disparate contexts. These studies include the national campaign for the human rights of Dalits in India, the fight for the right to early education in municipal Buenos Aires, and the monitoring of earthquake reconstruction in Pakistan.[40] The case studies of Brazil and South Korea in this volume further suggest that strong civil society engagement is likely to be critical for opening up avenues for broader participation in fiscal decisionmaking. Although it is again premature to reach universal generalizations from this set of case studies, the evidence is growing on the ways in which civil society actors have been able to affect government policies and processes related to fiscal transparency, participation, and accountability.

Third, in the past few years alone, various multistakeholder and cross-sectoral initiatives to bring together governments, international institutions, civil society groups, and the private sector have been established to promote transparency and accountability in various areas of government action. The Extractive Industries Transparency Initiative, for example, has spearheaded an overhaul of the systems through which governments and extractive industry companies deal with each other and provide public information on contracts, royalties, revenues, and so on.[41] In some countries, revenues from natural resource extraction constitute the main source of budget finance; their transparency fundamentally alters the power game around the allocation and use of public resources more generally in those societies.

---

39. Robinson (2008).

40. For information on the IBP efforts, see http://internationalbudget.org/what-we-do/major-ibp-initiatives/partnership-initiative/learning-program/case-studies/.

41. For information on the Extractive Industries Transparency Initiative, see www.eiti.org.

President Barack Obama launched the Open Government Partnership (OGP) in 2011,[42] and more than fifty governments from across the globe have prepared action plans to increase transparency and citizen engagement in various areas of public policy, including fiscal decisionmaking. Independent review mechanisms are being set up for civil society to monitor the implementation of these action plans. In another initiative related to the OGP, the governments of Brazil and the Philippines, together with the World Bank, the IMF, the IBP, and other key actors, have set up the Global Initiative for Fiscal Transparency (GIFT),[43] a multistakeholder effort aimed at advancing global norms and strengthening incentives for fiscal transparency, participation, and accountability around the world.

Fourth, transparency has also become a priority for international donors. Aid programs are increasingly linked to minimum standards of budget transparency in recipient countries. For example, former World Bank president Robert Zoellick declared in April 2011 that the Bank "will not lend directly to finance budgets in countries that do not publish their budgets."[44] As a consequence, some of the Bank's internal operational guidelines were revised, asking that countries applying for so-called Development Policy Operations be subject to a preliminary screening for budget transparency. The United Kingdom's Department for International Development has included a benchmark related to budget transparency in its guidelines for providing direct support to a country's budget, and this benchmark was included in the United Kingdom's commitments to the OGP action plan. The European Commission (EC) has recently added a similar benchmark for countries to qualify for EC budget support.

The need to establish transparent public financial management systems in countries receiving aid has been clearly stated in the declaration coming out of the fourth High-Level Forum on Aid Effectiveness held in Busan (South Korea) in late 2011 and endorsed by more than 100 governments and international institutions. Finally, the push for increased transparency, participation, and accountability in fiscal matters is receiving increasing support by several new donors such as the Hewlett and Gates foundations, alongside some of the ones that have been active in this field for longer, like the Ford and Open Society foundations. Some of these organizations, together with the U.K. Department for International Development, have recently set up the Transparency and Accountability Initiative, with the aim of highlighting the work being done in this field and evaluating its impact more rigorously.

---

42. For information on OGP, see http://www.opengovpartnership.org.

43. For information on GIFT, see http://fiscaltransparency.net.

44. Zoellick (2011). A few months later, the Bank issued more specific guidance for its budget support operations.

Part of the broad press for increasing fiscal accountability comes from the widespread perception that the global financial crisis of 2009 and subsequent debt challenges of several European countries—most notably Greece—can be attributed at least in part to the lack of government fiscal transparency. Just as the Asian financial crisis of 1997 led to the promulgation of the IMF Code of Good Practices on Fiscal Transparency, the 2009 crisis and its aftermath pressured governments as well as stakeholders to prioritize reforms in fiscal decisionmaking. These factors and trends together create an increasingly dense global environment of organizations, networks, norms, and initiatives that makes government action toward greater transparency in the management of all public resources increasingly likely. This, in turn, opens up more space for and further empowers domestic actors to access relevant information, engage in fiscal decisionmaking processes, and work toward holding governments accountable.

Strategic Lessons, Future Prospects, and Research Agenda

This volume offers lessons for policy and practice for those who seek to advance fiscal transparency, participation, and accountability around the world. What stands out most clearly is that punctuated and often large advances can be achieved during windows of opportunity that are triggered by major political changes (transitions to democracy, campaigns and elections, and alternations of parties in power), fiscal crises, and corruption scandals. Promoters of fiscal accountability should be attentive to these opportunities and seize them to press for major legal and institutional reforms and actual changes in government practices (including the publication of budget documents, development of a citizen's budget, and creation of greater opportunities for legislatures and citizens to engage in fiscal decisionmaking). It is even possible for fiscal transparency to advance at least partially in nondemocratic settings through a combination of fiscal crises, corruption scandals, and the motivation of government officials to be seen as good public financial managers by their peers in other countries and at the international level.

There clearly is no magic wand or privileged actor that, by itself, can advance fiscal transparency, participation, and accountability. The opportunities for much greater collaboration among government reformers, civil society advocates, international agencies, and even the private sector to promote change have never been greater. For example, more and more governments are motivated to signal to public actors (such as bilateral aid agencies) and private actors (such as bond and credit rating agencies) that they are worthy of increased foreign direct investment and aid because transparency constitutes a component of their sound public financial management systems. Conversely, lenders, donors, and counterparties impose increasingly costly sanctions on governments that are found to be covering up poor fiscal policy and positions. Strengthening these positive and negative incentives for fiscal transparency is likely to be critical in the future.

In addition, while there are now much more elaborated sets of international norms, the guidance being provided to governments about appropriate practices is not as effective as it might be, given the existence of multiple codes and assessments. At the same time, gaps in critical areas still exist, such as standards on legislative oversight or public participation. Further development of a more coherent global architecture of norms (principles, standards, and assessments) will directly and indirectly contribute to improvements in fiscal transparency, participation, and accountability. The various multistakeholder initiatives, including EITI, OGP, GIFT, and others, have great potential to strengthen such norms and incentives.

Important achievements have already been made in increasing fiscal transparency, and this moment offers opportunities to expand and deepen these achievements. Those active in the transparency field now recognize that their next challenges will be to develop similarly forceful and systematic methods of assuring that budget information is well used by local and international actors and that adequate opportunities exist for citizens and other actors to engage meaningfully in different stages of the budget process—what we have called participation—and that such participation produces increased accountability.

There is no question that strengthening the capacity of oversight actors—especially legislatures, audit institutions, civil society groups, and the media—is essential to increasing the use of budget information. These actors can be much more influential in advancing fiscal transparency and using its fruits if they have resources, experience, expertise, and support. Beyond mere strength, however, is the challenge of orientation and organizational strategy. Even when significant budget information is not available, these actors will not use that budget information unless they develop agendas and strategies through which the information can help them to advance their particular objectives—winning elections, advocating for policies, or selling newspapers. This is one of the critical frontiers of the transparency and accountability field.

Another frontier, which may be more daunting still, is to develop a systematic understanding of how transparency and participation in fiscal matters can be converted into increased public accountability and what methods can increase the conversion rate. Cases like Brazil and South Korea show how increasing participation by strong civil society organizations on the ground is critical for advancing the downstream goal of greater government fiscal accountability. Civic and political groups often analyze budget information and employ it in their advocacy and campaign strategies, but their efforts are frustrated by entrenched, insulated, and powerful interests. How can policymakers and activists pave the road that leads from participation to accountability? Part of the answer may lie in the construction of formal mechanisms in which social actors can trigger action and sanction through the use of information. Procedures for public hearings and investigations, public audit and transparency institutions, and independent judiciaries capable of prosecuting malfeasance fall into this category. But a wide range of less formal mechanisms and practices, such as social audits, public expenditure tracking surveys, and data-driven tools, can increase the conversion rate from participation to public accountability.

This volume builds on the growing, but still quite scant, body of research on fiscal transparency and public accountability. Scholarship in this domain just scratches the surface of what needs to be known about the political economy of fiscal transparency, participation, and accountability. The possibilities for more sophisticated statistical research using time-series data will soon become a possibility. The evolving global environment means that more research rigorously analyzing the emerging interactions between domestic and international factors and mechanisms will be needed. As this field develops, we should be especially attentive to the unintended consequences and possible regressions in fiscal transparency, participation, and accountability. There is no teleological necessity that makes governments throughout the world inexorably become more transparent and accountable.

This field, then, faces enormous challenges and opportunities. Those advocating greater fiscal transparency and activists seeking to use new information to improve the quality of governance and public service delivery now enjoy favorable winds from the proliferation of transparency norms, the policies of international organizations, and domestic pressures for openness. In the future, it will be critical to discover how best to leverage transparency and promote the substantive values of accountability and development it is meant to secure. In this distinctive moment, scholars of development, governance, and transparency can produce rigorous work that is highly relevant and practically significant by studying the conditions, pathways, and methods that determine the nature of that leverage so that it can be used to foster human progress.

References

Abers, Rebecca. 2000. *Inventing Local Democracy: Grassroots Politics in Brazil.* Boulder: Lynne Rienner.

Alt, J. E., and D. D. Lassen. 2006. "Transparency, Political Polarization, and Political Budget Cycles in OECD Countries." *American Journal of Political Science* 50, no. 3: 530–50.

Alt, J. E., D. D. Lassen, and S. Rose. 2006. "The Causes of Fiscal Transparency: Evidence from the U.S. States." *IMF Staff Papers* 53 (special issue): 30–57.

Baiocchi, Gianpaolo. 2005. *Militants and Citizens: The Politics of Participatory Democracy in Porto Alegre*. Stanford University Press.

Baiocchi, Gianpaolo, Patrick Heller, and Marcelo K. Silva. 2011. *Bootstrapping Democracy: Transforming Local Governance and Civil Society in Brazil*. Stanford University Press.

Bastida, F., and B. Benito. 2007. "Central Government Budget Practices and Transparency: An International Comparison." *Public Administration* 85, no. 3: 667–716.

Bellver, A., and D. Kaufmann. 2005. "Transparenting Transparency: Initial Empirics and Policy Implications." Unpublished manuscript.

Benito, B., and F. Bastida. 2009. "Budget Transparency, Fiscal Performance, and Political Turnout: An International Approach." *Public Administration Review* 69, no. 3: 403–17.

Brautigam, D. A. 2000. *Aid Dependence and Governance*. Stockholm: Almqvist and Wiksell.

Brautigam, D. A., and S. Knack. 2004. "Foreign Aid, Institutions, and Governance in Sub-Saharan Africa." *Economic Development and Cultural Change* 52, no. 2: 255–85.

de Renzio, P., and D. Angemi. 2012. "Comrades or Culprits? Donor Engagement and Budget Transparency in Aid-Dependent Countries." *Public Administration and Development* 32, no. 2: 167–80.

de Renzio, P., P. Gomez, and J. Sheppard. 2009. "Budget Transparency and Development in Resource-Dependent Countries." *International Social Science Journal* 57 (issue supplement s1): 57–69.

de Renzio, P., and H. Masud. 2011. "Measuring and Promoting Budget Transparency: The Open Budget Index as a Research and Advocacy Tool." *Governance* 24, no. 3: 607–16.

Egorov, Georgy, Sergei Guriev, and Konstantin Sonin. 2009. "Why Resource-Poor Dictators Allow Freer Media: A Theory and Evidence from Panel Data." *American Political Science Review* 103, no. 4: 645–68.

Ferraz, C., and F. Finan. 2008. "Exposing Corrupt Politicians: The Effects of Brazil's Publicly Released Audits on Electoral Outcomes." *Quarterly Journal of Economics* 123, no. 2: 703–45.

Florini, A. 2007. *The Right to Know: Transparency for an Open World*. Columbia University Press.

Fox, Jonathan. 2007. "The Uncertain Relationship between Transparency and Accountability." *Development in Practice* 17, no. 4: 663–71.

Frankel, J. 2010. "The Natural Resource Curse: A Survey." NBER Working Paper 15836. Cambridge, Mass.: National Bureau for Economic Research.

Fukuda-Parr, S., P. Guyer, and T. Lawson-Remer. 2011. "Does Budget Transparency Lead to Stronger Human Development Outcomes and Commitments to Economic and Social Rights?" IBP Working Paper 4. Washington: International Budget Partnership.

Fung, Archon, Mary Graham, and David Weil. 2007. *Full Disclosure: The Perils and Promise of Transparency*. Cambridge University Press.

Glennerster, R., and Y. Shin. 2008. "Does Transparency Pay?" *IMF Staff Papers* 55, no. 1: 183–209.

Goetz, A. M., and R. Jenkins. 2001. "Hybrid Forms of Accountability: Citizen Engagement in Institutions of Public Sector Oversight in India." *Public Management Review* 3, no. 3: 363–83.

Hameed, F. 2005. "Fiscal Transparency and Economic Outcomes." IMF Working Paper WP/05/225. Washington: International Monetary Fund.

———. 2011. "Budget Transparency and Financial Markets." IBP Working Paper 1. Washington: International Budget Partnership.

IBP (International Budget Partnership). 2013. *Open Budget Survey 2012.* Washington.
IMF (International Monetary Fund). 2007a. *Code of Good Practices on Fiscal Transparency.* Washington.
————. 2007b. *Manual of Good Practices on Fiscal Transparency.* Washington.
————. 2012. "Fiscal Transparency, Accountability, and Risk." IMF Board Paper prepared by the Fiscal Affairs and Statistics Departments. Washington, November.
Islam, R. 2006. "Does More Transparency Go Along with Better Governance?" *Economics and Politics* 18, no. 2: 121–67.
J-PAL (Abdul Latif Jameel Poverty Action Lab). 2011. "Governance Review Paper." J-PAL Governance Initiative. Cambridge, Mass.
Karl, Terry Lynn. 1997. *Paradox of Plenty: Oil Booms and Petro-States.* University of California Press.
Khagram, Sanjeev, James V. Riker, and Kathryn Sikkink. 2002. *Restructuring World Politics: Transnational Social Movements, Networks, and Norms (Social Movements, Protest, and Contention).* University of Minnesota Press.
La Porta, Rafael, Florencio Lopez-de-Silanes, Andrei Shleifer, and Robert Vishny. 1999. "The Quality of Government." *Journal of Law, Economics, and Organization* 15, no. 1 (April): 222–79.
Lassen, D. D. 2000. "Political Accountability and the Size of Government: Theory and Cross-Country Evidence." EPRU Working Paper 00-20. University of Copenhagen.
McGee, Rosemary, and John Gaventa. 2010. "Review of Impact and Effectiveness of Transparency and Accountability Initiatives: Synthesis Report." Paper prepared for the Transparency and Accountability Initiative.
Meyer, John W., John Boli, George M. Thomas, and Francisco O. Ramirez. 1997. "World Society and the Nation-State." *American Journal of Sociology* 103, no. 1: 144–81.
Moss, Todd, Gunilla Pattersson, and Nicolas van de Walle. 2006. "An Aid-Institutions Paradox? A Review Essay on Aid Dependency and State Building in Sub-Saharan Africa." Working Paper 74. Washington: Center for Global Development.
O'Donnell, Guillermo A., and Philippe C. Schmitter. 1986. *Transitions from Authoritarian Rule: Tentative Conclusions about Uncertain Democracies.* Johns Hopkins University Press.
OECD (Organization for Economic Cooperation and Development). 2002. "Best Practices for Budget Transparency." Paris.
OECD, Development Assistance Committee. 2009. "Better Aid: Managing Aid Practices of DAC Member Countries." Paris.
Petrie, M. 2003. "Promoting Fiscal Transparency: The Complementary Roles of the IMF, Financial Markets, and Civil Society." IMF Working Paper WP/03/199. Washington: International Monetary Fund.
Rajkumar, A. S., and V. Swaroop. 2008. "Public Spending and Outcomes: Does Governance Matter?" *Journal of Development Economics* 86, no. 1: 96–111.
Reinikka, R., and J. Svensson. 2004. "The Power of Information: Evidence from a Newspaper Campaign to Reduce Capture." Policy Research Working Paper 3239. Washington: World Bank.
Robinson, Mark. 2008. *Budgeting for the Poor.* New York: Palgrave Macmillan.
Rosendorff, B. P., and J. R. Vreeland. 2006. "Democracy and Data Dissemination: The Effect of Political Regime on Transparency." Unpublished manuscript.
Ross, M. 1999. "The Political Economy of the Resource Curse." *World Politics* 51 (January): 297–322.

————. 2011. "Mineral Wealth and Budget Transparency." IBP Working Paper 2. Washington: International Budget Partnership.

Santos, Boaventura de Sousa. 1998. "Participatory Budgeting in Porto Alegre: Toward a Redistributive Democracy." *Politics and Society* 26, no. 4: 461–510.

Stevens, P., and E. Dietsche. 2008. "Resource Curse: An Analysis of Causes, Experiences, and Possible Ways Forward." *Energy Policy* 36, no. 1: 56–65.

Triesman, Daniel. 2000. "The Causes of Corruption: A Cross-National Study." *Journal of Public Economics* 76, no. 3 (June): 399–457.

Wampler, Brian, and Leonardo Avritzer. 2004. "Participatory Publics: Civil Society and New Institutions in Democratic Brazil." *Comparative Politics* 36, no. 3 (April): 291–312.

Wehner, J., and P. de Renzio. 2013. "Citizens, Legislators, and Executive Disclosure: The Political Determinants of Fiscal Transparency." *World Development* 41 (January): 96–108.

You, Jong-Song, and Sanjeev Khagram. 2005. "A Comparative Study of Inequality and Corruption." *American Sociological Review* 70, no. 1: 136–57.

Zoellick, Robert B. 2011. "The Middle East and North Africa: A New Social Contract for Development." Remarks delivered at the Peter G. Peterson Institute for International Economics, Washington, April 16. www.piie.com/publications/papers/paper.cfm?ResearchID=1802.

2

What We Know Can't Hurt Them: Origins, Sources of Sustenance, and Survival Prospects of Budget Transparency in South Africa

STEVEN FRIEDMAN

A sustained and high level of budget transparency flowing not from a gov-ernment's vulnerability to public pressure but from its insulation from it seems counterintuitive. This, however, may provide an accurate picture for the country rated by the International Budget Partnership (IBP) as the most trans-parent in the world—South Africa.

This chapter discusses the sources of budget transparency in South Africa, arguing that transparency has been introduced and sustained not because of the presence of overt public pressure on government officials, but because of its absence. It suggests that, while the government never faced direct pressure to pro-vide budget information and a transparent budget process, the fact that it did so and that openness has not faced any significant counterpressure is a result of an unusual context in which the balance of forces in the economy and society created an environment conducive to transparency. It also suggests that the very factors that ensure high levels of transparency also ensure that transparency has little role in empowering the citizenry and is far more useful to government than to citizens.

The State of Budget Transparency in South Africa

According to IBP's 2010 Open Budget Index (OBI), South Africa's level of budget transparency is the highest of all the countries surveyed, with a score of ninety-two out of 100.[1] South Africa publishes all eight of the key budget documents required by the survey—and for seven of the eight it received an A for level of information, indicating that "extensive" information is available. Its audit report is the only exception; it received a B score, indicating that "'significant" information is available. However, the survey also found that the executive's budget proposal lacks information on quasi-fiscal activities, tax expenditures, and financial and other assets. It added, "Despite laudable efforts to improve monitoring and evaluation systems, the budget proposal still lacks information on outputs and outcomes."[2] Despite these reservations, the survey reached a strongly favorable conclusion on the degree of budget transparency in South Africa.

Nonetheless, the IBP measure may significantly overstate the degree of effective transparency. It assesses only the performance of national government; provincial and local governments are not nearly as transparent, even in the formal sense.[3] An IBP study on parastatals in South Africa, which has not yet been published, found weaknesses in transparency in the use of public funds.[4] And at the national level, while South Africa's Auditor General's office meets all the formal standards of independence and transparency, it is repeatedly forced to issue qualified audits for some government departments that have supplied insufficient accurate information.[5] Although this confirms the autonomy of the auditing institution, it shows that information on how government departments spend their money is not always available. Thus an unpublished research report by Neil Overy for the IBP notes, "South Africa's budget documents provide very little detailed information about what happens to . . . money once [it is] transferred out of the national fiscus. . . . The documents released by the relevant parastatals do even less to fill this void in South Africa's budget transparency picture."[6] A government official eager to defend the transparency regime asserted, "Our budget at national level is far more transparent, user friendly, clear, accurate, and honest than the United Kingdom's"—a significant statement given that the standards of the former colonial power are often cited in South African debates as those against which achievement should be measured. He added, "The estimates of national

1. IBP (2010).

2. See the summary for South Africa in IBP (2010).

3. As only one of many examples, in 2008 the Public Service Accountability Monitor was obliged to use legal action to force the Eastern Cape government to release a report assessing citizens' assessment of its performance. See judgment in *Public Service Accountability Monitor and N Mkhize* v. *Director-General, Office of the Premier, Eastern Cape Provincial Government and Premier, Eastern Cape Provincial Government*, High Court of South Africa, Eastern Cape Division, Case no. 6047/07, May 29, 2008 (www.saflii.org/za/cases/ZAECHC/2008/70.rtf).

4. Personal communication to author by IBP, October 17, 2010.

5. See, for example, Parliamentary Monitoring Group (2010).

6. Cited in Dlamini and Wildeman (2010).

expenditure is an outstanding document by international standards, and I do think that we deserve a fairly high score by international standards." But he noted, too, "Australia and Canada are not in the list of countries surveyed by the IBP. If they were included, I am sure that they would come out on top."[7]

More generally, government procurement processes are not particularly transparent. Individual departments have their own systems, and these are not readily accessible to the public. In one view, this is a license for misuse of public funding because decentralized procurement systems need a great deal of transparency if they are to be subject to effective public control.[8] Generally, critics suggest that transparency is often honored in form rather than substance and that the IBP criteria may flatter a country such as South Africa because they tend to favor an Anglo-Saxon parliamentary model rather than the processes followed in Francophone countries.[9]

Some analysts also point out that budget transparency in South Africa means that government is willing to supply information about its finances, but not that citizens have a strongly protected right to demand information from government.[10] While legislation does allow citizens to file requests for government information, there is no guaranteed right to budget information,[11] and transparency rests purely on the government's willingness to disseminate information. Despite legislation enforcing citizens' right to access information from government, South Africa is not a particularly strong performer in respecting the right of citizens to ask government what it is doing. A 2006 study of access to information in fourteen countries found that 62 percent of requests for information to government agencies met with "mute refusal" to respond, the third worst performance among the countries researched.[12] It also found, "Only 19 percent of the requests submitted yielded a compliant outcome and only 13 percent yielded information. . . . This is by far the lowest score of the seven monitored countries with freedom of information laws."[13]

This does not mean that budget transparency in South Africa is a mirage. While one interviewee said that the data are so comprehensive that it is possible to establish whether money has been spent on a particular school, others in the field challenge this view.[14] South Africa achieved its high rating from the IBP

7. Communication, Treasury official, January 27, 2011.

8. Interview, Alta Folscher, consultant and former activist, Cape Town, November 25, 2010.

9. Interview, Folscher.

10. Interview, Folscher.

11. Interview, Albert van Zyl, International Budget Project, Cape Town, November 25, 2010.

12. Open Society Justice Initiative (2006, p. 43).

13. Open Society Justice Initiative (2006, p. 69).

14. Interview, van Zyl; interview, Folscher.

because the Treasury does indeed publish a wide range of data that enable researchers, journalists, or active citizens to learn a great deal about how public money is allocated and spent. In 1998 the Treasury introduced the medium-term expenditure framework (MTEF), which "indicates(s) the size of the financial resources needed during the medium term (three to five years) in order to carry out existing policy commitments."[15] In 1999 Parliament enacted the Public Finance Management Act, which contains a detailed set of procedures compelling government officials to provide financial information and to account for their actions.[16] The law applies to the nine provinces as well as to national government.[17] Recognizing that transparency has been far more evident at the national than the subnational level and seeking to ensure that local government complies with the same norms, Parliament enacted the Municipal Finance Management Act in 2003.[18] For the past few years, the National Treasury has initiated a program to ensure that local government is as transparent as its provincial and national equivalents.[19] This entails measures requiring local governments to make information available to citizens: section 75 of the Municipal Finance Management Act requires each municipality to publish specified key information on its website. The National Treasury and provincial treasuries have also created processes aiming to improve the quality and accuracy of municipal financial information.[20] The Municipal Finance Management Act makes it an offense (with a five-year prison sentence) for a municipal official deliberately or negligently to provide incorrect or misleading information in any document that must be made public. The Treasury cites this as one indication of the government's seriousness in enforcing transparency in local government.[21]

Despite the qualifications offered here, then, the national government clearly has made a significant commitment to budget transparency that has proved remarkably robust despite an inhospitable political environment. First, since 1994, when the country became a democracy, the ruling African National Congress (ANC) has not faced any serious challenge to its control of national government and is now firmly in control of all but one province. Voter support largely shields it from pressures for greater accountability. Second, while the adop-

15. Idasa (n.d., p. 1).

16. Public Finance Management Act no. 1 of 1999; See also, for example, Department of Health (2002).

17. Public Finance Management Act, ch. 3.

18. Municipal Finance Management Act 56 of 2003 (www.info.gov.za/acts/2003/a56-03/index.html).

19. Telephone interview, Conrad Barberton, National Treasury, November 28, 2010.

20. Interview, Barberton. Communication, National Treasury, March 9, 2011.

21. Communication, National Treasury. See section 171(1)(d) of the Municipal Finance Management Act.

tion of measures enabling transparency was certainly the product of a particular set of political circumstances, it was not the result of pressure by interest groups, and so public pressure is not what is keeping the regime in place.[22] Third, perhaps the most important challenge to South African democracy is the pervasive role of money in politics.[23] Part of the problem is that key politicians and officials exert substantial pressure in the hopes of gaining access to public funds. Important political and government actors have a strong interest in ensuring that the transparency of public finances is kept to a minimum.

Budget transparency in South Africa has, therefore, been almost exclusively a national government project. To the extent that there has been pressure from civil society, it has been muted and indirect. Many of the people who are currently engaged in researching or supporting budget transparency (including the current director of the IBP) cut their teeth in the Budget Information Service of the Institute for Democracy in South Africa (Idasa), the country's largest nongovernmental organization (NGO) promoting democracy. But Idasa's purpose was not to press for budget transparency; it aimed to monitor the budget and the extent to which it catered to the poor. While this gave it an indirect interest in transparency—it could not monitor spending if it was denied the information it needed to do that—it did not initiate the push for openness. While it did assist the National Treasury in drafting measures ensuring greater transparency, this role was limited and did not entail nudging the government in a new direction. Idasa simply "helped the Treasury do what it wanted to do."[24]

Why, then, was government interested in budget transparency at all? While theories vary, transparency is clearly a product of the advent of democracy in 1994. Interest in transparency was evident in the National Treasury even during the last years of apartheid: reformist officials in the apartheid state were said to have been interested in introducing an MTEF in the mid-1980s.[25] However, there is general agreement that budget transparency has been a project of the post-1994 National Treasury. There are two explanations for why officials favored transparency. The first is the reformist zeal of the first generation of officials serving a new democracy. In this view, the officials in the post-1994 Treasury were veterans of or sympathizers with the fight against apartheid and eager to democratize government. This was not unique to the Treasury: in the first few years of democracy, all government departments were staffed by officials who had fought apartheid and hoped that working in government could change the world. What

22. Interview, van Zyl; interview, Folscher; telephone interview, Barberton.
23. Butler (2010b).
24. Interview, van Zyl.
25. Interview, van Zyl.

is unusual is that many of those officials remain in the Treasury today (while in many other departments they have moved on).[26] Transparency, it is argued, is a product of their democratic reformism.

The second explanation locates the beginnings of the transparency regime in a potential fiscal crisis toward the end of 1996. While the Treasury was able to control national finances, the provinces created by the new constitution were a far greater challenge. An analysis of the dynamics of the period suggests that regional elites left over from the apartheid era used the provinces to continue the patronage politics of apartheid's "homeland" system, while new regional elites lacked the expertise and sometimes the will to control provincial finances. For its part, the National Treasury stresses, first, that establishing provinces meant devolving functions and budgets and establishing financial management systems. Second, provinces were responsible for paying social grants, and there was great uncertainty about how to budget for this function. Consequently, in 1996–97 some provinces overspent their budgets massively.[27] Provincial budgets were "out of control,"[28] and "the only people who knew their true financial situation was their bank manager."[29] The Treasury felt that it did not have an appropriate system for monitoring spending patterns. Establishing clear budget formats and in-year financial reporting (which enhanced transparency) became crucial tools in its attempt to impose discipline on the provinces.[30] In effect, the Treasury could not manage provincial spending if it lacked the information that would enable it to determine the size of the problem. And requiring provinces to disclose spending made it possible to win political support for fiscal discipline: "The Treasury depended on transparency to win the debate on fiscal prudence: it is not something which enjoys much political support, and transparency made it possible to win the argument despite that."[31] Armed with the information it needed, an independent student of the process believes that the Treasury used the Budget Council, a committee of the national finance minister and the nine provincial ministers, "to manage provincial treasuries from afar."[32] The Treasury rejects this interpretation, insisting that, once the necessary budget and reporting processes were established, it worked with provincial treasuries to achieve common goals: ensuring more accurate budget projections and better management of spending. This, it says, largely resolved provincial overspending problems.[33] While the Trea-

26. Interview, Barberton.
27. Communication, National Treasury.
28. Interview, van Zyl.
29. Interview, Barberton.
30. Communication, National Treasury.
31. Interview, Barberton.
32. Interview, van Zyl.
33. Communication, National Treasury.

sury's view and independent analysis may differ in their understanding of the national-provincial dynamic, both agree that problems in provincial fiscal management were a significant spur to greater transparency.

There is no need to choose between reformist zeal and a desire to improve provincial budgeting as motives for greater transparency. Both explanations may capture aspects of the dynamic that produced measures enforcing transparency. They may have combined to ensure that reformist officials could pursue their program with the necessary political support. The measures to control government spending were a key feature of the project of the minister of finance, Trevor Manuel, whose considerable political influence helped to support the transparency regime. Indeed, one interviewee associates the beginning of attempts to introduce transparency to Manuel's appointment and insists that the role of a "strong minister" was crucial in establishing and sustaining it.[34] In any case, budget transparency clearly has been the result not of a hard-fought campaign by organized citizens, but of a deliberate strategy by government politicians and officials. This, of course, makes the question of why it has survived the pressures discussed earlier all the more interesting.

Sources of Transparency and Participation

Before developing the main argument of this chapter, it is necessary to point out that segments of the citizenry may play a greater role in sustaining the transparency regime than the preceding analysis suggests, but that they have exerted this influence indirectly. South African democracy was established in an unusual set of circumstances. A majority government that took office in 1994 inherited a country unlike any other on the continent: it boasted an economy that, while highly unequal, included a private sector that was far larger and more diversified than any other in Africa. In virtually all other African countries, majority governments inherited economies with few formal privately owned businesses, and so business activity depended on links with government. In South Africa, business owed its growth to links with the previous system or, in many cases, with the international economy.[35] Business leadership was, in 1994, almost exclusively white, and, despite a decade and a half of government policies designed to enhance black ownership of formal businesses, whites continue to dominate both asset ownership and executive posts.[36]

The economy that the National Treasury sought to manage was, therefore, one in which powerful market actors had an interest in obtaining accurate information

34. Interview, Folscher.
35. Mbeki (2009).
36. Doneva (2010) and Dlanga (2010).

about public finances. Because these actors were either wary of or hostile to the post-1994 political elite, an absence of information would have been more likely to persuade them to think worse of government than to give it the benefit of the doubt. The influence of racial attitudes on economic actors is illustrated by the fact that the appointment of the first black minister of finance in the country's history, Manuel, in February 1996, precipitated a currency crisis.[37] He was later to become an almost iconic figure among domestic white business, but the initial response made it clear that most market actors had no confidence in a black-run Finance Ministry. In this context, budget transparency was a crucial means of winning over the business support that was crucial to the new democracy's operation. While this may not have been a conscious motive—and no source of information suggests that officials were influenced directly by this reality—transparency may well have been a more viable option for both officials and politicians in a context in which winning and retaining the cooperation of white business people (abroad as well as at home) was a priority. Transparency may have played a role in securing favorable investment grades and in reassuring international business, which derived much of its information on South Africa from local white business, that the economy remained viable despite majority rule.

Of course, we do not know how formal business would have reacted had it been prevented from knowing how public money was being spent. But the dynamics of governance in post-1994 South Africa suggests that, if the government had officially refused to share information, the business sector would have complained loudly; after all, affluent citizens concerned about crime frequently denounce the government's decision to limit the release of crime statistics.[38] It seems likely that the government's desire to retain the cooperation of business would have prompted a greater readiness to release budget information than it has shown when pressed to release crime statistics.

To explain the reasons why the transparency regime has persevered, it is useful to divide the post-1994 political order into two periods, pre- and post-2008. The divide is crude but serves our explanatory purpose. From 1994 until September 2008, government was under either de facto or de jure control of Thabo Mbeki, who became first deputy president under Nelson Mandela in 1994 and president in 1999. During his presidency, Mandela was preoccupied with the need to ensure a smooth transition between his presidency and Mbeki's, and so the latter became the de facto head of government very early in the post-1994 order and remained so for fourteen years.

---

37. Handley (2002, pp. 9–10).
38. Parker (2009).

The Mbeki period was singularly conducive to the Treasury officials' experiment in budget transparency. It was marked by very weak accountability within the ruling party: no ANC president had contested an internal election for fifty years, and it was assumed that leadership of the ruling party insulated the incumbent from removal. The perception that political leadership was immune from pressures that might force it to accommodate politicians and interest groups was enhanced by the ANC's large electoral majority, which seemed to guarantee its right to govern for decades. Mbeki was therefore assumed to enjoy enough leeway to impose his stamp on the movement, which he did: power within the ANC was centralized, and those who challenged Mbeki usually found themselves relegated to the fringes. His approach to government was preoccupied with a concern to demonstrate that a black administration was as good at doing what white opinion was assumed to value as whites were assumed to be.[39] This entailed a stress on technical and managerial governance and in particular on state-of-the-art techniques of governing, which were assumed to demonstrate the modernity and sophistication of the majority government. It also meant a particularly high degree of sensitivity to white business; although the relationship between it and government was often acrimonious, there was little doubt that government took business's opinion very seriously indeed. Ironically, one consequence of majority rule was a government elected in the main by poor black people that was obsessed with demonstrating its competence to the advantaged minority.

It should take no great leap of the imagination to see how a form of budget transparency that relied on the goodwill of government rather than citizen activism thrived in this environment. First, it was clearly a "cutting-edge" public management technique that demonstrated the sophistication and modernity of the administration. Second, it promised to enhance the administration's credibility among business and professional groups, internationally as well as at home. Third, it was primarily useful to elite groups that the administration took seriously rather than to the grassroots citizens who voted for it. It offered substantial benefits with few if any costs by providing a resource to those whose approbation the government valued, without empowering significantly those who might have turned transparency into a hindrance or threat. Fourth and finally, it faced no substantial political threat. Budget transparency was not a particularly potent weapon in the hands of the ANC's opponents because its guaranteed base of support ensured that its share of the vote would not be threatened by opposition politicians quoting budget numbers. Transparency therefore offered the ANC leadership substantial advantages and few disadvantages; as long as Mbeki and his

39. Friedman (2010b).

allies remained in charge, there was no reason why the reforms should face sub-stantial challenge.

The lack of a challenge was enhanced by some key features of South African politics and society. Post-apartheid civil society has been energetic, vocal, and engaged, but it has also been shallow, in the sense that the majority of citizens lack the resources to participate in the interest group associations that engage with government. By far the largest and most organized civil society organization (CSO), the Congress of South African Trade Unions (Cosatu), is a formal ally of the ANC: although it often challenges its ally, it obviously does this within the limits imposed by its concern to maintain the ANC in office. Cosatu is by far the most representative CSO, but it does not represent the millions of poor people who cannot secure work in the formal economy. Civil society, the most likely user of budget transparency, may therefore have been an irritant to the govern-ment at times, but hardly a threat. This significantly reduced the costs of main-taining transparency since it meant that budget information was unlikely to pro-vide weapons to citizens who could make life uncomfortable for the political leadership. In essence, no individuals were going to lose their job or their hold over power because of budget transparency, and so the pressures it faced were weak if they existed at all.

All this changed, at least potentially, in 2007, when Mbeki was defeated in his attempt to win a third term as ANC president, and then in September 2008, when his party asked him to resign as state president because he no longer enjoyed its confidence. The change introduced a degree of accountability within the ANC that had been absent. Leaders were now aware that they could be voted out of office by movement activists, and they became far more concerned about the opinions of active ANC members. But, because the ANC remains electorally dominant, this was not accompanied by an equivalent pressure toward account-ability to the citizenry.[40] In effect, then, the context moved from one unusually favorable to budget transparency to one particularly unfavorable—from one in which government was largely insulated from the pressures of politicians who had found transparency bothersome to one in which those pressures now had to be taken seriously, but in which the large ANC majority meant that nothing much seemed to need doing to reassure the citizenry. The threat was exacerbated by the reality that the opening up of ANC politics following Mbeki's removal not only unleashed pressures for accountability, but also gave enhanced leeway to politicians and officials who saw political power as a conduit to personal wealth and wealth as a conduit to more power, which could be achieved by dispensing

40. Friedman (2009).

patronage.[41] Transparency was clearly a potential problem for these increasingly influential actors, and their relative ascendancy could have been expected to place new pressure on the transparency regime.

These events have had some impact on the transparency regime despite South Africa's high IBP score in 2010: "There has been some going backwards over the last two years. Two years ago it was possible to find out what government was transferring to Eskom [the national electricity utility]; today it is not."[42] One commentator, expressing concern about the implication of government transfers to the electricity utility, argued that the budgeting system that has held sway under the transparency regime has been marked by "three virtues": public finances have been negotiated through a medium-term framework, budgets have been informed by prior decisions about government priorities, and Treasury representatives "have followed spending proposals from their initiation in departments . . . through to the full cabinet." These measures have "introduced a culture of justification into conflicts over scarce resources," one in which politicians and officials have been forced to justify their demands for resources. He argued that this was now under threat from a government approach that excludes the finance minister and his officials from some government committees, thus allowing some politicians and officials "space to generate expenditure ideas that serve personal rather than governmental objectives." Allocations to Eskom were cited as an example of a tendency to place the real or perceived needs of government officials or agencies ahead of transparency and predictability.[43] This, he argued, is no isolated trend. The parastatal sector, "where public borrowing now virtually equals that of the government itself," is increasingly seen as a realm in which the transparency practiced by the Treasury is ignored.[44] The size of the sector makes this a significant threat to the transparency regime.

Two points are worth stressing about this analysis. The first is that it understands the transparency regime as a vehicle not for citizen empowerment but for effective maintenance of fiscal discipline: while the ultimate beneficiaries are assumed to be the citizenry, citizens are not seen as agents of transparency nor is transparency seen as a way of enhancing their agency. The notion that transparency's purpose is not to enable citizens to get their government to do what they want but to enable Treasury officials to watch over profligate actors denies transparency's utility as an instrument of democratic accountability and citizen agency and thus makes it not a key instrument of democracy but a mere tool of public

41. Butler (2010b).
42. Interview, van Zyl.
43. Butler (2010a).
44. Butler (2011).

management. While this may be normatively disturbing to democrats (including this one), it is an accurate account of transparency's rationale in South Africa and of its concrete impact on government behavior. The second is that transparency is significantly vulnerable to changes in elite politics within the ruling party and consequent changes in government style: the chief reason for the shift is said to be that the current president, Jacob Zuma, has "brought into national government the habits of mind of a provincial baron."[45] It was, of course, the profligacy of those barons that, in 1996, provided an important impetus toward transparency. Logically, we would expect a transparency system built on the need to refine public management technique rather than respond to the demand of citizens' groups for greater accountability to crumble as soon as the wind blows in a new direction.

But, while the trends discussed here are real and may well become more explicitly so in the future, subjecting transparency to intolerable pressure, perhaps the most interesting feature of the past few years is how robust it has proved to be in the face of these pressures. The chief reason is that the trend toward a politics of patronage has been strongly contested within the ruling ANC. The reasons for this are complex, but for our purposes it is sufficient to stress that there are significant pressures against patronage politics in the ANC[46] and that this is a strong force for continued transparency. It is also worth noting that, while the change in government leadership also prompted a change in finance minister, this has not altered the Treasury's public commitment to the transparency regime. On the contrary, the current minister, Pravin Gordhan, made a point, in his late 2010 medium-term budget review, of mentioning that South Africa had topped the OBI survey.[47] According to government insiders, this was a deliberate intervention designed to shore up political support for transparency among political leaders.[48] This suggests that transparency was not simply the preference of a particular politician, Manuel, but a strategic imperative of the Treasury. Gordhan's chief role since he became minister in 2009 has been to maintain fiscal discipline in the face of pressures from politicians seeking to use public funds to dispense patronage, and the transparency regime is clearly an important weapon in his arsenal. Although, as the evidence presented here shows, he has not always succeeded, the fact that he is a former South African communist party activist and is politically close to the president ensures that he is better able to maintain both discipline and transparency than the unfavorable context might suggest. Indeed, to some extent, the transparency regime has, despite the trends discussed here, been extended into new areas of government over the past two years, as the attempt to apply it

45. Butler (2010a).
46. See, for example, Molele (2010).
47. Gordhan (2010).
48. Discussion with government officials, December 2010.

to local government has gained momentum.[49] One reason why it has endured may be the manner in which modes of acting become institutionalized within the public service—sometimes in a very short time: "Traditions emerge fairly quickly."[50]

Whether the formal transparency regime will survive in the future remains unclear. Perhaps it will remain, but will apply to a diminishing portion of public revenues. This would happen if a growing parastatal sector, marked increasingly by lack of transparency, became the playground of those within government eager to avoid transparency without being seen to do so. Yet it is hard to imagine the transparency regime surviving if the patronage politicians defeat their opponents or succeed in dominating decisionmaking. And, while their current opponents might champion openness, there is no guarantee that they would continue to do so if they emerged as dominant, particularly since some current opponents of patronage politics have faced unwelcome attention to their own lifestyles and spending patterns.[51] Continued divisions ensure that some officeholders will always have a reason to expose others to public scrutiny and thus maintain an interest in transparency.

A reason for maintaining the transparency regime, however, may be that it continues to be far less of a threat to politicians who wish to avoid public scrutiny than it may seem. The transparency regime has not ensured an empowered citizenry willing and able to use it to hold government to account, and so the costs to patronage politicians of maintaining it have been far lower than conventional wisdom might assume. This does not mean that transparency has had no impact at all. Despite the points made here, it has had an effect on the relationship between government and citizens, even if it has not yet become a major constraint on unaccountable officials and politicians. This chapter now turns to the nuanced impact of transparency on citizen and government action.

Transparency and Its Impact

Perhaps the most revealing evidence of the transparency regime's lack of impact on governance in general, and on management of the economy in particular, is that, far from feeling besieged by citizens' groups using transparency to make the

49. Interview, Barberton.
50. Interview, Barberton.
51. An obvious example is the minister of higher education and general secretary of the South African communist party, Blade Nzimande, who has been the subject of press reports on his lifestyle and who has seemed to sympathize with controls on the media as a consequence. "Red Card for Blade's Stay at the Mount Nelson," *IOL News*, July 17, 2010 (www.iol.co.za/news/politics/red-card-for-blade-s-stay-at-the-mount-nelson-1.490106); "Nzimande: SA Media Is Threat to Democracy," *Mail and Guardian*, August 2,

government's life difficult, Treasury officials complain that they are disappointed with the limited impact it has had on the national debate.

Parliament is a key user of budget information; indeed it and the media are the two immediate targets of the information in the hope that both will ensure a better-informed public.[52] This obviously has had some impact on the national debate and on public perceptions, since parliamentary business is reported on in the media and interest in politics in the society is high.[53] Parliament does use budget information. It is used by members, who ask questions of ministers, and by the Select Committee on Public Accounts, which monitors government finances.[54] But there are distinct limits to the role that Parliament can play. Almost two-thirds of the members represent the ANC and therefore have an obvious incentive not to ask the government too many embarrassing questions. Internal strife within the ANC saw a significant increase in willingness by its members of Parliament (MPs) to hold ministers to account from 2007 onward, but there are signs that this may be curtailed by the ANC leadership—chairs of parliamentary committees who had been active in holding ANC ministers to account were replaced in late 2010 by presumably more compliant chairs. Even during the high point of active oversight, budget information played a very limited role in the efforts of ANC MPs. The opposition has tended to be more active in using the information, but this has had far less impact than conventional constitutional theory might suggest. Obviously, parliaments can use budget information to hold governments to account only when a set of political circumstances exist that make this feasible, and in South Africa such circumstances are still largely absent.

A senior Treasury official, when told about this project, said that trying to understand the impact of budget transparency is a useful intervention because transparency has not fostered a better-informed national debate. He singled out the media for complaint: despite the availability of copious data, media coverage is, in his view, often ill informed, and this clearly has been a source of deep frustration to the Treasury.[55] One of his colleagues endorsed this view, noting that the "biggest disappointment" of the transparency regime is that it has not led to an informed public debate and better media coverage of the budget: "Ordinary people have responded better to transparency than the media."[56] The national media

2010 (www.mg.co.za/article/2010-08-02-nzimande-sa-media-is-threat-to-democracy). While the minister did later support freedom of the media, there is no guarantee that he would continue to do so if divisions in the ANC ceased.

52. Interview, Barberton.

53. For one piece of evidence that, despite a lack of formal education, grassroots citizens do use the media to inform themselves, see Charney (1995).

54. Interview, van Zyl.

55. Telephone discussion, senior Treasury official, November 2010.

56. Interview, Barberton.

do give saturation coverage to the annual budget speech by the finance minister, but the coverage is largely superficial: most reporters restrict themselves to the speech itself and to the reaction of political parties and CSOs; few delve into the reams of printed information released with the speech in order to dig out trends.

Of course, the failure of the media to use the information appropriately may say more about the state of journalism in South Africa than about transparency. This raises an obvious question: has the Treasury been energetic enough in disseminating information? Its preoccupation with the media could be read as an implicit acknowledgment that newspapers, radio, and television have been saddled with the task of conveying government financial information to the public. This renders transparency hostage to the competence of journalists, besides, of course, excluding those citizens who do not get their information from the media. It could be argued, then, that transparency has not changed the way in which citizens respond to government because the authorities have not adopted an energetic dissemination strategy.

A Treasury official acknowledged that there is scope to improve how budget and expenditure information is disseminated. Thus far dissemination has occurred largely on the National Treasury website and in printed form. This, he said, is a result not of lack of will but of capacity constraints: "We are stretched and are not able to move beyond our present functions." But he was skeptical that a more energetic campaign would produce a different result, noting that attempts to reach the middle class have had little impact. Currently, the National Treasury produces a people's guide to the budget in five of the country's eleven official languages as well as booklets summarizing the budget tax proposals.[57] For a time, the budget review and estimates of national expenditures were made available through a prominent chain of suburban bookstores, but with little uptake—the practice of making them available at bookshops was discontinued because of lack of public interest.[58] The reason, the Treasury official suggested, is that citizens do not see how budget information affects them. While everyone pays tax—value added tax is levied on the purchase of goods and services—only some 5 million out of more than 20 million adults pay income tax and so directly experience paying taxes. Most citizens, in this view, therefore do not see budget issues as a source of immediate concern: there is a "lack of familiarity with the subject matter."[59]

This does not mean that budget information simply nestles on a website or that its only impact is its contribution to the government's international reputation. It does have an impact on domestic economics and politics. On the first score, the budget information is used by business—by organized business to lobby but also by

57. Communication, National Treasury.
58. Interview, Barberton.
59. Interview, Barberton.

financial analysts and by, for example, civil engineering firms that are directly affected by government spending patterns and use the information to assess risk.[60] This presumably means that economic decisions are made on the strength of more accurate information and that the market economy functions more effectively. In this guise, budget information does not ensure more active citizenship but does enable higher levels of economic efficiency.

It also has some impact on the way in which citizenship is exercised. Cosatu uses the data to inform the national debate and is often strongly critical of the government's approach. Activists who have compiled alternative budgets designed to highlight the circumstances of the poor or vulnerable social groups—the people's budget or the women's or the children's budget exercises that have been launched by NGOs at times with Cosatu's support—have also relied on the information that transparency makes available.[61] A far more direct link to concrete change is the use of budget information by researchers who assist CSOs in bringing court actions against the government seeking social and economic rights. For example, budget information was used in a celebrated case that secured the distribution of anti-retroviral treatment in public hospitals to prevent mother-to-child transmission of HIV (human immunodeficiency virus) and AIDS (acquired immune deficiency syndrome) and in cases in the Eastern Cape Province dealing with school maintenance.[62] The fact that the data are available to researchers means that better-informed academic economic analysis is fed into the national debate.

Budget transparency also plays an important role in enabling a set of NGOs to secure greater government accountability. The most obvious example is Idasa, whose attempts to influence budget priorities played a role at the inception of the transparency regime. This work continues in the Economic Governance Programme, which remains a major voice in the national debate on budget processes and priorities.[63] Another significant voice, which relies heavily on information that is available because of the transparency regime, is the Public Service Accountability Monitor, which, although it is based in the Eastern Cape Province and tends to monitor government accountability and effectiveness in that province only, is often an important participant in national debates.[64] Both these organizations are largely influential among the elites who participate in the national debate and therefore are more likely to influence policy actors than grassroots citizens. But another NGO, the Centre for Economic Governance and AIDS in

60. Interview, van Zyl; interview, Barberton.

61. Interview, van Zyl.

62. Interview, van Zyl.

63. For details of current programs, see www.idasa.org.za/our_work/programme/economic_governance _programme/.

64. For activities, see www.psam.org.za.

Africa, does use budget information to work with grassroots activists: its IBP-supported project promoting community monitoring of health spending is a partnership with the Treatment Action Campaign, whose efforts to win a comprehensive government response to HIV and AIDS is often seen as the most successful example of civil society activism in post-apartheid South Africa (and was responsible for bringing the court case seeking antiretrovirals in government hospitals noted above).[65] With this partial exception, NGOs do not mobilize grassroots citizens to hold government to account, but they are an important check on it at the elite level.

While Parliament's role is limited, it is not irrelevant. For example, where opposition MPs use information to alert media to weaknesses in government performance, the subsequent coverage may well strike a chord among most citizens, even if they do not support the opposition parties from whence the information came. So transparency does contribute to economic efficiency as well as to citizen activism and national dialogue, which are essential to enhanced government performance. The problem is that this impact is far less significant than advocates of budget transparency might hope.

Although the argument that this is a consequence of a lack of citizen familiarity with tax and budget issues may have some merit, it does not tell the whole story. Government income and expenditure are, in a way, an obsession in the mainstream South African debate. Affluent, largely white, business and professional people regale each other with a steady diet of tales of government waste and corruption, and this is reflected in media coverage and in the preoccupations of the official opposition.[66] As implied earlier, Cosatu, while officially an ANC ally, frequently weighs in with similar concerns,[67] and there is a growing sense among ANC voters too that politicians are more concerned with their own bank accounts and status than with the needs of citizens.[68] At the local level in particular, activism directed at municipal governments that are not seen to spend their money in the interests of citizens crosses racial and political barriers. Among some white suburbanites, it has been expressed through payment boycotts (and incessant grumbling among those who do pay); among black residents of low-income townships, it has been expressed in eight years of public demonstrations.[69] There is, therefore, no lack of interest in budgetary issues. What seems to be lacking is intervention that can translate the data into a form that citizens can understand and use.

---

65. See www.cegaa.org/projects.php. For a study of the Treatment Action Campaign, see Friedman and Mottiar (2005).

66. See, as just one of myriad examples, Ipoc (2010).

67. Fengu (2010).

68. Friedman (2010a).

69. See, for example, Harvey and Hollands (2010) and Parliamentary Monitoring Group (2009).

Despite the Treasury's perspective mentioned above, the authorities could do more if they really were serious about disseminating budget information. To name one important example, many local activists in townships and shack settlements might find the budget information very useful if they received it in a form they could understand. While the popular budget initiative does seek to address this, far more is needed to ensure that citizens can access the information. Besides ensuring that it reaches the areas where most people live, more thought may be needed about how to get budget information to people who do not use print media (including books). However, this task may well be more suited to social movements and CSOs than to Treasury officials. And the reason these organizations do not do more to ensure that citizens receive budget information in a form that can contribute to activism stems from the nature of interest group politics, which remains largely the preserve of the connected middle class and is still dominated by historical racial divides (despite the commonalities in concern about corruption). This ensures that politics is far more about sweeping statements expressing group identities (albeit often expressed in code) than about data-driven campaigns. The obvious implication is that the connection between budget transparency and citizen empowerment is hardly automatic. Information fuels activism for accountability only when the data are disseminated in an appropriate context for collective action. In South Africa, this activism has not yet emerged.

In the peculiar conditions of post-apartheid politics, in which the ANC remains electorally dominant but deeply riven by internal factionalism, budget transparency may have another, no doubt unintended, role—as a resource in battles between competing factions within the ruling party. Thus in 2010, for example, the Johannesburg branch of the ruling party drew up a seventy-page dossier detailing the purported governance failures of the mayor, Amos Masondo, in support of its demand that he step down and be replaced by another ANC mayor. A key feature of their attack was a detailed record "in particular (of) spending it disagreed with."[70] It is not clear whether the mayor's detractors used the municipal budget information available from the Treasury to draw up their case against him. What is clear is that they would not have been able to produce a litany of his allegedly flawed spending decisions if the information that the transparency regime requires had not been available. The impact on governance is open to debate. On the one hand, the mayor's critics were clearly more interested in removing him and replacing him with their candidate than in pressing for more accountable government. On the other, this is further evidence that divided political elites are extremely functional to transparency and the results it seeks to achieve, both because more information becomes available and because politi-

70. Shoba (2010).

cians are forced to be more accountable (and because it gives influential politicians a motive to allow transparency to continue). Since there is no sign that the tensions within the ANC are abating, there may well be other cases in which budget information is used against incumbent mayors and municipal representatives—not by their constituents or the opposition but by rivals in their own party.

Another key factor, however, is the access of citizens to organizations able to influence decisions. More affluent suburban residents are usually represented by ratepayer associations. Treasury receives a growing number of requests from these associations for information on municipal budgets—twenty to thirty letters a year[71]—and some have become authorities on municipal budgets, which they regularly use to fight campaigns. The information has, however, been largely available to affluent, largely white, suburban associations rather than to the poor, black, majority. This is the result not of official policy—on the contrary, the Treasury insists that it wants information to reach groups representing grassroots citizens, including those in rural areas[72]—but of highly unequal access to the means of organization that has persisted into the post-apartheid era. There are tentative signs that at least some black citizen groups operating in the townships where the poor live are beginning to learn that information on municipal budgets is available from the Treasury. Thus the Treasury has begun to receive requests for information from township groups,[73] but these requests are far too few to offer any sense of whether a trend is emerging.

At this stage, budget transparency at the local level mostly benefits businesses seeking opportunities, financial analysts concerned about solvency, and affluent ratepayer associations eager to ensure that they retain control over the suburban environment despite the advent of majority rule. At the national level, its use by trade unionists, some NGOs, and some MPs ensures that its impact is less restricted to economic elites but more limited on the polity. In the absence of the sort of politics that may give budget information more impact but also ensure that it is far more of a threat to public power holders, the transparency regime remains robust but ineffective, and its robustness may well be a direct consequence of the (relative) ineffectiveness.

Budget Transparency and Government Performance

A key point of agreement between the Treasury and its critics is that transparency has not improved the effectiveness with which government services are provided to citizens. The view among activists that transparency has not improved the value

71. Interview, Barberton.
72. Interview, Barberton.
73. Interview, Barberton.

that citizens receive for their taxes was cited earlier.[74] A researcher and activist said, "I don't know of any studies which show that transparency had led to more equitable government spending or better government service."[75] What is perhaps more interesting is the reported observation of a senior central bank official that government strategists had thought that the transparency regime would lead to better service, but that it did not.[76]

One of the reasons cited is a technical one: a 2006 study of government service provision "could not establish any links between budgets and strategic plans." In this view, the effect of the transparency regime on government departments and agencies was to induce formal compliance with "masses of paper" requiring information but not an understanding of the substance of what was required.[77] Thus a Treasury official insisted that the rationale of the transparency regime is to ensure better public service. Fiscal discipline is, in this view, an important means to an end. It safeguards the medium- to long-term ability of the government to continue delivering services because a bankrupt government cannot finance services. It is thus a minimum requirement for effective government. But improving the quality of government remains the goal of transparency.[78] Government critics argue, however, that the way in which it is implemented within government ensures that it does not have this effect. Top-down control by the Treasury may be effective in ensuring fiscal discipline, but not in delivering more accountable and responsive government. Information does not automatically make government work better when its workings are generally not conducive to adequate service, which is often the case in South Africa. Even if people have the necessary information, the needed response from government is often not available. Transparency in South Africa "does not translate into an effective state."[79]

It is, however, implausible to see the lack of connection between greater transparency and better government service as largely a problem of inadequate public management techniques. The rationale behind the transparency regime is that citizens apply the most effective pressure for better government service; to do so they require information so that they can hold government to account and force it to respond. This reasoning is impeccable. While governments always need technical and managerial skills if they are to provide the efficient services that citizens need, this is never enough because only citizen action can ensure that officials are concerned about what the public needs in the first place.[80] The prime rationale for

74. Dlamini and Wildeman (2010).
75. Interview, Folscher.
76. Interview, Folscher.
77. Interview, Folscher.
78. Interview, Barberton.
79. Interview, Folscher.
80. See, for example, Friedman, Hlela, and Thulare (2005, pp. 51–68).

budget transparency is not that it will produce better public sector management techniques, but that it will empower citizens to hold government to account and force it to respond. The transparency regime has, all parties acknowledge, not done this in South Africa to anything like the extent hoped—despite the fact that the Treasury insists that it wants transparency to produce a more informed and activist citizenry and that it works actively to achieve this goal.

Part of the problem, of course, may be a point made several times in this chapter: transparency cannot produce more accountable government if it is restricted to national-level budgetary information. Thus a government official sought to place budget transparency in a wider context: "The budget reform agenda was driven by a simple philosophy," he noted. "Let managers manage, but hold them accountable for performance by forcing them to report on what they do. In this way, the public, the media, Parliament, and society at-large can exert a positive influence over the running of public services and the allocation of resources. The public can become custodians of the public finances."[81] Clearly, more than a transparent national budget is needed to realize this vision.

Transparency has not yet had the same impact on local government. As with the provinces in the mid-1990s, the Treasury is using transparency as a management tool to improve the administration of public finances.[82] But, while the transparency regime has standardized the way in which municipalities report their finances, it has not and cannot ensure uniformity in the way they respond to pressure to manage those finances competently. The degree to which municipalities embrace transparency does not, as might be expected, depend on size and affluence: one of the country's major cities has responded "dysfunctionally," even while others have risen to the challenge.[83] Nor has it managed to nudge municipalities to better financial management. The government acknowledges that local financial management remains a major problem: "Local government was also bedeviled by a lack of adequate financial management skills due primarily to political appointments. Such appointees tended to have insufficient technical skills," a national government statement declared in 2009.[84]

The key question confronting the transparency regime at national and provincial levels is whether local government's present is its future—in other words, whether transparency will come in time to act as a bulwark against patronage politics. But the transparency regime on its own is unable to counter patronage politics. While adequate provincial financial management systems may be in place, the new political pressures are taking their toll: provincial budget deficits

81. Communication, government official, January 27, 2011.
82. Interview, Barberton.
83. Interview, Barberton.
84. Department of Cooperative Governance and Traditional Affairs (2009).

are now the largest they have been since 1996.[85] For that task—ensuring that money is spent in the interests of citizens rather than politicians and officials—a conducive set of political realities is required, and it is by no means clear that these exist. At present, the fight between those who seek to use public funds for private purposes and those who seek to prevent this rages on and will for some time. Without political actors and organized citizenry willing and able to use budget information to protect the integrity of public funds and the accountability of those who spend them to those on whose behalf they are meant to govern, transparency may be a useful tool for business people, researchers, and some activists, but not a guardian of government probity, let alone of services that meet the needs of citizens.

Conclusion

The peculiar features of the South African case hold important lessons for students of budget transparency who see it as an important means to active citizenship and accountable government willing and able to serve citizens appropriately.

On the one hand, it shows that budget transparency can take root in unlikely circumstances. Perhaps the only feature of the current South African polity that makes transparency a plausible option is the zealotry of public officials and the tacit relationship between government and business leaders who do not trust each other but know they must work together. And yet this has proved sufficient to sustain a transparency regime that, although not nearly as open as the OBI survey claims, remains far more open than that of many middle-income countries and certainly far more open than political realities might suggest. The regime has thus far proved robust even as political circumstances have seemed increasingly to threaten it.

On the other hand, the reason why the regime has taken root and proven more resilient than the context might suggest is equally instructive. Transparency has shown surprising resilience because it has not yet posed a serious threat to anyone in government, including those it should be expected to threaten most: the politicians and officials who see public funds as a source of personal wealth and power. Precisely because transparency has been largely a project of officials in the Treasury and, for a variety of reasons, has not fueled effective pressure for accountable spending, it has avoided the potential political storms. The clear implication, made at several points in this chapter, is that transparency on its own is not an automatic force for more accountable and responsive government. It needs politicians and citizens to understand its utility and to act on it, and it needs a con-

85. Interview, van Zyl.

ducive political environment. Just as the vote is no guarantee of power unless citizens use it to ensure that political power serves them,[86] so too is information power only if citizens and politicians are able to use it effectively to ensure that government is more accountable and responsive to them. This does not minimize the importance of transparency, but it does argue for an approach that is concerned not only with whether budgets are transparent, but also with the context in which they are transparent.

Understanding budget transparency as a resource for active citizenship without which it cannot achieve its purpose also suggests an approach that focuses not only on whether governments release budget information but on how, in what form, and to whom they do so. South Africa is not the only society in which it is possible to release information in ways that reach only the elite. Many other African societies may also be prone to this because their formal economies are relatively small and because so many grassroots economic activities—and those who engage in them—are beyond the reach of central banks and national treasuries.

These observations are not only intended for scholars and practitioners of budget transparency around the globe. They are also important pointers for the future direction of budget transparency in South Africa. If the transparency regime is to become a force for more accountable and effective government, it will need to reach far more citizens in a more usable form. This counsels paying attention not only to engaging in wider and more energetic dissemination, but also to conveying the information in ways that enable grassroots civic activists and social movements to use it. Much more debate and research is needed on how that could be done.

If this approach were adopted, budget transparency might well prompt far more pressure on government to perform more accountably and responsively. That would make the South African regime far more significant and effective, but also far more dangerous to those who would prefer that citizens not know how public money is used. When and if that happens, the proponents of transparency in the Treasury may well find that they need strong allies in the citizenry to protect transparency and the sort of governance it is meant to support. This argues for a strategic approach that begins actively building allies now, not when intense pressure makes it too late. If the Treasury wants to maintain the transparency regime and make it work for better government, it must move beyond providing information to a relatively small circle and engage much more actively with the society it serves.

Finally, civil society organizations concerned to ensure accountable and responsive government, particularly of a sort that includes the poor and weak, need

---

86. Friedman (2002).

to begin realizing the potential that budget transparency offers for citizen action and to begin acting on it now—not only to use transparency, but also to prepare to defend it if it begins to do its work in government and society.

References

Butler, Anthony. 2010a. "New Eskom Fiasco Is a Gamble with Public Funds." *Business Day,* November 19.

———. 2011. "Parastatals: 'Budgets for Dummies' the Way to Go." *Business Day,* March 18.

———, ed. 2010b. *Paying for Politics: Party Funding and Political Change in South Africa and the Global South.* Johannesburg: Jacana.

Charney, Craig. 1995. *Voices of a New Democracy: African Expectations in the New South Africa.* Johannesburg: Centre for Policy Studies.

Department of Cooperative Governance and Traditional Affairs. 2009. "Cooperative Governance to Develop Local Government Turnaround Strategy in October." Cape Town (www. sabinet-law.co.za/provincial-local-and-traditional-government/articles/cooperative-governance-develop-local-government).

Department of Health. 2002. *Financial Management: An Overview and Field Guide for District Management Teams, 2002.* Pretoria (www.doh.gov.za/docs/reports/2002/finance/section2.pdf).

Dlamini, Thembinkosi, and Russel Wildeman. 2010. "SA Is Torn between the Paths of Secrecy and Transparency." *Business Day,* October 27.

Dlanga, Khaya. 2010. "It's Still Too White at the Top." *Mail and Guardian,* December 23 (www.mg.co.za/article/2010-12-23-its-still-too-white-at-the-top).

Doneva, Svetlana. 2010. "JSE Still off Black Ownership Target." *Fin24,* September 1 (http://www.fin24.com/Companies/JSE-far-off-black-ownership-target-20100901).

Fengu, Msindisi. 2010. "SA: Vavi in Scathing Attack on ANC." Woodstock: Ipoc, May 17 (www.ipocafrica.org/index.php?option=com_content&view=article&id=489:sa-vavi-in-scathing-attack-on-anc&catid=85:conflicts-of-interest-news&Itemid=99).

Friedman, Steven. 2002. "Equity in the Age of Informality: Labour Markets and Redistributive Politics in South Africa." *Transformation* 57, no. 5: 31–55.

———. 2009. "An Accidental Advance? South Africa's 2009 Elections." *Journal of Democracy* 20, no. 4 (October): 108–22.

———. 2010a. "Get Grassroots into Fight against Corruption." *Business Day,* November 17.

———. 2010b. "Seeing Ourselves as Others See Us: Racism, Technique, and the Mbeki Administration." In *Mbeki and After: Reflections on the Legacy of Thabo Mbeki,* edited by Daryl Glaser. Johannesburg: Wits University Press.

Friedman, Steven, Kenny Hlela, and Paul Thulare. 2005. "A Question of Voice: Informality and Pro-Poor Policy in Johannesburg, South Africa." In *Urban Futures: Economic Growth and Poverty Reduction,* edited by Nabeel Hamdi, pp. 51–68. Rugby: ITDG.

Friedman, Steven, and Shauna Mottiar. 2005. "A Rewarding Engagement? The Treatment Action Campaign and the Politics of HIV/AIDS." *Politics and Society* 33, no. 4: 511–65.

Gordhan, Pravin. 2010. "Medium-Term Budget Policy Statement 2010." Speech by Pravin Gordhan, minister of finance. South African Government Information, October 27 (www.info.gov.za/speech/DynamicAction?pageid=461&sid=14081&tid=2329).

Handley, Antoinette. 2002. "Business and Economic Policy: South Africa and Three Other African Cases." Occasional Paper 2/2002. Johannesburg: South Africa Foundation.

Harvey, John, and Barbara Hollands. 2010. "Ratepayers Flex Muscles." *Herald,* September 7.

IBP (International Budget Partnership). 2010. *The Open Budget Survey 2010.* Washington.

Idasa. n.d. "A Short Introduction to Medium-Term Expenditure Frameworks." Pretoria (www. idasa.org.za/gbOutputFiles.asp?WriteContent=Y&RID=549).

Ipoc (Information Portal on Corruption and Governance in Africa). 2010. "SA: ANC's Wasteful Expenditure Has Reached R1bn Mark—DA." Woodstock, April 8 (www.ipocafrica. org/index.php?option=com_content&view=article&id=398:sa-ancs-wasteful-expenditure-has-reached-r1bn-mark-da&catid=85:conflicts-of-interest-news&Itemid=99).

Mbeki, Moeletsi. 2009. *Architects of Poverty: Why African Capitalism Needs Changing.* Johannesburg: Picador Africa.

Molele, Charles. 2010. "Warning of 'Predator State': Cosatu Will Not Give Its Support to ANC 'Political Hyenas.'" *Times,* August 26.

Open Society Justice Initiative. 2006. *Transparency and Silence: A Survey of Access to Information Laws and Practices in Fourteen Countries.* New York: Open Society Institute.

Parker, Faranaaaz. 2009. "Cele Lashed over Crime-Stats Stance." *Mail and Guardian,* August 5 (www.mg.co.za/article/2009-08-05-cele-lashed-over-crimestats-stance).

Parliamentary Monitoring Group. 2009. *Report on Current Service Delivery Protests in South Africa.* Cape Town, October 5 (www.pmg.org.za/node/18556).

———. 2010. *Auditor-General on the Audit Outcomes for 2008/09.* Cape Town, January 26 (www.pmg.org.za/report/20100126-auditor-general-audit-outcomes-200809).

Shoba, Sibongakonke. 2010. "Joburg ANC Draws up Long List of Masondo's 'Failures.'" *Business Day,* August 24.

3

Accountability from the Top Down? Brazil's Advances in Budget Transparency despite a Lack of Popular Mobilization

JORGE ANTONIO ALVES AND PATRICK HELLER

The Brazilian public sector is large by international standards. According to the Organization for Economic Cooperation and Development (OECD), it is the fourteenth largest in the world, bigger than developed democracies such as the United Kingdom or Spain. Tax revenues have continued to rise since financial stabilization in the mid-1990s, reaching a high point of 34.8 percent of gross domestic product (GDP).[1] The importance of public sector spending has only increased since democratization, first through the expansion of social programs such as health care and education and later through the extension of the government's social assistance conditional cash program, Bolsa Família. These circumstances magnify the importance of budget transparency, both for public oversight and for the management of public finances.

As illustrated by the relatively high scores in the Open Budget Index (OBI) of the International Budget Partnership (IBP)—74 percent in 2006 and 2008 and 71 percent in 2010—the Brazilian public sector provides a considerable amount of information regarding budget development and execution.[2] Contrary to the minor decline in the latest IBP score, Brazil's transparency efforts have increased substantially in recent years. Of note, the public sector now releases a vast array of disaggregated expenditure information shortly upon disbursement. On the federal government's transparency portal, one can access—albeit with different

---

This chapter is the product of research and writing conducted primarily by Jorge A. Alves, with support and advice from Patrick Heller.

1. OECD (2010).

2. Available at www.internationalbudget.org/what-we-do/open-budget-survey. The decline in the score was credited to less-detailed year-end and audit reports.

degrees of difficulty—information ranging from federal transfers to states and municipalities, expenditures tabulated by government ministries or by program, and even wages for public employees.[3] Clicking through the hierarchy of expenditures, one can reach information on the payee and date of payment and even report errors or malfeasance. Legislative branches report expenditures and reimbursements by individual members of Congress, down to proof of payment. In recent years, state and municipal governments have also launched transparency portals with similar fine-grain information.[4]

Brazil's high ranking in budget transparency (eighth overall in 2009 and ninth in 2010 in the OBI) is puzzling in that it defies conventional social science explanations. Most structural predictors of government accountability such as socioeconomic indicators would yield contrary forecasts. Brazil ranks relatively low on income measures such as GDP per capita (fifty-five in the International Monetary Fund's *World Economic Outlook*) and fares particularly poorly with regard to income inequality (seventy-five in the United Nations Development Programme's *Human Development Report*).[5] Cultural and historical predictors—a Portuguese patrimonial bureaucratic heritage and modern history of state corruption—do not favor transparency. Transparency International's Corruption Perception Index ranks Brazil sixty-nine in the world (up from seventy-five in 2009) in perceived corruption.[6] And though not unique to Brazil, the domestic narrative through the media is far from positive, as a constant bombardment of corruption scandals (both large and petty), misuse of funds, and ineffective spending has created popular animosity for both the political class and state employees.[7]

And yet, since redemocratization in the 1980s and macroeconomic stabilization in the 1990s, Brazilian governments have enacted legislation that has increased accountability, expanded participation, and introduced stringent transparency standards for the public sector. Despite political resistance from elected officials and the need to generate new administrative capacities for compliance, the public sector has largely met these new requirements. But as with most things in Brazil, the national-level narrative clouds a great heterogeneity in local experiences. In this chapter, we provide an overview of the current state of budget transparency in

3. www.tranparencia.gov.br. Although the disclosure of individual wages is common practice in a wide range of countries, it is highly contested in Brazil. Public sector unions are particularly combative on the issue and have used the judicial system to prevent governments from disclosing such information. See, for example, "Prefeitura de SP volta a publicar salários de funcionários na web," *Folha de São Paulo,* January 19, 2011.

4. Brazil is a three-tier federal system consisting of a federal government, twenty-six states, one federal district, and 5,564 municipalities.

5. IMF (2010) and UNDP (2009).

6. www.transparency.org/policy_research/surveys_indices/cpi/2010/results.

7. See, for example, the congressional scandal monitor by the *Folha de São Paulo*'s Fernando Rodrigues, available at http://noticias.uol.com.br/escandalos-congresso/.

Brazil, which we argue is significantly advanced and yet troublingly uneven. Although extensive information is now made publicly available, its dissemination is shaped by the interests and demands of the actors involved—the federal executive, political opposition, a limited number of high-capacity civil society organizations (CSOs), and the media. Concurrent processes of decentralization and participatory governance have done a great deal to disseminate transparency subnationally. However, the use of public information by civil society and the population at-large is still underdeveloped. We describe the current level of transparency, the budgetary process, and the major changes in the last twenty years, highlighting the major actors (reformist presidents, finance bureaucrats, legislators, CSOs, and the media), the importance of the development of democratic practices, and the role of systemic crises—both financial and of public opinion—in galvanizing domestic actors and speeding the process along.

The Open but Distorted Budget Process in Brazil

Brazil is a three-tier federal system, with an analogous and well-established budgetary process for national, state, and municipal governments (figure 3-1). The annual budget (Lei Orçamentária Anual, LOA) is subsidized by two guiding documents: a four-year budgetary plan (Plano Plurianual, PPA) and a yearly Budgetary Guidelines Law (Lei de Diretrizes Orçamentárias, LDO). Upon taking office, a new administration develops a PPA that will apply for the subsequent four years.[8] Within the guidelines of the multiyear plan, the planning and finance ministries develop an LDO for the upcoming year, specifying financial assumptions, policy goals, as well as fiscal targets—of particular note for Brazil's federal government are projecting the national minimum wage and setting goals for the primary surplus.[9] Following approval of the LDO, the executive presents a budget proposal (PLOA) to a joint commission of the Chamber of Deputies and the Senate (Comissão Mista de Orçamento),[10] initiating a series of discussion cycles that include a study of revenues by the Treasury Department and an extensive number of legislative amendments (*emendas parlamentares*). Legislators have the opportunity to attach amendments to the budget—up to twenty-five amend-

8. Brazilian executives are elected for four-year terms. Overlapping the multiyear plan with the first year of the subsequent administration emphasizes continuity and allows the incoming executive to develop the next PPA.

9. For the federal government, the LDO must be submitted to Congress by April 15 and must be approved by July 17. Formal rules state that Congress is forbidden from taking the midyear recess before approving the LDO.

10. The lower house (Chamber of Deputies) provides population-based representation, while the upper house (Senate) provides territorial-based representation. Subnational governments have a single legislative assembly.

Figure 3-1. *The Budget Process in Brazil*

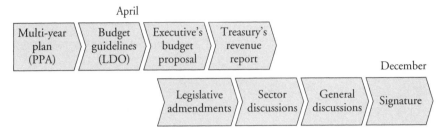

Source: Comissão Mista do Orçamento.

ments each—submitted through cross-party state delegations.[11] Amendments and sector-specific portions of the budget are discussed with ministries and (indirectly) with civil society in a sectoral cycle and then in a general cycle, when the joint commission finalizes the budget proposal. The budget is signed into law close to the end of the year (the official deadline for approval is December 22).

While the stages of budgetary development include the legislature and are open to popular access (if not participation), two characteristics of the budget process make participation and oversight difficult. First, Brazil's 1988 constitution specifies a large portion of the state's operational responsibilities, including transfers to subnational governments, pensions, and earmarks for specific sectors. Almost 75 percent of each of the previous four budgets was composed of obligatory expenditures, leaving most of the budgetary cycle to debate the much smaller public investment budget.[12] Therefore, though extensive and inclusive, the budgetary process makes only marginal changes to the overall amounts of the initial proposal (table 3-1). Legislative amendments, on average, amount to a very small portion of the budget proposal: 1.9 percent of the PLOA and 3.3 percent of the "effective budget" (net financial expenses) for the period 2005–11.[13] Legislators are allowed to pursue individual amendments, funded out of an equal predetermined quota per member of Congress.[14] While this strategy ensures every representative equal opportunity and thus

11. Delegations have additional collective amendments, as do specific commissions of both houses. This adds up to more than 9,000 amendments per budget.

12. Although high, this is a *decrease* from the early years of the new democracy. From 1988 to 1993, more than 90 percent of the federal budget consisted of obligatory spending. Since then, the government has reissued legislation (the Fund for Fiscal Stabilization or Fundo de Estabilização Fiscal and later the Detachment of Union Resources or Desvinculação de Recursos da União, DRU) to guarantee control over at least 20 percent of the yearly budget (Alston and others 2008).

13. Cambraia (2011). At the same time, Cambraia argues that they are a significantly higher proportion of the *discretionary* portion of the budget proposal (34.5 percent, on average, for the period 2005–11).

14. The equalization of amendment funds per legislator followed in the aftermath of a political scandal exposing a scheme in which legislators diverted public funds to fake nonprofits. Media scrutiny during

Table 3-1. *Total Changes during the Budget Cycle in Brazil, 2002–11*
R$ million unless otherwise noted

Year	PLOA	LOA	Change (percent)
2002	629,705	642,041	2.0
2003	1,009,532	1,036,056	2.6
2004	1,457,687	1,469,087	0.8
2005	1,574,500	1,606,403	2.0
2006	1,627,909	1,660,772	2.0
2007	1,504,499	1,526,143	1.4
2008	1,344,646	1,362,268	1.3
2009	1,575,879	1,581,448	0.4
2010	1,729,634	1,766,022	2.1
2011	1,930,628	1,966,016	1.8
Average			1.6

Source: PLOAs and LOAs from Orçamento Brasil (www.camara.gov.br/orcamento).

minimizes conflict within the joint commission, it also has negative effects, as most amendments tend to fund pork-barrel projects that yield political dividends for local constituencies but pulverize public spending and fund low-quality projects.[15] These amendments are generally approved (particularly those with individual-legislator sponsorship), allowing legislators to claim immediate political credit with the target constituencies (table 3-2). Collective amendments (presented jointly by cross-party state delegations and legislative commissions) tend to contemplate higher-quality, larger-scale public projects but, due to their diffuse heritage, suffer more harshly from cuts during the budget process.

In part, legislators are granted such freedom in determining individual amendments because the executive has practically unfettered control over implementation of the budget.[16] This latitude over the authorization but also the timing of dis-

---

this time revealed that politicians who controlled different budget commissions (referred to as the *anões do orçamento*) used the great latitude in allocating budgetary amendments to provide preferential treatment to their political allies and extract kickbacks from large contractors (Limongi and Figueiredo 2005).

15. These amendments are derided as yielding low-quality public spending (Alston and others 2008) and have repeatedly been exposed as sources of corruption among legislators, nonexistent nonprofits, and overpricing contractors. Sodré and Alves (2010) argue that municipalities that receive funds through legislative amendment are 25 percent more likely to experience corruption. Furthermore, once "pacified" by a set amount of amendment funding, legislators spend most of the time allocating their individual quotas rather than debating the priorities of the budget proposal itself (Cambraia 2011), a discussion kept for the select few committee rapporteurs (Figueiredo and Limongi 2002).

16. Limongi and Figueiredo (2005) argue that this transfers the conflicts between the executive and the legislature and the competition between legislators themselves from the allocation to the implementation phase. A similar level of executive discretion is identified in Mexico, the subject of chapter 5 in this volume.

Table 3-2. *Legislative Amendments in the 2011 Budget in Brazil*
Amounts in R$ million

Type of amendment	Number of authors	Proposed		Approved		Approved after vetoes	
		Number	Amount	Amount	Percent	Amount	Percent
Collective	58	610	64,409	13,406	21	12,126	19
Individual	593	9,193	7,707	7,707	100	7,119	92
Total	651	9,803	72,116	21,112	29	19,245	27

Source: Siga Brasil (www9.senado.gov.br/portal/page/portal/orcamento_senado/SigaBrasil).

bursements yields a series of economic and political distortions, including magnifying the effect of short-term economic fluctuations and the use of disbursement authorization as a political bargaining chip.[17] But the executive's discretion over disbursements generates more distortions to accountability than just "hollowing out" amendments. When fiscal discipline was necessary (as was the case through most of the two decades since democratization), the executive made widespread use of budgetary curtailment (*contingenciamento*) in order to rein in public sector spending. This solution became prevalent when Brazil pursued structural adjustment programs with support from international financial institutions, which attached sizable primary surpluses as conditionality. As marginal and lesser-quality expenditures, legislative amendments were especially vulnerable to the ax, with execution falling as low as 40 percent in the hardest-hit years.[18] The extent of executive latitude is also evident in the low overall rates of budgetary execution—on average less than 75 percent for the previous decade (table 3-3).

Executive control over the budget is also achieved through a series of accounting maneuvers undertaken by the planning and finance ministries. One such strategy is the purposeful understatement of future revenues in order to cap budgetary growth, even when the budget fails to cover all existing expenditures. This shortfall is then addressed during execution by the inclusion of additional budgetary credits throughout the fiscal year.[19] Fiscal year manipulation is also customary: capital and social sector expenditures are withheld until financial benchmarks have been achieved and then are cleared toward the end of year, spiking every December in what is commonly referred to as "Christmas packages."[20] This creates serious implementation problems for subnational governments and agencies, which must then

17. Pereira and Mueller (2002) and Alston and others (2008).

18. CONOF (2011) and Limongi and Figueiredo (2005).

19. Purposeful underbudgeting in constitutionally mandated social sectors such as health and education is common practice, to the extent that actors know to expect additional credits multiple times during the year.

20. Protásio, Bugarin, and Bugarin (2004).

Table 3-3. *Budget Execution in Brazil, 2001–10*

Year	Approved budget (R$ million)	Additional credits (percent)	Executed (percent)
2001	950,202	2.9	59
2002	650,410	9.0	93
2003	1,036,056	6.2	77
2004	1,469,087	2.6	59
2005	1,606,403	1.7	66
2006	1,660,772	4.2	66
2007	1,526,143	2.5	75
2008	1,362,268	13.9	76
2009	1,581,448	7.8	78
2010	1,766,022	4.7	77
Average		5.5	72.5

Source: Siga Brasil.

rush to spend allocations in a short period of time, at the risk of having to return monies to the federal government and failing to fulfill their constitutional requirements. Needless to say, this overtaxes even the best-intentioned government agents and provides ample opportunity for corruption for those less well intentioned.[21]

The (Otherwise) Extensive Transparency Tools

Despite the obfuscating effects of budgetary maneuvering by both the executive and legislative branches, the state of transparency in Brazil is nonetheless quite advanced. Budget documents (pre-budget statement, budget summary, budget proposal, and enacted budget) are published in the official press (*Diário Oficial da União*) and disseminated electronically throughout the budget process. Both the Senate and the Chamber of Deputies publish updated versions of the budget on the Internet at each stage of the process and host an extensive list of historical documents online. The Senate hosts a web platform (Siga Brasil) where users can generate electronic reports down to specific amendments or line items. Brazil also produces and discloses reports on execution, including in-year reports, year-end

21. Curtailment is also made necessary because congressional rapporteurs respond to the Treasury's understatement by overstating public revenues, in order to expand the pool of resources available for amendments. This yields incongruous situations, the latest of which occurred in late 2010, when president-elect Dilma Rousseff announced plans to curtail up to R$50 billion ($31.2 billion) from the 2011 budget almost concurrently with its publication. See "Ministérios com maior número de emendas serão mais afetados pelo corte," *O Globo,* February 10, 2011.

reports, and independent audit reports. The government does not produce a mid-year review or a citizen's budget, although the Chamber's website has recently added a simplifying explanation of the budget process.[22]

Public disclosure was made much simpler by the fact that the quality and availability of budgetary information historically have been high for Brazil's federal government. Due to their perceived importance, finance-related bureaucracies generally have been shielded from patronage appointments and generally have outperformed other sectors of the state.[23] Highly developed budgetary documents were available as early as the *Estado Novo* regime in the 1930s, when President Vargas created the Administrative Department of the Public Service (DASP).[24] As economists and planners rose to prominence during Brazil's bureaucratic-authoritarian regime (1964–84), the DASP offices grew in power and resources and so did the quality of budgetary data.[25] However, by the end of the military government, the lack of downward accountability and the politicization of the bureaucracy had led to fiscal profligacy and lack of financial controls throughout the three levels of government.[26] Hyperinflation, which plagued the Brazilian economy through most of the 1980s and the early 1990s, significantly lowered the quality and comparability of budgetary information.

The state has three embedded oversight bodies: the Comptroller General (Controladoria Geral da União), the accounts tribunals (*tribunais de contas*), and the Public Prosecutor (Ministério Público).[27] These institutions have the mandate of overseeing expenditures and budgetary processes, as well as investigating the misuse of government funds. The effectiveness of these bodies has varied across both time and place. Due to their overlapping mandates, they have been hindered by a certain amount of bureaucratic infighting. There are also significant problems with political interference. Since the executive at different levels of government appoints the heads of the tribunals, their independence is compromised— particularly at the local level, where the personal selection of tribunal heads tends to lower the likelihood of negative reports. But executive interference occurs even at the top. With the implementation of infrastructure programs lagging prior to an election year, President Luis Inácio "Lula" da Silva publicly criticized the state's

22. "Entenda o Orçamento" (www2.camara.gov.br/atividade-legislativa/orcamentobrasil/cidadao/entenda).

23. Evans (1995) refers to these parts of the bureaucracy as "pockets of efficiency" among patronage-infested line ministries.

24. Viana (1947).

25. On bureaucratic authoritarianism, see O'Donnell (1973).

26. Abrúcio (2007).

27. The Public Prosecutor is an institution of independent public prosecutors with freedom to enforce laws and prosecute in defense of the state and the people.

oversight bodies for nitpicking and obstructing progress.[28] Recently, criticism through the media has resurfaced in the wake of the delay surrounding infrastructural projects for the upcoming World Cup and Olympics events.

Most important, domestic legislation now expands the dissemination of public budget information far beyond the budget development process, requiring federal, state, and larger municipal governments to disclose electronically disaggregated information on public revenues and expenditures shortly after their execution. In these "transparency portals," executives must disclose daily revenues, budget execution by category and by line item, and documentation for each individual expenditure, including information on payee and services rendered. While the federal government already provided some of this information over its multiple platforms, state and municipal governments have had to adapt in order to fulfill these requirements, with varying results.

A domestic nongovernmental organization (NGO) named Contas Abertas recently surveyed federal and state transparency portals and generated a ranking of the electronic tools.[29] The Contas Abertas survey provided an extensive test of information disclosure, evaluating ease of access and clarity, periodicity of updating, and comprehensiveness of information disclosed by federal and state governments. In the initial rankings, the federal government scored the highest mark, 7.56 out of ten possible points.[30] In addition to the scores, Contas Abertas provided analytical reports, in which it classified the federal government's offerings as fairly comprehensive, including daily updates for some information and monthly updates for the remainder. The report flagged accessibility as an area in need of significant improvement, since disparate websites and software platforms provide uneven levels of precision, making the manipulation and cross-tabulation of data cumbersome.[31]

As can be expected in a country as diverse as Brazil, the level of transparency in subnational governments varies significantly. The Contas Abertas Index places state governments in a broad range from a high of 6.96 (São Paulo) to a low of 3.04 (Piauí), with a national average ranking of 4.88. Not surprising, states in the more developed South and Southeast regions tend to rank relatively higher than states in the rest of the country (figures 3-2 and 3-3). However, individual cases show the importance of intrastate political environments, with the relatively poor

---

28. "Lula critica burocracia," *O Globo,* April 30, 2009, and "Lula critica TCU por paralisação de obras e defende mudanças em órgãos de fiscalização," *Folha de São Paulo,* October 23, 2009.

29. Índice de Transparência (www.indicedetransparencia.org.br).

30. The index has not been updated since its original publication, making it impossible to assess transparency improvements systematically.

31. Among other strong points, the Contas Abertas report praised the existence of an up-to-date database of ineligible companies linked to corruption investigations.

northeastern state of Pernambuco ranking second among states (third overall) and the northern state of Rondônia ranking seventh (eighth overall). State governments have continued to improve their transparency portals as they develop the technology and managerial practices, perhaps to a further extent than expressed in the rigorous standards of the Contas Abertas Index.

Within-country heterogeneity in levels of development and managerial capacities is augmented when municipal governments are considered. The National Confederation of Municipalities (Confederação Nacional de Municípios) decried the introduction of transparency requirements based on feasibility as well as affordability concerns. Current legislation phased in the requirement of "real-time"[32] electronic disclosure by municipal governments based on population categories, currently encompassing municipalities with more than 50,000 inhabitants (representing 11 percent of municipalities, but 65 percent of national population). In the first year under the law, the number of municipalities with populations larger than 100,000 failing to disclose information fell by almost half (from 14 to 7.5 percent).[33] For the smaller of the two categories of municipalities (representing 6 percent of the total), transparency rules have been effective since May 2011, with 70 percent of them meeting legal requirements at the time of writing. Due to relatively recent applicability of the law at the municipal level, the quality of local portals has not yet been systematically assessed.

Major Advances in Transparency

Budget transparency in Brazil was made possible by two broader societal transformations that created conditions conducive to its development: *democratization* (including the process of democratic consolidation) and *macroeconomic stabilization*.[34] Against this backdrop, three major legal benchmarks determined transparency advances: the citizen constitution (1988), the Fiscal Responsibility Law (2000), and the Transparency Law (2009).

Although not directly determining transparency, the regime transition in the 1980s, culminating with the 1988 constitution and the direct presidential elections in 1989, positioned the state for increased public sector accountability and

32. Although the current Transparency Law (Complementary Law 131 of May 27, 2009) mandates "real-time" disclosure of public expenditures, it does not specify the operational meaning of real time. After a year of delay, the executive issued a decree (Decree 7,185 of May 27, 2010) specifying it as forty-eight hours from disbursement.

33. Authors' update of National Confederation of Municipalities surveys. Original survey results available at http://portal.cnm.org.br/sites/5700/5770/27052010_tabelas_municipios.pdf and http://portal.cnm.org.br/sites/5700/5770/26052011_lista_transparencia.pdf.

34. There are also advances in information technology, such as the dissemination of personal computers and Internet access, since they provide the medium through which budgetary information is disseminated.

Figure 3-2. *Transparency in Subnational Governments in Brazil*

a. Contas Abertas Transparency Index
(state governments)

b. Municipalities with populations greater than 50,000
with transparency portals (percent by state)

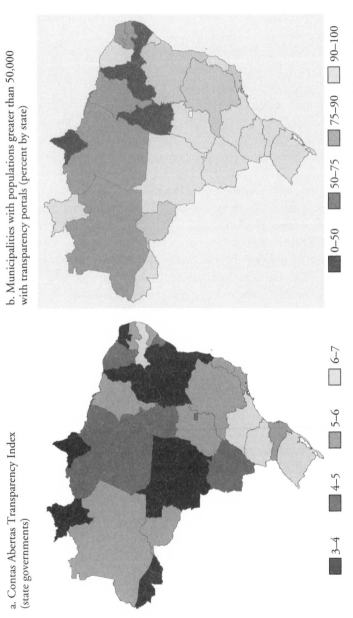

■ 3–4 ■ 4–5 ■ 5–6 ▢ 6–7

■ 0–50 ■ 50–75 ■ 75–90 ▢ 90–100

Source: Contas Abertas, Confederação Nacional de Municípios, and authors. For panel b, authors' update of National Confederation of Municipalities surveys.

Figure 3-3. *State-Level Transparency Scores versus Income in Brazil*

CA's Transparency Index (2008)

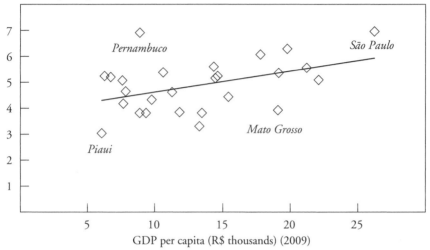

GDP per capita (R$ thousands) (2009)

Source: Contas Abertas and IBGE (2011).

transparency. The direct elections of public representatives served to reestablish the norm that the state served and should be accountable to the population. Likewise, the constitution's overt commitment to redress social inequalities through the provision of basic social services such as health, education, and social security reinforced this notion. By the same token, the process of democratization also relegitimized the participation of civil society in government without fear of persecution. A highly mobilized civil society played a critical role in directly shaping the new constitution, in particular by provisions guaranteeing civil society participation in sectoral policy formulation (for example, health) and budgeting (setting the stage for participatory budgeting in Brazilian municipalities).

Macroeconomic stability is also a prerequisite for transparency and something Brazil did not achieve until the *Real* Plan in 1994. Brazil experienced high rates of inflation through most of the 1980s and early 1990s—the average annual inflation rate between 1985 and 1994 was 1,024 percent, peaking at almost 2,500 percent in 1993.[35] Inflation of this magnitude has distortionary effects throughout the economy; since numbers quickly lose their meaning, overseeing accounts becomes practically impossible.[36] Officials in the three levels of government and parastatal

35. Figures for 2011 are available at Instituto Brasileiro de Geografia e Estadística (www.ibge.gov.br/home/estatistica/indicadores/precos/inpc_ipca/ipca-inpc_201105_1.shtm).

36. See, for example, "A inflação é de 5.500% por ano," *Veja*, January 24, 1994.

companies took advantage of the inflationary distortions in order to increase spending, continuing to feed the price spiral. After multiple failed stabilization attempts under the preceding governments, the *Real* Plan succeeded in curtailing inflation, curbing it to an annual rate of 10 percent by 1996 and reaching double digits again only once in the years since. Macroeconomic stability transformed the fabric of the Brazilian economy and society, aiding transparency in two major ways. First, stability made numbers significant once again, allowing publicly elected executives and legislators to oversee the functioning of the state. Second, halting inertial inflation exposed budgetary holes, which the executive then sought to eliminate in order to balance the federal and subnational budgets.

Legal Benchmarks

The 1988 constitution initiated a series of reforms that would set in motion the process of increasing public accountability. First, the emphasis on decentralization aimed to break the central government's hold on policy formation and history of curtailing civil society involvement. Embraced by social movements across sectors of the economy, decentralization opened new venues for policy experimentation and popular participation. Based on the principles of legality and oversight, the constitution also reempowered the accounts tribunals and public prosecutors. However, due to the multiplication of municipalities and political control of state and municipal accounts tribunals, the effects of these policy reforms were initially dampened.

The Fiscal Responsibility Law (Lei de Responsabilidade Fiscal, LRF) was the first legal benchmark that overtly forced national, state, and local governments to reveal and control their finances.[37] Created against a backdrop of ballooning state debts and the concentrated costs of financial stabilization, the law curtailed public spending by setting limits on expenditures for personnel (50 percent of revenues for the federal government and 60 percent for states and municipalities),[38] capping debt levels, and prohibiting further federal assumption of subnational debt. The LRF also prohibited the creation of new long-term financial commitments (maturities greater than two years) without a matching source of revenue. It also addressed predatory practices resulting from the electoral cycle, prohibiting the hiring of personnel and short-term debt financing in election years. This prevented the previously common practice in which outgoing executives ratcheted up spending, leaving insolvent cities and states for subsequent govern-

---

37. Complementary Law no. 101, May 4, 2000.

38. In reality, the LRF did not create the limits on personnel expenditures, but it did reaffirm the ones stated in a previous law (Complementary Laws 82/1995 and 96/1999, known as the Camata Law) before it came to term.

ments.[39] Finally, for the first time in Brazilian history, the LRF made executives (mayors and governors) personally liable for noncompliance.

Furthermore, the LRF mandated the public disclosure of budgetary documents—as "instruments of transparency in fiscal management"—as well as the dissemination of audit reports and simplified versions of budgets for public access (Article 48). This initiated the reporting of budget execution, since executives were mandated to publish and submit their yearly budget to the accounts tribunals at their level of government. The media was quick to expand its coverage of the process, especially reporting on cases where accounts were rejected, and opposition parties used these results to chastise the malfeasant incumbents. The LRF, however, did not specify how different branches of the government should disclose information publicly, which led to experimentation and the proliferation of independent platforms and standards of information across levels and branches of government.

The LRF remained virtually untouched as the legal base for budgetary transparency in Brazil until 2009, when Congress passed another complementary law (the Transparency Law) expanding the LRF's Article 48. The most visible change in the complementary law was the determination that the public sector must electronically disclose budgetary execution in "real time." The law was based on a 2003 proposal introduced by Senator João Capiberibe from the left-of-center Socialist Party of Brazil (Partido Socialista Brasileiro, PSB), which determined that all levels of government should actively and openly disclose (without requiring a password) information on revenues and particularly expenditures, including payee information and funding source. In response to subnational resistance, the law's final text allowed for a one-year grace period for federal, state, and 272 large municipal (populations greater than 100,000) governments to comply. Medium-size municipalities (populations between 50,000 and 100,000) were granted a two-year grace period and those fewer than 50,000, a four-year grace period. Under its framework, noncompliance is punishable by the freezing of federal voluntary transfers, which constitute a significant portion of the total revenue for poorer and smaller states and municipalities.

While the grace period for smaller municipalities is understandable from the point of view of fostering subnational compliance, an analysis of the stock of Brazilian municipalities nevertheless reveals the size of such a concession (figure 3-4). The lion's share of Brazilian municipalities (89 percent) have populations smaller than 50,000 and hence fit into the most lenient timetable for disclosure. And while the

---

39. The LRF also created budgetary curtailment as it exists today by determining that, if revenues fall short of budgetary predictions, expenditures should be trimmed to match the shortfall (CONOF 2011).

Figure 3-4. *Municipalities in Brazil, by Size and Population, 2010*

Percent

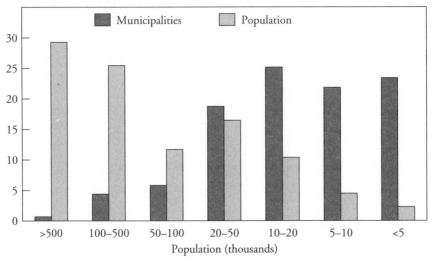

Population (thousands)

Source: IBGE (2010).

municipal proportion of public revenues is relatively small (about 1.5 percent of GDP) and concentrated in larger cities, municipal governments nonetheless provide a major portion of public services (22 percent of total government expenditures).[40] Every municipality is guaranteed a basic political and administrative staff and receives sizable federal transfers. The Office of the Attorney General recently observed in an audit report that most instances of corruption occur at the local level, through partnerships (*convênios*) made between the federal government, municipalities, and municipal providers in sectors such as health and education.[41] These partnerships are legal, but they are not properly developed tools for making federal transfers to municipalities. Since they are mostly small and disaggregated (even within municipalities), they are incredibly laborious to oversee. According to the federal government's transparency website, there are currently more than 38,000 municipal partnerships across the country (an average of seven per municipality). While individually small, their large numbers add up to significant diversion of public funding.

40. STN (2011).
41. See "Governo perde R$ 2,1 bilhões para a corrupção" (www.indicedetransparencia.org.br/?p=1490).

The Process behind Transparency Advances

Despite the presence of a vibrant civil society sector and a few high-capacity CSOs specializing in budgetary issues, most transparency advances in Brazil have been driven by actors within the federal government. Major advances in transparency legislation have occurred when the longer processes of debate within the bureaucracy and Congress have been augmented by elected officials taking advantage of catalytic opportunities and behaving strategically in the direct aftermath of economic crises or public scandals. As CSOs and the independent media build up their reaction to the crises, progressive members of the public sector succeed in overcoming the resistance of conservative and opposition forces and pushing through reforms.

Transparency as a Tool for Fiscal Responsibility

The Fiscal Responsibility Law was voted against a backdrop of domestic financial instability and international financial institution rescue programs. Following the democratic transition, politicians took advantage of weak oversight institutions to engage in a period of electoral largesse, catering to constituencies by inflating the minimum wage and expanding patronage appointments within the public sector; this deficit spending greatly increased the stock of subnational debt.[42] The orthodox economic policies anchoring monetary stabilization (including high real interest rates) exposed and worsened subnational positions, with more than 55 percent of municipalities running deficits by 1998,[43] state governments borrowing heavily to cover operational expenses, and both paying hefty interest charges on their debt. Accosted by an attack on the *real* in international markets and having to run to the international financial institutions for help, President Fernando Henrique Cardoso's economic team saw that bringing public sector expenditures under control would not be possible without curtailing the excesses of subnational governments. State governments in particular were in a precarious financial position, as stabilization exposed a series of financial tricks used to cover up excessive spending, including taking out large loans from state-owned banks and failing to repay them.[44]

---

42. The chaotic state of subnational finances was an effect of a political backlash to national-level centralization during the military regime. Since elections for state governors preceded all others during redemocratization, state governors became extremely powerful during the constituent assembly (Samuels and Abrúcio 2000). They used this legitimacy to strengthen their hold over local electoral arenas, aggressively expanding public sector hiring and statewide construction projects.

43. "Déficit atinge 55,53% das prefeituras," *Folha de São Paulo,* January 31, 2000.

44. The bailout of state banks cost the federal government more than R$90 billion. "Socorro custou R$110 bi," *Folha de São Paulo* (http://www1.folha.uol.com.br/folha/dinheiro/banespa_ajuda.shtml).

As state governments ran out of credit and in some cases fell into arrears with suppliers and employees, President Cardoso used this leverage to impose fiscal responsibility on subnational governments. In exchange for the federal government assuming state debts and reopening lines of credit, states had to accept budgetary prudential limits for overall and personnel expenditures, deficit spending, and levels of indebtedness. As a result of this policy, the federal government was able to rein in the sources of the most egregious subnational financial profligacy, including states' ownership of banks and the ability to borrow in the open market. At the same time, the LRF curtailed a major source of patronage by limiting the portion of subnational revenues that could be spent on personnel.[45] To ensure compliance, the federal government included Article 48 in the LRF, which dealt directly with the dissemination of budget data and reempowered the accounts tribunals to oversee compliance. With insolvency on the horizon and taking a beating from public sector unions and the press, subnational governments agreed to greater accountability and transparency in exchange for one last bailout.

The negotiations leading to the LRF occurred mostly within the public sector, between the federal and subnational executives and between the top finance bureaucrats and national legislators. Bureaucrats from the ministries of planning and finance introduced the bill in April 1999 to a Special Committee on Fiscal Adjustment, and after spending most of the year within the committee, the bill was introduced to the floor in December. President Cardoso called a special session of Congress for January and February 2000, with the main goals of voting two fiscal reforms: making obligatory spending more flexible (the DRU, which freed 20 percent of the federal budget) and passage of the LRF. The executive faced a complicated negotiation in Congress, since resistance came not only from opposition parties in the left but also from legislators in the second largest partner in the coalition, the rightist Party of the Liberal Front (Partido da Frente Liberal, PFL). With ties to subnational executives in the less-developed Northeast region, the PFL leadership in Congress sided with governors and mayors in arguing for relaxing its most stringent points (such as the cap on personnel spending) and imposing a slower timetable for implementation. Cardoso's economic team took advantage of the unstable macroeconomic conditions in order to convince political actors of the operational inevitability as well as the moral imperative of the reforms.[46] Likewise, the media, covering the public sector's dire straits and reporting on the very human costs of fiscal profligacy, reinforced the executive's narrative.

45. "A pedra na engrenagem," *Veja*, February 2, 2000.
46. Loureiro and Abrúcio (2004).

This approach shifted the alternatives for viable resistance, and subnational actors moved from outright rejection to delaying tactics. The timing of implementation was such a prominent issue of contention because mayors were facing an electoral year. Hence, they were particularly vocal against the immediate implementation of the LRF, lobbying legislators and the federal government through their constituencies and through encompassing associations. After failing to attract support from the opposition parties, the federal government nonetheless pushed for the vote in the Chamber of Deputies and, after getting the PFL delegation on board—and the second largest opposition party, the Democratic Labor Party (Partido Democrático Trabalhista, PDT)—passed the bill with a 75 percent approval rate.[47] Still eyeing the electoral calendar, the executive pushed for quick approval of the LRF in the Senate, while state and municipal governments continued to decry the law as unconstitutional (since it imposed on federal sovereignties) and attempted to delay its implementation. Despite municipal efforts, the Senate approved the bill in April 2000, once again by a large majority. And though the implementation of the fiscal targets would not be applicable until the following year, the measures curtailing electoral spending were made effective immediately. In return, a tacit agreement had Cardoso delay signing the bill into law until the end of the regulatory two-week period, allowing some highly indebted states and municipalities to roll over their existing debt prior to the LRF's enactment. A few states and municipalities managed to roll over R$14.5 billion in short-term maturities—$10 billion for the city of São Paulo alone—a move criticized by the opposition and the press.

Civil Society Inclusion but Limited Advances in the Early Lula Administration

Years later, when Lula, the perennial leader of the Workers' Party (Partido dos Trabalhadores, PT), won the presidential election, many civil society organizations were hopeful about the prospect of greater accountability and outright inclusion in development of the federal budget. Lula's government made the first attempt at this type of civil society participation in the development of its first multiyear budgetary plan in 2003. In this process, the Brazilian Association of Nongovernmental Organizations mediated the participation of more than 2,200 CSOs, which made suggestions throughout development of the PPA. The process included a wide sample of groups, ranging from high-capacity organizations with budgetary expertise to

47. www.camara.gov.br/internet/votacao/default.asp?datDia=25/1/2000&numSessao=16. The Workers' Party (PT), the Communist Party of Brazil (PCdoB), and the socialist PSB closed ranks and voted against the bill, based on the fact that it provided caps for all types of expenditures except interest payments. The opposition introduced a series of amendments and proposed voting the law in parts rather than as a whole, but the executive's majority held through all the votes.

broader representation of social movements.[48] After jumping at the opportunity to participate, CSOs were disappointed with the PPA's final results, which they argued had ignored their input and maintained the usual preferences of federal planning and finance bureaucrats. The relationship between civil society organizations and the administration was further strained when the government reneged on a promise to grant CSOs access to its financial management system, the *sistema integrado de administração financeira* (SIAFI).[49] When the Lula administration suffered a negative media blitz due to a scandal related to bribing congressmen in exchange for favorable votes,[50] many CSOs abandoned the budget process in protest. At this time, however, Contas Abertas managed to obtain permission (and the passwords) of legislators who were sympathetic to the cause of transparency and proceeded to access SIAFI information and disseminate it on its website.

The initial fallout between CSOs and the Lula administration highlights the overall trends we identify. First, finance bureaucrats from within the executive continued to have a prominent position in the budget process. Faced with a choice between greater inclusion (with potentially significant changes to the budget process and allocations) and continuity (with access to financial markets and economic windfalls), President Lula's political core chose the latter. Two factors facilitated this choice: Lula's inner circle clearly understood the popular consensus around responsible and transparent economic management, closing the door in Brazil to the Chavez-type leftist style of populism. Second, as Avritzer (2009) identifies, Lula's wing of the PT was not directly connected to subnational

48. Brazil has a vibrant civil society sector, including a few highly capable CSOs in the public finance sector, aiming to disseminate good budgeting practices, educate the public about budget issues, and advocate for greater government transparency. Two of these institutions, the Instituto de Estudos Socioeconômicos and the Instituto Brasileiro de Análises Sociais e Econômicas, have partnered with international NGOs such as IBP in the past, helping to develop the country's budget transparency report. These institutions have also served jointly as part of the Brazil Budget Forum (Fórum Brasil Orçamento)—a structure though which the federal government has attempted to bring a variety of civil society representatives into the budgetary process. Two other CSOs work directly with the disclosure or misuse of public funds and encourage discussions about public transparency: Transparência Brasil and Contas Abertas. The latter develops and publishes the transparency rankings for national and subnational executives. As part of the strategy to disseminate budgetary and expenditure information and increase popular oversight, these institutions hold training sessions for budgetary literacy with the Brazilian Association of Investigative Journalism in order to improve the press's ability to digest and report on the multitude of data currently available. The Forum for the Right to Access Public Information has advocated for an access to public information act, recently signed into law by President Dilma Rousseff.

49. The SIAFI is the main tool governing the state's public expenditures and serves as the baseline and main information feed for the federal transparency portals. Highly specialized SIAFI technicians (known as *os ratos do SIAFI*, the SIAFI rats) navigate the system's complex interface and feed information on public expenditures to the media and political parties.

50. For an overview, see "Entenda o 'mensalão,'" *Folha de São Paulo* (www1.folha.uol.com.br/folha/brasil/ult96u70256.shtml).

participatory experiences, which explains in part why the national-level PT was not as proactive in introducing the participatory budget practices that the party had developed in its local experiences in government. Therefore, while civil society actors were activated, the lack of a catalyzing moment meant that the early Lula administration failed to pursue more active transparency practices. Operational-type transparency practices continued to improve, however, as demanded by financial and managerial controls.

Conditions in Alignment Once Again

Further transparency-enhancing legislation did not come to the fore again until early 2009, when a series of political scandals aligned the slow-burning process of reform with short-term political necessity. The first sparks were set off after the two main parties in President Lula's cabinet could not compromise over who would take over as president of the Senate.[51] The competition between former president José Sarney, from the catchall Partido do Movimento Democrático Brasileiro (PMDB, the Brazilian Democratic Movement Party), and Tião Viana (PT) quickly soured, with both sides leaking accusations of corruption and misuse of public funds to the national press. While the first accusations were relatively mild (pertaining to minor misuses such as lending official mobile phones to family members), public embarrassment quickly escalated the dispute. In retaliation for the first set of leaks, PT aides exposed Sarney's strongman within the Senate bureaucracy as living in an undeclared R$5 million ($3 million) mansion. Once the media pursued the story, reporters began unearthing a series of opaque practices by the Senate's staff, known as the "secret acts."[52] New discoveries dominated the national media for most of the first semester of 2009, paralyzing legislative activity in the Senate.

At the same time, corruption scandals derailed the Chamber of Deputies. The troubles started when the head of the Internal Affairs Commission was found to have sold a medieval-style castle in his home state worth R$25 million ($15 million), while failing to report the transaction to tax authorities.[53] As images of the castle proliferated across the national media, the same deputy was found to be directing his reimbursement allowance to pay for services from companies of his

---

51. Informal norms determine that the largest party nominates the president and the second largest nominates the first vice president in each legislative house. As the largest party in both houses, the PMDB fielded concurrent candidates for both contests. In doing so, it broke a standing power-sharing agreement with the PT in which the parties agreed to support each other in alternating candidacies for each house.

52. Among the more than 600 secret acts were appointing cronies and family members and raising salaries above constitutional limits. See "Entenda o escândalo dos cargos e benesses do Senado," *Estado de São Paulo*, June 9, 2009.

53. "Líderes de sistem de aprovar proposta para divulgar notas fiscais com gastos de deputados," *Folha de São Paulo*, February 10, 2009.

ownership.[54] Once the media's attention had been called to legislators' reimbursements, new stories surfaced almost daily, ranging from questionable to outright illegal use of the public coffers. Shortly thereafter two unrelated stories broke regarding misuse of the legislators' airfare allowances: in one, a large number of deputies used their quotas on family and friends (including international vacations), while in another, deputies sold their unused tickets to travel agencies, who in turn dealt them to unknowing travelers.[55]

In the immediate wake of these scandals, progressive legislators proposed statutory changes to ameliorate Congress's public standing and increase public transparency. A conservative strategy was to impose stricter rules on the benefits available to members of Congress, which attacked the visible symptoms, while fending off calls from the media and civil society for deeper reform. But others took advantage of the situation to push forth deeper changes. Deputy José Aníbal, from the opposition Party of Brazilian Social Democracy (Partido da Social Democracia Brasileira, PSDB), called for urgent voting on a bill (PLP 217/2004) that had been in "congressional limbo" for five years. The bill, originally proposed by Senator João Capiberibe and Deputy Janete Capiberibe, sought to expand the transparency requirements of the LRF to real-time disclosure over the Internet of budgetary execution across the branches and levels of government. The selection of this particular bill illustrates the complicated confluence of events that lead to improved transparency.[56] The Capiberibes had introduced twin bills in the Senate and Chamber back in 2003, based on the senator's previous experiences while governor of the northern state of Amapá. The bill was unanimously approved in multiple committees in the Senate and Chamber by the end of 2005, but no further action was taken until 2007. With João Capiberibe no longer in the Senate, Deputy Janete Capiberibe pursued multiple attempts to bring the bill to the floor, with little success. Once on the floor, the bill remained without a vote for two years, being tabled for items of immediate interest to the executive. In the meantime, the Capiberibes rallied support for the bill by chairing discussions with academic, professional, and civil society organizations, as well as the federal comptroller general (Jorge Hage) in the hopes of gathering political momentum and bringing the amendment to a vote. When the sustained

54. "Câmara vai proibir uso de verba indenizatória em empresa pertencente a deputados," *Folha de São Paulo*, March 31, 2009.

55. "Após 'farra das passagens,' Câmara anuncia medidas moralizadoras para a casa," *Folha de São Paulo*, April 22, 2009; "Gabinetes negociam bilhetes de deputados com agências," *Folha de São Paulo*, April 24, 2009; and "Sinais de vida," *Veja*, May 6, 2009.

56. According to Contas Abertas, many other proposals were in Congress at the time. Committee reports specifically attached six similar proposals that were canceled with passage of the Capiberibe-sponsored bill.

scandals brought public scrutiny to the issue, the bill jumped from the back burner to immediate approval, passing unanimously on the same day the vote was requested in the Chamber (May 5, 2009). The Senate approved the law by month's end, and President Lula sanctioned the law in early June.[57]

Riding the credibility crisis of the legislature and the political class, strategic reformist politicians like the Capiberibes and sectors of the state like the Comptroller General's office under Hage were able to defeat strong opposition to the measure's implementation. Once again, mayors were vocal in criticizing the law. Organized through two national associations, they marched on Brasília arguing that they lacked the technical capacities and the resources to upgrade their financial and management systems for real-time disclosure. In response, the final text of the law granted grace periods for governments to arrange their accounts and acquire the necessary technologies to make detailed expenditure information available in real time. Public sector unions also openly opposed the disclosure of salary information. Arguing that publicizing their wages violated their right to financial privacy and would make them susceptible to violence, public employees fought the disclosure in the courts, eventually shutting down websites that provided individual information.[58]

The Opportunities and Challenges of Decentralization

In addition to the processes occurring in the federal arena, fiscal and administrative decentralization generated opportunities for experimentation with different models of transparency in a localized fashion. Decentralization became a popular strategy in Brazil's democratic transition as an alternative to the centralized policy process during the country's authoritarian regime (1964–84). Proponents of decentralization praised these reforms for increasing democratic accountability—bringing government closer to the citizenship would allow for greater oversight by local constituencies, the development of civic and democratic capacities, and subnational innovation—while also increasing efficiency in the management of the public sector.[59] The opportunities presented by decentralization resulted in a variety of experiments with institutional forms and yielded two types of institutions for participatory governance that were particularly successful: participatory budgeting (*orçamento participativo*) and community health councils (*conselhos de saúde*).[60]

---

57. Law no. 131, May 27, 2009.
58. "Prefeitura de São Paulo tira salários de funcionários da internet por decisão da Justiça," *Folha de São Paulo,* January 6, 2011.
59. Fung and Wright (2003) and Heller (2001).
60. At the same time that it unshackled subnational actors to experiment with delivery, decentralization also reinforced existing differences in local capacity and allowed local political bosses to exploit power differentials, forming subnational authoritarian enclaves (Gervasoni 2006 and Gibson 2005).

Brazil's most publicized contribution to governance—the development of participatory budgeting in the southern city of Porto Alegre, later expanded to other municipalities with mayors linked to the PT—highlights the extent to which local government can make a difference with regard to citizen inclusion and public transparency. The PT administrations in Porto Alegre created a process in which community representatives could participate directly in budget development, indicating priorities for public investments in their communities. Participatory budgeting brought positive results for Porto Alegre, including higher levels of citizen participation and the redistribution of public investments to less-developed neighborhoods.[61] Participatory budgeting models allowed for a completely different process of transparency development than the bureaucratically driven process at the federal level, which perhaps accounts for its greater dissemination to civil society actors.[62]

Other participatory governance models also had positive effects on public sector transparency and accountability, such as the health councils across levels of government. Health councils are legally mandated institutions that support the public Unified Health System (Sistema Único de Saúde), responsible for setting health care priorities and overseeing their implementation. Their institutional design represents the historical forces and participatory nature of Brazil's public health care movement, grounding high-level state policymaking in the health care community and combining representative and participatory forms of governance.[63] Although their mission exceeds the budgetary arena, approving the health sector's portion of subnational budgets is one of their main responsibilities. As a result, the relationship between health councils and their executives is largely conflictual, and their level of institutionalization varies greatly. Even if their track record with regard to policy deliberation is mixed, their power to deny local executives access to federal health resources has nonetheless led to the dissemination of budgetary information and, as a result, made governments more accountable to local constituencies. As a concrete example, municipal governments must present multiyear health plans (stating policy goals and the resources available for their operationalization) to their health councils in order to be eligible to receive federal transfers. In addition, they must present year-end reports (*relatórios anu-*

---

61. Avritzer (2009) and Baiocchi (2005).

62. Avritzer (2009) highlights, however, that there are limits to participatory budgeting even where it is fully backed by municipal governments. In particular, while it has changed the *distribution* of public investments, it has not affected the *amount* of resources available, which is determined by the finance departments.

63. Half of the voting seats are assigned to civil society representatives, one-quarter to management (including private contractor representation), and one-quarter to health sector workers (including the public health scientific community). For a more detailed account of the public health care system's institutional structure, see Alves (2012)).

ais de gestão) in which they analyze policy actions and execution of the health budget. As a result, budget transparency is more extensive and more developed in health than in other sectors. While only 11 percent of municipalities have to provide transparency portals under the current legislation, 78 percent had year-end reports approved by health councils for the 2009 exercise.[64] Therefore, while the broader process of public sector transparency and accountability might be relatively lagging at the local level, local experiences in health care can be expanded to other sectors.

Clearly, the institutional engineering of participatory institutions cannot single-handedly transform subnational realities. Since their initial rise to prominence, a second generation of studies has problematized the exportability of participatory models to different social and political environments. Comparing four Brazilian capitals, Avritzer (2009) highlights the importance of the interaction of dense civil society with reformist political actors for participatory models to flourish. Likewise, Wampler (2008) argues that participatory models are more likely to succeed in municipalities where mayoral support coincides with a history of noncontentious strategies by civil society. Alves (2012) argues that the proliferation of participatory councils is deflated by the removal of policy discussions (and therefore financial allocations) to technical forums. Finally, Baiocchi, Heller, and Silva (2011) examine four matched pairs of municipalities with and without participatory budgeting and find that the adoption of participatory budgeting did, in fact, increase the activity and effectiveness of civil society in shaping municipal budgets. While recognizing the importance of local contexts, these institutional experiences nonetheless illustrate the importance of subnational levels of government as multiplying spaces for contact between the state and civil society, increasing participation, accountability, and transparency, while also mobilizing a different set of users of information in ways that are not as feasible at higher levels of aggregation.

The Initial Outcomes of Transparency in Brazil

Although the implementation of transparency-enhancing reforms is relatively recent—and in the case of the 2009 Transparency Law, still incomplete—some early outcomes are potentially related to increased transparency. Of first importance, the parallel development of transparency practices and democratic consolidation has no doubt generated a positive reinforcement mechanism in which the population begins to associate the two processes. The "active" transparency practices, relating to the automatic disclosure of public budgetary information, are

---

64. See http://portal.saude.gov.br/portal/arquivos/pdf/dados_2009_210611.pdf.

clearly established at the national level and are slowly, if unevenly, trickling down to local governments. LRF requirements for the annual presentation of executive accounts have empowered oversight bodies within the state such as the accounts tribunals, and the increased oversight has curbed fiscal profligacy in state and municipal governments, while greatly diminishing the worst effects of the electoral cycle on public finances. Likewise, the creation of sectoral and local participatory institutions such as neighborhood participatory budgeting committees and municipal health councils has galvanized civil society groups and generated increasing capacities to understand and challenge public expenditures. In health care in particular, mobilization across levels of government has allowed state and municipal associations to use the access to publicly disclosed budget planning documents to perform their own studies pointing out budgetary shortcomings or misallocations and to lobby the legislature for more funding for the Ministry of Health.

In addition, the availability of public data has created an ample source of information to reinforce the national media's "watchdog" role within society. "Exposé-ism" (*denuncismo*) drove the national narrative incessantly in the months preceding passage of the Transparency Law. Investigative reporters and their media channels, both locally and nationally, have the time, the resources, and the incentives required not only to navigate the extensive and complex data provided on public transparency websites, but also to follow through and look for discrepancies (for example, calling up or searching for addresses for payees). Major media outlets have used these resources to tighten their supervision of public sector programs and to expose the lavish entitlements of the Brazilian political class. CSOs and the media have partnered in this process, sharing their capacities and resources and aiding in the dissemination of studies and specific discoveries.[65] In a recent interview, the head of Transparência Brasil highlights the relative importance of such actors, especially considering the low demand for information from civil society: "The demand [for these numbers] is poor; [transparency is] not just a question of publishing [data]. The only actors who seek these data are the private sector, which needs to know about the state to develop its strategies, the press, and the NGOs, who have even greater difficulty."[66]

---

65. Although the top-down, bureaucratically driven nature of the national transparency process is very similar to the South African experience, examined in chapter 2 of this volume, the presence of an active (though not immune from connections to those in power) media sector that processes public information and disseminates it has undoubtedly contributed to a changing consensus on what are acceptable practices by elected representatives and public sector employees.

66. "Governos dão acesso precário a dados públicos, dizem especialistas" (http://noticias.uol.com.br/politica/2010/07/15/governos-dao-acesso-precario-a-dados-publicos-dizem-especialistas.jhtm). The translation is ours.

In this environment of relatively low civil society engagement, transparency advances continue to reflect the demands of the actors prominently involved in reforms, namely, bureaucratic actors within the federal government. As their main goals have been to have access to information in order to ensure fiscal discipline from different sectors of the state as well as subnational governments, the face of public transparency illustrates these highly technical demands, with a proliferation of platforms and fine-grain information that is nonetheless quite complex to the casual user. In the meantime, political parties use transparency platforms to dig up and expose their opponents to the media and society. The increasingly stringent requirements for the disclosure of public accounts are also forcing a positive externality in the form of stronger managerial and technological capacities in state and local governments as they seek to fulfill legal requirements, as attested by the increasing numbers of municipalities that have developed the capacity to provide fine-grain expenditure information in a relatively short period of time.

While celebrating these first-generation reforms, it is important to raise the difficult issues regarding public sector transparency that remain unresolved. For one, the budget process itself continues to allow for budgetary distortions in allocation, atomization of investment spending into low-quality pork-barrel amendments, and manipulation of the fiscal calendar, with detrimental results for transparency and for public programs. There are still a series of "black boxes" in the public budget, including the use of corporate credit cards by the presidential office and closed budgets in the Foreign Service Ministry and, especially, parastatal companies. Furthermore, the voluntary provision of information ("active" transparency) has been disassociated from other forms of public transparency that increase the responsiveness of the state to society. Much like in South Africa, "passive" transparency, or the response to requests for not readily available information, is quite underdeveloped in Brazil. Citizens, researchers, and civil society organizations have great difficulty in getting responses or information from different state offices, even when they know how to navigate the dense bureaucratic channels involved. Up until recently, Brazil had the unlikely confluence of providing highly detailed budgetary information, while not having legislation that ensures access to public information. Despite pressure from CSOs like the Forum for the Right to Access Public Information (Fórum de Direito de Acesso a Informações Públicas),[67] debate over the legislation was delayed under the Lula administration, as conservative politicians such as former presidents José Sarney and Fernando Collor de Mello publicly defended indefinite confidentiality of some public documents, and the national executive sought a special regime to expedite and maintain secret any information regarding the infrastructure projects related to the upcoming World

67. See www.informacaopublica.org.br.

Cup and Olympics to be held in Brazil.[68] While President Rousseff has since signed the bill into law, it is too early to tell whether the state will respond in a timely and substantive manner to requests for information.

Conclusions

Budgetary transparency in Brazil has continued to improve—though at uneven pace and reach—since the 1980s. Although democratic consolidation does not necessarily yield increases in transparency and accountability, for Brazil at least, it appears to have done so. Redemocratization and macroeconomic stabilization were two major changes in the fabric of Brazilian society that paved the way for transparency reforms during the 2000s. A capable public bureaucracy, empowered by President Cardoso's reformist state-building agenda and later by President Lula's understanding of the popular consensus surrounding the issues of macroeconomic stability and good governance, was able to take advantage of catalytic opportunities—fiscal crises and corruption scandals—to force greater transparency standards on other levels of government and on the political class in general. The federal government, determined to rein in fiscal profligacy, has been proactive in imposing discipline and greater transparency on subnational units.

While the amount of information at the public's disposal is extensive and updated regularly, the current demand by civil society is frustratingly low. Given the costs in time and expertise required to navigate the complexities of budgeting, accessing and digesting this information have been limited to high-capacity CSOs, academics, the business class, and the media. Yet the mere public disclosure of budgetary information is nonetheless an important and necessary first step toward developing the capacities of civil society and the general public—the clients of this information—and enabling the state to become accountable.

Transparency has not lowered the perceptions of corruption in Brazil. If anything, media access to information and the constant exposés run in newspapers and on television have made the presence of corruption and misuse of public funds more obvious in daily life. Perhaps because of this, the repercussions, especially for politicians, have been relatively small, as the population seems unable or unwilling to maintain interest once the media has moved on to the next scandal.[69]

68. For the debate over freedom of information, see "Senado deve votar 'sigilo eterno' até dia 15 de julho," *Estado de São Paulo*, June 25, 2011; for the World Cup projects, see "Governo quer manter em sigilo orçamentos da Copa de 2014," *Folha de São Paulo*, June 16, 2011.

69. Power and Taylor (2011). Although this too might be changing, as the Supreme Court recently convicted top political insiders (including President Lula's former chief of staff) in the widely publicized "*mensalão*" trial. Domestic and international media have defined this as a potential turning point for Brazil's judicial and political systems. See, for example, "A Blow against Impunity," *The Economist*, November 15, 2011.

At the same time, the public sector has continued to develop its disclosure capacities, albeit unevenly and in some cases half-heartedly. But this has allowed for major reforms in the social sector, including expansion of health care services (through family health teams) and a massive cash transfer program (Bolsa Família), to be rolled out with relative effectiveness. Although it is difficult to show a direct correlation, there is little doubt that greater transparency in budgeting has limited leakage and rent seeking in these sectors. The tougher standards of the 2009 Transparency Law have yet to take effect in some states and in the vast majority of local governments, but they will undoubtedly help to shed light on budgetary and expenditure processes. In that sense, the initial resistance of subnational governments to transparency reforms only underscores their potential for uprooting opaque public management practices.

References

Abrúcio, Fernando L. 2007. "Trajetória recente da gestão pública brasileira: Um balanço crítico e a renovação da agenda das reformas." *Revista de Administração Pública* (Edição Comemorativa): 67–86.

Alston, Lee, Marcus Melo, Bernardo Mueller, and Carlos Pereira. 2008. "Who Decides on Public Expenditures? The Political Economy of the Budget Process in Brazil." Draft, March 28.

Alves, Jorge A. 2012. "Coordinating Care: State Politics and Intergovernmental Relations in the Brazilian Healthcare Sector." Ph.D. dissertation, Brown University.

Avritzer, Leonardo. 2009. *Participatory Institutions in Democratic Brazil.* Johns Hopkins University Press.

Baiocchi, Gianpaolo. 2005. *Militants and Citizens: The Politics of Participatory Democracy in Porto Alegre.* Stanford University Press.

Baiocchi, Gianpaolo, Patrick Heller, and Marcelo K. Silva. 2011. *Bootstrapping Democracy: Transforming Local Governance and Civil Society in Brazil.* Stanford University Press.

Cambraia, Túlio. 2011. "Emendas ao projeto de lei orçamentária anual: Algumas distorções." COFF Working Paper. Brasilia: Câmara dos Deputados, Consultoria de Orçamento e Fiscalização Financeira, February.

CONOF (Consultoria de Orçamento e Fiscalização Financeira). 2011. "Orçamento impositivo, contingenciamento e transparência." Brasilia: Câmara dos Deputados.

Evans, Peter B. 1995. *Embedded Autonomy: States and Industrial Transformation.* Princeton University Press.

Figueiredo, Argelina, and Fernando Limongi. 2002. "Incentivos eleitorais, partidos políticos e política orçamentária." *Dados* 45, no. 2: 303–39.

Fung, Archon, and Erik Olin Wright. 2003. *Deepening Democracy: Institutional Innovations in Empowered Participatory Governance.* New York: Verso Books.

Gervasoni, Carlos. 2006. "A Rentier Theory of Subnational Authoritarian Enclaves: The Politically Regressive Effects of Progressive Federal Revenue Redistribution." Prepared for delivery at the 2006 annual meeting of the American Political Science Association, Philadelphia, August 31– September 4.

Gibson, Edward L. 2005. "Boundary Control: Subnational Authoritarianism in Democratic Countries." *World Politics* 58, no. 1: 101–32.

Heller, Patrick. 2001. "Moving the State: The Politics of Democratic Decentralization in Kerala, South Africa, and Porto Alegre." *Politics and Society* 29, no. 1: 131–63.

IBGE (Instituto Brasileiro de Geografia e Estatística). 2010. *Censo demográfico 2010.* Brasília (www.ibge.gov.br/home/estatistica/populacao/censo2010/sinopse/default_sinopse.shtm).

———. 2011. *Contas regionais do Brasil, 2005–2009.* Brasília. (www.ibge.gov.br/home/estatistica/economia/contasregionais/2009/contasregionais2009.pdf).

IMF (International Monetary Fund). 2010. *World Economic Outlook.* Washington.

Limongi, Fernando, and Argelina Figueiredo. 2005. "Processo orçamentário e comportamento legislativo: Emendas individuais, apoio ao executivo e programas de governo." *Dados* 48, no. 4: 737–76.

Loureiro, Maria R., and Fernando L. Abrúcio. 2004. "Políticas e reformas fiscais no Brasil recente." *Revista de Economia Política* 24, no. 1: 50–72.

O'Donnell, Guillermo. 1973. *Modernization and Bureaucratic Authoritarianism: Studies in South American Politics.* University of California, Institute of International Studies.

OECD (Organization for Economic Cooperation and Development). 2010. *Revenue Statistics 1965–2009.* Paris.

Pereira, Carlos, and Bernardo Mueller. 2002. "Comportamento estratégico em presidencialismo de coalizão: As relações entre executivo e legislativo na elaboração do orçamento brasileiro." *Dados* 45, no. 2: 265–301.

Power, Timothy J., and Matthew M. Taylor, eds. 2011. *Corruption and Democracy in Brazil: The Struggle for Accountability.* University of Notre Dame Press.

Protásio, Carla G., Mauricio S. Bugarin, and Mirta S. Bugarin. 2004. "À espera da reforma orçamentária: Um mecanismo temporário para redução de gastos públicos." *Estudos Econômicos* 34, no. 1: 5–41.

Samuels, David, and Fernando L. Abrúcio. 2000. "Federalism and Democratic Transitions: The 'New' Politics of the Governors in Brazil." *Publius* 30, no. 2: 43–61.

Sodré, Antonio Carlos, and Maria Fernanda Alves. 2010. "Relação entre emendas parlamentares e corrupção municipal no Brasil: Estudo dos relatórios do programa de fiscalização da Controladoria-Geral da União." *Revista de Administração Contemporânea* 14, no. 3: 414–33.

STN (Secretaria do Tesouro Nacional). 2011. *Resultado primário do governo geral.* Brasilia (http://www.tesouro.fazenda.gov.br/hp/downloads/ResGovGeral.xls).

UNDP (United Nations Development Programme). 2009. *Human Development Report 2009: Overcoming Barriers; Human Mobility and Development.* New York: Palmgrave Macmillan.

Viana, Arizio. 1947. *Budget Making in Brazil.* Ohio State University Press.

Wampler, Brian. 2008. "When Does Participatory Democracy Deepen the Quality of Democracy? Lessons from Brazil." *Comparative Politics* 41, no. 1: 61–81.

4

A Mutually Reinforcing Loop:
Budget Transparency and Participation
in South Korea

JONG-SUNG YOU AND WONHEE LEE

South Korea (hereafter simply Korea) is hailed as a rare case of achievement in both economic development and democratic transition among developing countries in the second half of the twentieth century. Korea is considered a success in terms of budget transparency as well. According to the Open Budget Index (OBI), published by the International Budget Partnership (IBP), Korea is one of the top performers in budget transparency in the Asia-Pacific region.[1]

During the authoritarian era in Korea, budget information, as well as overall government information, was not widely shared. Secrecy, rather than transparency, was often deemed necessary for efficiency. Citizen participation in the budgetary process and in policymaking more generally was forbidden. Even members of the National Assembly had only limited access to budget information. Hence, political democracy permitted the development of fiscal democracy in Korea.

However, not all inchoate democracies have successfully implemented budget transparency and participation. This fact suggests that political democratization does not automatically lead to fiscal democracy and that other conditions may be required for fiscal transparency. We examine the Korean example to explore this issue in depth.

Our findings suggest that the democratic transition of 1987 led to some fiscal transparency, but progress was limited. Important improvements were made as civil society exerted increasing pressure, in particular after the change of government in the midst of the financial crisis of 1997. Although the crisis made

1. IBP (2010).

105

transparency reforms urgent, the requisite changes could not have been implemented without the incoming liberal government, which was responsive to the demand for reform from civil society and was not tied, as prior governments were, to the practices of secrecy and collusion with the conglomerates (chaebols). Furthermore, improvements in good governance and budget transparency could not have occurred without the efforts of nongovernmental organizations (NGOs), which pressed tirelessly for sweeping reforms in fiscal democracy.

In this chapter, we first assess the positive achievements and limitations in budget transparency and participation in Korea. Then we trace historical processes to identify key milestones and watershed moments that allowed for breakthroughs. We provide detailed accounts of how fiscal democracy has been institutionalized through various reforms. We further attempt to explain the factors and mechanisms that have facilitated these processes and examine the roles of various actors, such as presidents, legislators, the judiciary, and, in particular, civil society organizations (CSOs) and the media. We also analyze how budget information was used and the effects of enhanced budget transparency on budgetary priorities, government efficiency, and corruption. We conclude, emphasizing the role of CSOs in promoting and maintaining virtuous circles of fiscal democracy.

Overall State of Budget Transparency and Participation in Korea

Korea was the top performer from Asia on the Open Budget Index 2010, with a score of seventy-one out of 100. It ranked second in the Asia-Pacific region, behind only New Zealand, and ninth out of the ninety-four countries covered by the 2010 OBI. Korea's OBI score indicates that the government provides the public with significant information on the central government's budget and financial activities during the course of the budget year. Although Korea's budget is not yet fully transparent, the amount of information published is generally sufficient for citizens to assess how their government is managing public funds.

The OBI measures the availability and adequacy of eight key budget documents. As table 4-1 indicates, the Korean government publishes a comprehensive set of budget documents that includes a pre-budget statement, an executive budget proposal, an enacted budget, a citizen's budget, a year-end report, and an audit report. Major deficiencies in Korea's budget transparency are the failure to publish a midyear review and the inclusion of insufficient information in in-year reports. Even though the Korean government publishes monthly reports on the fiscal deficit and on budgetary implementation, these are far from comprehensive. Additionally, there is no comparison of actual with estimated expenditures and revenues. The executive's budget proposal is fairly comprehensive, although it does not present information on the impact of different macroeconomic

Table 4-1. *Adequacy and Availability of Eight Key Budget Documents in Korea*^a

Document	Level of information	Publication status
Pre-budget statement	A	Published
Executive's budget proposal	B	Published
Enacted budget	A	Published
Citizen's budget	A	Published
In-year reports	D	Published
Midyear review	E	Not produced
Year-end report	A	Published
Audit report	A	Published

Source: International Budget Partnership [[AQ: IBP (2010)?]].

a. An average score of 0–20 (scant information) is graded as E; 21–40 (minimal) is graded as D; 41–60 (some) is graded as C; 61–80 (significant) is graded as B; and 81–100 (extensive) is graded as A.

assumptions on the budget. Furthermore, it provides insufficient data on extra-budgetary activities, including special funds, guarantees, and loans.

Strong Areas

Let us elaborate the positive achievements that Korea has made in budgetary transparency and participation. The Korean government has a modern budget process and an effective accounting system. It produces timely statistics for the consolidated central government budget that conform to international standards. In addition, Korea has clear standards for procurement and public employment as well as an independent, active, and professional National Audit Office.[2]

Budget transparency in Korea has a solid legal basis. As stipulated in Article 59 of the constitution, taxes, duties, fees, and charges must have an explicit legal basis and be approved by the National Assembly. Tax laws are accessible, and the Ministry of Planning and Finance provides a summary of tax legislation. The Basic Law for National Tax contains details of taxpayer rights, tax dispute procedures, and the application of tax laws. Additionally, the newly enacted National Fiscal Act plays a role in integrating the budget and other special funds.

Consolidated central government fiscal data are available on the D-Brain information technology system.[3] All budget and audit reports approved by the National Assembly are accessible on this website. Data for each local government are accessible on another website.[4] After the National Fiscal Act was enacted in 2006, all documents related to the preparation, execution, and reporting of the

2. IMF (2001).

3. www.digitalbrain.go.kr.

4. http://lofin.mopas.go.kr.

budget became relatively open to the public. The budget guidelines that are distributed by the Ministry of Strategy and Finance (MoSF), the central budget agency, to each line ministry are also open to the public. All transactions relating to execution of the budget are recorded and available for both internal and external audit.

There is strong oversight by an independent audit institution. The Board of Audit and Inspection (BAI), a constitutionally independent body that reports to the president and the National Assembly, provides audited annual reports of central government operations and government-invested organizations. The BAI has about 900 staff members, many of whom have been trained as lawyers and certified accountants. The head of the organization is appointed for a four-year term by the president with the consent of the National Assembly and cannot be dismissed except by impeachment. The BAI examines the final revenue and expenditure accounts of the state mainly for financial compliance but also for performance. If irregularities are found in the course of audit, the BAI can order the imposition of disciplinary actions on civil servants, request corrective measures, or refer the case to the Public Prosecutor's office. The BAI also conducts various other financial compliance audits, regularity audits, and performance audits, with the scope and topics of the audit decided by the BAI's Council of Commissioners.

Participatory budgeting, which originated in Brazil, is being diffused throughout the local governments in Korea. In June 2002 nationwide local elections were held. During the campaign, the leftist Democratic Labor Party introduced participatory budgeting as the party's platform and, although the party itself enjoyed minimal success, the concept gained national popularity. As of 2010, ninety-nine local governments out of 246 had adopted participatory budgeting and had their own ordinances. With this system, citizens have a right to access the budget.

Weak Areas

Despite significant improvements in budget transparency and participation in Korea, many weaknesses persist.

It is still difficult to grasp the Korean budget due to many kinds of extra-budgetary special funds. The consolidated central government budget is made up of one general account, five public enterprise special accounts, thirteen other special accounts, and sixty-five extra-budgetary funds. The proliferation of extra-budgetary funds, which are managed by line ministries, and the extensive ear-marking of various revenue sources have complicated the management of overall public finances. This makes it difficult for the public to understand the whole budget. By reducing the compartmentalization of the budget, the government could improve transparency, accountability, as well as allocative efficiency.

For efficient management of the budget, reliable and detailed cost estimates of each program are necessary. But budget documents in Korea do not explicitly distinguish the costs of continuing government programs from the costs of proposed initiatives. There is no statement on the changes in tax and expenditure policy from year to year or quantitative evaluation of their fiscal effects. Projects costing more than $45 million cannot be included in the budget without a preliminary feasibility test or a preliminary investigation of the project's costs and benefits. But such a preliminary feasibility test is often exempted without scientific grounds.

"Sacred territories" or "national security costs" are shielded from public scrutiny. They include the KCIA (intelligence services), the military, and the contingency budget. The budget contains a contingency account amounting to 1 percent of total budget spending. The KCIA can use half of the contingency budget without any oversight from the National Assembly. Even though many critics think that spending on the military is unreasonable, detailed information on the military budget is not provided—in the name of national security.

In Korea, the correct total amount of national debt is still a subject of debate. The budget does not contain a report on government contingent liabilities and potential future obligations, such as the actuarial imbalances in the occupational pension schemes. In 2010 the official debt was equivalent to W40 trillion, but some CSOs and some members of the National Assembly insisted that it was actually W100 trillion. This debate demonstrates the need for information on contingent liabilities. The report on contingent liabilities (including but not limited to government guarantees) should indicate the nature of each contingent liability, its beneficiaries, and the expected cost. In addition, there should be a clear reporting of contingent liabilities that resulted in expenditure during the previous year's budget.

Each year government prepares a supplementary budget as a tool of fiscal policy. Even though the National Fiscal Act of 2006 prohibits supplementary budgets in ordinary times, supplementary budgets are still introduced and justified as necessary for managing an economic crisis. The problem is that the supplementary budget is often not reviewed in the context of its expected impact on fiscal outcomes and tends to reduce transparency, making it difficult to undertake aggregate control and set strategic priorities.

The complicated relationships between the central government and local governments make it difficult to get a complete picture of the budget. Central government revenues constitute about 80 percent of the national budget, while local government revenues constitute about 20 percent. Central government expenditure is 45 percent, whereas local government spending is 55 percent. This means that about 40 percent of central government revenue is transferred to local governments. This system makes it hard to hold local government accountable for the delivery of public services.

The budget process is more transparent within the executive branch than in the past, but is seriously flawed within the National Assembly. The most crucial stage of deliberating on the budget is drafting the budget resolution by the Special Subcommittee on Budget and Accounts, and its meetings are not open to the public. The subcommittee does not produce any record except the final draft budget resolution, and so the public does not have access to the deliberation process. This represents a serious problem given the possibility of pork-barrel politics.

Historical Overview of Changes in Budget Transparency and Participation

Although Korea has performed fairly well in budget transparency in recent years, the budgetary process was opaque and closed off during the military authoritarian regimes led by Park Chung-hee (1961–79) and Chun Doo-hwan (1980–87). During this era, political rights as well as civil liberties were suppressed, and transparency and participation in any government process were nonexistent. The budget was formulated and discussed by a small number of officials within the political and bureaucratic elite. The deliberative function of the National Assembly was superficial, and budget documents provided to members of the National Assembly lacked sufficient information. The audit function of the Board of Audit and Inspection was quite strong, but it was used strictly to control internal bureaucratic corruption, and its audit reports were not released to the public.

Ever since the Student Democratic Revolution of April 1960, which was interrupted by the military coup led by Park Chung-hee in May 1961, Koreans have fought continuously for democracy. After the military force led by Chun Doo-hwan violently suppressed the Kwangju democratization movement in 1980, the move toward democratization was temporarily halted. In 1987, however, mass demonstrations against the military regime spread to the whole country, and the Chun Doo-hwan government was forced to surrender to popular demands for direct presidential elections and other democratic reforms.

Democratization forced the government to be more open and responsive to the people, and demands for transparency and citizen participation in government affairs increased. Although Roh Tae-woo, Chun's handpicked candidate for the ruling party, won the presidential election in December 1987 due to the split of opposition candidates, the National Assembly elections in April 1988 produced a divided government, with three main opposition parties occupying an absolute majority of the National Assembly seats. The opposition parties, with their legislative power, and the president, with his veto power, reached a compromise on several politically significant issues. One important reform was to restrict private contracts for large government projects through an amendment to the Budget Accounting Law in 1989—one of the early reforms enacted by the opposition-dominated National Assembly.

After the three-party merger between the ruling party and two opposition parties in 1991, further democratic reforms stalled for the rest of Roh Tae-woo's presidency (1988–92). However, Kim Young-sam, a former opposition leader, succeeded in capturing the merged ruling party's nomination for presidential candidate. He became the first civilian president by defeating Kim Dae-jung, who used to be his long-time rival within the opposition, in December 1992. President Kim Young-sam (1993–97) launched an ambitious reform agenda to promote transparency and curb corruption, including implementation of a "real-name" financial transaction system (banning "false-name" and "borrowed-name" accounts) in 1993, asset disclosure of high-level public officials in 1993, and enactment of the Information Disclosure Act in 1996. However, there was little reform in the area of budget transparency and participation during his presidency. His anticorruption drive fell far short of curbing political corruption, which was vividly revealed by his own son's involvement in a big corruption scandal. Kim Young-sam's failure to reform the chaebols and financial sectors not only sustained the cozy relationship among the government, banks, and the chaebols but also contributed to bringing about a series of failures of overleveraged chaebols, followed by the financial crisis of 1997.

In the midst of the financial crisis and International Monetary Fund (IMF) bailout, long-time opposition leader Kim Dae-jung was elected president in December 1997. His administration (1998–2002) pursued the "parallel development of democracy and market economy" and declared the end of government-business collusion or crony capitalism. He launched the so-called "IMF-plus" reforms, a comprehensive reform program that went beyond IMF-mandated reforms.[5] Structural reforms were carried out in the financial, corporate, labor, and public sectors. The chaebol reforms sought to enhance transparency and accountability in corporate governance and accounting practices. Financial reform strengthened financial safety nets and consolidated financial supervisory functions. These reforms increased openness and competition in the economy. Now, many new economic players such as banks, foreign investors, and institutional investors are acting independently of both the government and the chaebols. Overall, the degree of economic openness and transparency significantly improved after the crisis.[6]

5. You (2010).
6. Mo and Weingast (2009) and You (2012).

Table 4-2. *Stages of Development in Budget Transparency and Participation in Korea*

Stage	Period	Policy orientation
Dark age	1961–1987	Bureaucratic-authoritarian rule
Takeoff	1987–1997	Democratization, increasing transparency
Development	1998–2007	Institutionalization of budget process reforms
Maturing	2008–	Diffusion and settlement

Source: Authors.

Kim Dae-jung's liberal government also implemented substantial reforms to enhance budget transparency and participation. An incentive system was introduced first for citizens in 1998 and then for public employees in 1999 to encourage them to report cases of budget waste by awarding those whose reports resulted in budget savings and by providing protection for whistle-blowers. Introduction of preliminary feasibility studies (1999), a performance-based budget system (1999), pilot projects for (or study of) a double-booking and accrual-based booking system (1999, fully implemented in 2010), a resident audit request system (2000), and a policy for reducing the quasi-taxes (2000) as well as enactment of the Basic Law for Management of Special Funds (2001) were intended to improve transparency of the budgetary process and encourage citizen participation. In particular, preliminary feasibility studies significantly enhanced transparency and improved efficiency in budget making, and resident audit requests produced tangible results by exposing cases of budget waste and fraud. Table 4-2 presents the stages that Korea has passed through in its efforts to improve transparency and participation.

Another liberal president, Roh Moo-hyun, and his "participatory government" (2003–07) made real changes in public financial management with the so-called Three plus One reforms. A top-down budgeting system was adopted to encourage innovations in budget allocation at each ministry within sectoral ceilings. A National Fiscal Management Plan was introduced, which was based on the five-year medium-term expenditure framework. These systems were interrelated with the performance management system, which emphasized goals for and indicators of performance. All renovations were introduced simultaneously, and the National Fiscal Act was enacted in 2006 to support this new system. In particular, these systems were backed by the D-Brain system. The Three plus One reforms institutionalized budget transparency and participation.

In addition to the two liberal governments under Kim Dae-jung and Roh Moo-hyun, civil society organizations also contributed significantly, advocating and pressuring for reform in fiscal transparency. Since the democratic transition of 1987, many NGOs have blossomed. In particular, the resumption of local elections has prompted NGOs to push for transparency and participation at the local level. After the financial crisis of 1997, NGOs focused their efforts on the central government, including monitoring government budget waste and advocating fiscal reforms for transparency and participation.

Institutionalization of Budget Transparency and Participation

This section describes some of the major reforms in the realm of budget transparency and participation that have been undertaken since the democratic transition.

Restriction on Private Contracts

During the authoritarian period, there were many problems with governmental contracts. After the opposition parties took a majority of seats in the National Assembly in 1988, parliamentary investigations of former president Chun Doo-hwan's corruption uncovered the prevalent abuse of private government contracts. To block future corruption in private (so-called "negotiated") contracts, the opposition-dominated National Assembly eliminated two articles of the Budget Accounting Law that had provided a legal basis for Chun's abuse of private contracts: the "public interest corporation contract" clause and an article authorizing the use of private contracts depending on "the purpose or characteristics of a project" and requiring approval by the National Assembly of future private contracts only in clearly delineated, exceptional cases.

James Schopf's recent research shows that, after the law was amended, there was a steep decline in both the overall number and individual size of private contracts used by central and local governments, public organizations, and government enterprises. Central government private contracts fell from 58 percent of the amount of total contracts in 1985 to only 7.7 percent in 1997. Government enterprise private contracts declined from 65 percent in 1982 to 6 percent in 1991, public body private contracts declined from 47 percent in 1983 to 15 percent in 1993, and local government private contracts declined from 54 percent in 1982 to 12 percent in 1991.[7]

Business Expenses

In Korea, every ministry and local government has an item called "business expenses" in its budget, and this is a discretionary item. These expenses are usually used to pay for meals with guests. In the past, ministers, governors, and mayors

7. Schopf (2011).

used this item without any regulations or scrutiny. The expenditure often was not supported by a receipt or a list of participants. Government executives customarily used business expenses for dinner with friends without any specific job-related purposes. Sometimes executives considered the money to be supplementary salary. They often gave money from the budget item to newspaper reporters in cash without receipts. When there were local elections, incumbent mayors and governors often used that money for electoral purposes such as dining with constituents and buying support from influential persons. This type of abuse went on for decades.

Beginning in 1998, NGOs asked the central and local governments to release the details of the business expenses item. Many newspapers published stories of abuse, and many whistle-blowers surfaced from within bureaucracies. When the ministries and local governments refused to release detailed information about business expenses, some NGOs took the issue to court, and court rulings were crucial to reform. An NGO called People's Solidarity for Participatory Democracy (PSPD) sued the mayor of Seoul Metropolitan City requesting the release of detailed information about business expenses. Initially, the local district court dismissed the request on the grounds that publicizing a list of the mayor's guests would encroach on the privacy of citizens. However, in 2001 the higher court argued that the request had due grounds, considering the intent of the Information Disclosure Act of 1996, and ruled in the NGO's favor. In 2004 the Supreme Court upheld that ruling, ordering that PSPD be given a copy of the receipts of business expenses of the mayor of Seoul Metropolitan City. In 2005 a similar case involved another city.

After the court rulings, transparency improved, but discretionary power did not decline. Many cases of misuse are still reported, and the total amount of this budget item has not declined. There has been strong resistance from elected provincial and local executives, because they are the beneficiaries. In 2009 the Public Employees Union researched the publication of business expenses on the Internet. It found that the president published the total amount of business expenses each month, without any details. The speaker of the National Assembly did not even have a menu of expenses on the website. This revelation further raised people's concerns about the abuse of business expenses. At the end of 2010, the central government published the standards and guidelines for business expenses. Real improvement will probably only be made through court decisions and detailed administrative guidelines.

Preliminary Feasibility Studies

During the early period of rapid economic development, the political elite made almost all the decisions about important projects. Without any oversight assessing the feasibility of such projects, some of the projects undertaken were not economically sound and subsequently failed. Even when feasibility studies were conducted, they were only physical feasibility studies conducted by individual ministries that were spearheading the project. Physical feasibility studies dealt only with construction design; projects were not evaluated for their "economic validity based on cost-benefit analysis." The need for such cost-benefit analysis was widely accepted. Moreover, as the size of the economy and budget grew, the opportunity cost of undertaking one project at the expense of another became increasingly important, and the planning stage of economic projects began to receive much more scrutiny.

In 1999 the Kim Dae-jung government mandated "preliminary feasibility studies" for all upcoming projects. The main goal of a preliminary feasibility study is to assess the economic validity of the proposed project in budget preparation. The feasibility study requires that economic planners ascertain whether the given project makes economic sense based on cost-benefit analysis.

At first, this requirement did not have a legal basis; it was proclaimed by presidential decree. All the social overhead capital (SOC) projects above W50 billion (roughly equivalent to $45 million) were subject to the test. Another significant change from the past was that responsibility for the budget was given to the MoSF, which now had power over line ministries in budget making.

In 2000 the government established the Center for Public Investment Management at the Korea Development Institute to conduct feasibility studies of all projects. If the result of the feasibility study is not favorable, the project cannot go forward to the next budgeting step. Some exceptions were made—for instance, some projects that had promoted equity goals were passed even if they did not pass the benefit-cost component of the feasibility test. Overall, this system is viewed as one of the great contributions to the development of budgetary management. In 2006, when the National Fiscal Act, the new basic law regarding the budget, was enacted, the feasibility study was included in the law. Furthermore, the target was expanded to include not only SOC projects, but also research and development projects.

"Three plus One" Reforms in 2004

Both the demand for social welfare and the sharp increase in the national debt increased the importance of managing public debt, and civil society organizations began to demand greater participation in the budgeting process. To meet these demands for fiscal transparency, in 2004 the government began to implement significant budgetary reforms, which included the introduction of a National Fiscal Management Plan, top-down budgeting, a performance management system, and a digital accounting system (see figure 4-1). Simultaneous

Figure 4-1. *"Three plus One" Reforms in Korea, 2004*

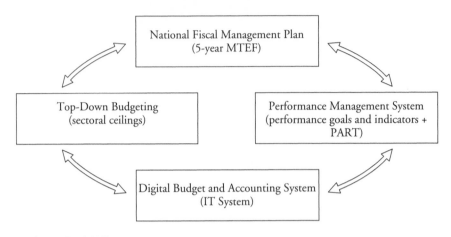

Source: Lee (2007).

implementation of interrelated reforms proved to be very effective. All of these budgetary reforms were aided by implementation of the digital information technology system (D-Brain), which enabled the public to access budget information with relative ease.

The traditional five-year economic development plan that had emphasized the role of the state in resource allocation during the authoritarian era was ended during the Kim Young-sam government, and emphasis was placed on the market economy. After the financial crisis of 1997, demand for a new midterm fiscal policy arose. In response, the Roh Moo-hyun government introduced the National Fiscal Management Plan (NFMP) and the medium-term expenditure framework (MTEF). The NFMP is a basic plan representing the aggregate plan for fiscal management, while the MTEF is a five-year fiscal management plan presenting the national policy vision and direction as well as sectoral expenditure programs in the medium-term perspective. The NFMP is a rolling plan that is subject to adjustment each year. It permits wide participation, including NGOs and experts, from the initial stage of formulation and is submitted to the National Assembly for deliberation.

Introduction of the "top-down budgeting" contributed to significantly improving the efficiency of the budget process. Before adopting the top-down budgeting system, the MoSF was fully authorized to allocate funds in public spending. It screened all projects that line ministries requested. The budget for all projects was ultimately determined by the MoSF, which had overriding power over line ministries. This, however, created perverse incentives for moral hazard on the part of line ministries. They requested many projects without valid reasons and often inflated the total amount required, anticipating substantial cuts by the MoSF. On the one hand, the sheer volume and number of projects, as well as the huge budgets requested, weakened the capacity of the MoSF. On the other hand, line ministries did not worry much about performance, because the overburdened agency was unable to undertake performance reviews.

After adoption of the top-down budgeting system, the budgetary process was divided into two steps. In the first stage, the MoSF sets overall ceilings by sector, and in the second stage line ministries allocate the budget for programs in detail within the ceilings. With this new procedure, the national plan and budget are connected more effectively with each other in accordance with ceilings authorized by the cabinet. Before the introduction of this system, the budgetary process was considered a black box. Now it is easier to understand the inner process, and relevant materials concerning negotiations between ministries are available to the public.[8]

Another significant reform measure was the introduction of performance management. Under the old budget system, it was difficult to understand the detailed contents of projects. Fraud, waste, and misuse were difficult to detect. As there was no process for evaluating performance, the budget was considered a blueprint for the MoSF. With the introduction of performance management, the main programs and projects became subject to review every three years. Line ministries monitor and review programs, which is called self-assessment. If this review detects inappropriate or wasteful spending, the MoSF can request an in-depth review, directly carrying out a meta-evaluation of the program and reflecting the results in budgeting for the subsequent year. All of these processes are open to the public on the website of MoSF. From the Internet, citizens can learn about budgetary performance. Furthermore, during program monitoring and review by line ministries and program evaluation by the MoSF, there is widespread participation by experts and NGOs. Thus the decision is not limited to bureaucratic politics but is influenced by the wider policy community. With increased transparency and participation, there is enhanced democratic control and accountability of the bureaucracy.

Last, but not least, introduction of the digital accounting system helped to enhance budget transparency. The budget is considered an annual process, and accumulated budget data were not provided until recently. Without accumulated data, it was hard to understand budget policies and processes. The government

---

8. After the top-down method was implemented, line ministries stopped making excessive budget requests. For example, the rate of increase of budget requests by line ministries dropped sharply, from 30.8 percent in 2004 to 11.7 percent in 2005, and some line ministries restructured their spending, because they were now responsible for their own programs.

then organized a Budget and Accounting System Reinvention Office to design a new system in consultation with the Ministry of Planning and Budget, the Ministry of Finance and Economy, the Ministry of Government Administration and Home Affairs, and the Board of Audit and Inspection. Since this office was established in May 2004, many studies have been carried out to set the direction of the new system and prepare detailed plans. The primary purpose of establishing the digital accounting system was to build a system for managing the performance of fiscal operations in the public sector. Another purpose was to improve the credibility of the government by introducing double-entry bookkeeping and accrual accounting with information on assets, debt, and costs. It also tried to integrate and connect fiscal information systems in line ministries, local governments, and public enterprises. With these policy goals, a new fiscal management paradigm has developed to enhance efficiency, transparency, and public participation in national fiscal management. The digital budget enables more accurate analysis of fiscal data and information, which provides policymakers with real-time support for policy formulation. Many observers say that the digital system has been functioning relatively well so far. It is the cornerstone of transparency and participation.

Factors and Mechanisms Affecting Change

In Korea democratization was probably the most important factor that contributed to enhancing budget transparency and participation. Democratic institutions such as electoral competition and political rights created pressures to open state practices to public scrutiny. After the democratic transition, the opposition-dominated National Assembly enacted laws to restrict private contracts and to require open bidding for government projects and procurements, and the first civilian president implemented many reforms to improve transparency and accountability of the government and public officials. The most significant reforms for budget transparency and participation, however, took place only after the change of government parties in 1997. In addition to the political will of liberal governments, the growth of a vibrant civil society and free media played important roles in advancing transparency reforms. Decentralization and local autonomy, with regular mayoral and gubernatorial elections as well as local and provincial council elections, also facilitated the growth of local NGOs and spread participatory budgeting throughout the nation.

Korea's meritocratic and competent bureaucracy also enabled it to control bureaucratic corruption and enhance transparency. Korea's historically low level of inequality and absence of powerful classes or interest groups in early years of economic takeoff were particularly important in establishing a meritocratic bureaucracy. Countries with high inequality and powerful economic elites, such as a landed class, often have difficulty establishing a meritocratic bureaucracy because the elites assert strong political pressures for patronage jobs.[9]

Watershed Moments and Breakthroughs

In Korea three watershed events produced significant momentum for (budget) transparency and participation: the democratic transition in 1987, the reintroduction of full local government autonomy in 1995, and the financial crisis and change of government parties in 1997. The democratic transition in 1987 played a decisive role in enhancing political transparency by empowering the citizenry and the legislature. There was inertia, however, and the old practices of secrecy in budgetary processes did not disappear easily. The financial crisis highlighted the importance and urgency of undertaking reforms in both the public and private sectors. In addition, the overall demand for change in this political environment resulted in the election of a government from the opposition party for the first time since 1987. The new liberal government undertook sweeping reforms to increase transparency and citizen participation in government policymaking and corporate governance. Finally, local autonomy empowered grassroots local NGOs, and the monitoring of budget waste and the practice of participatory budgeting spread throughout the country over time. The three events reinforced and accelerated democratic reforms, including budget transparency and participation. These events empowered both the legislature and the citizens, and the increasingly vocal civil society played a major role in promoting budget transparency and participation. Figure 4-2 shows how these three events contributed to budget transparency and participation through their influence on various actors.

Major Actors and Their Strategies

After the democratic transition, many agents of change contributed to budget transparency and participation. The most notable are NGOs, presidents, and members of the National Assembly, among others.

CIVIL SOCIETY ORGANIZATIONS. After the democratic transition in 1987, many CSOs were created and citizens' demand for transparency in government increased. Among the newly organized CSOs, the Citizens' Coalition for Economic Justice (CCEJ) and the People's Solidarity for Participatory Democracy were particularly active and influential.

The CCEJ was founded in July 1989 to fight for legal and institutional reforms such as the "real-name" financial transaction system, the Freedom of

9. You (2012).

Figure 4-2. *Major Events and Mechanisms for Change in Korea*

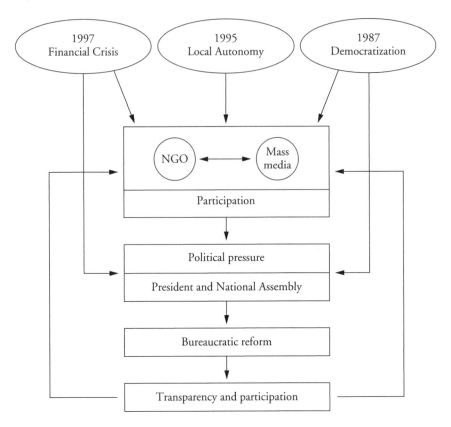

Source: Authors.

Information Act, whistle-blower protection, and corporate governance reform. By 1997, membership had grown from 500 to 20,000, and there were forty local chapters throughout Korea. Similarly, the PSPD served as a watchdog in the realm of abuse of power. Founded in 1994 by more than 200 members, the PSPD is dedicated to promoting justice and human rights through people's participation.

After the financial crisis in 1997, civic movements for transparency in government, corporate governance, and business-government relationships expanded. In particular, new organizations and activities for budget monitoring were launched. Citizens against Budget Waste (CABW) was founded as one division of CCEJ in March 3, 1998. The CABW declared March 3, the day on which the National Tax Administration was established in 1966, as Taxpayers

Day. It sought to show cases of budgetary waste and reward government officials who implemented efficient budgets; each year it announced ten worst cases and taxpayers' "friend" awards. In addition, it sought to enhance budgetary literacy. Citizens wanted to know about the budget, but they thought it was too difficult to understand. To improve the basic knowledge of an average Korean citizen on fiscal matters, the CABW began holding classes on understanding the government budget. The enhancement of budget literacy was an important catalyst in the movement toward transparency and participation.

Another influential civil society organization was the Citizens' Action Network. Established in 1999, it specialized in the online anti-budget-waste movement. In particular, its monthly "broken jar award" was given to organizations deemed to have misused public funds. Even though the named organizations always refused to accept the "award," the announcement itself was widely publicized and influential. The Citizens' Action Network's main success was in linking up the various organizations working for budget transparency and participation. For example, it worked with women's groups to monitor the National Assembly's legislative activities and budget deliberations regarding women's issues and programs. When the social welfare budget was at issue, it worked with organizations concerned with social welfare to increase the overall size of the social welfare budget and improve the efficiency of welfare spending.

The PSPD also joined the budgetary transparency movement. With the Center for Administration Watch and the Center for Tax Reform, the PSPD became involved in activities to promote budgetary transparency, focusing on taxpayers' lawsuits. The PSPD submitted a petition on "the law for the taxpayers' lawsuit" to the National Assembly in December 2000, but its petition was not successful.

Additional pressure for reforms came from the Korean Taxpayers Union, which was founded in June 1999, with the mission of making the tax system fairer. The founders were professors of fiscal policy, accountants, and lawyers, all of whom possessed the knowledge and the skills to monitor and assess government budgetary bureaucracies.

All of these CSOs shared some characteristics. First, many professors and experts, especially those who had taken part in the student democratization movement during the authoritarian era, participated in CSO activities and worked to promote transparency and participation. Second, these organizations were nonpartisan and independent voluntary organizations, enjoyed widespread support from citizens, and were politically influential. Third, they had some sort of "division of labor." Even though the main concern of most organizations was budgetary waste, each organization focused on different areas and often collaborated with each other. Fourth, their activities were often inspired by international organizations such as the World Bank and the IMF, whose reports and guidelines urged governments to enhance transparency. Many NGOs in Korea established collaborative relationships with foreign and international organizations such as Citizens Against Government Waste (CAGW), the National Taxpayers Union, the Project on Government Oversight, and the IBP.[10]

PRESIDENTS. Some reform-minded presidents played an important role in promoting transparency in the budget process and overall government affairs. The first civilian president Kim Young-sam, the first opposition-turned-president Kim Dae-jung, and the liberal president Roh Moo-hyun took various initiatives for promoting transparency. President Kim Dae-jung, for example, launched the so-called "IMF-plus" reforms, which went beyond IMF conditionality. He vigorously pursued a vision of parallel development of democracy and market economy and embraced various reforms for budget transparency and participation.

President Roh Moo-hyun pursued the vision of government innovation and launched several initiatives to promote transparency, participation, and openness, evaluation and internal audit, and so forth. To make a roadmap for reforms and monitor the implementation process, the Presidential Commission on Government Innovation and Decentralization was established. Many academics and staff at the civil organizations were invited to the commission. The philosophy and leadership of President Roh were crucial because he pushed for the new systems of transparency and participation.

NATIONAL ASSEMBLY. During the authoritarian regime, the National Assembly did not play an important role in policy and budget decisionmaking. The decisionmaking process was monopolized by the president and the bureaucracy, and there was very little substantive deliberation of the budget among lawmakers. With the onset of democracy, however, the role of the National Assembly began to assume increasing importance. Furthermore, the National Assembly was under pressure from CSOs to promote budget transparency and participation. In 2005 the National Assembly Act was revised to stipulate public hearings on budget bills.[11] When civil organizations published ten cases of budget waste, some

10. Professor Wonhee Lee, a founding member of the CABW, was a visiting fellow at CAGW in 2000 and 2001. This was an important turning point for the CABW, enabling it to establish cooperative relationships with civil organizations in the United States.

11. Article 84-3 (Public Hearing on Budget Bill and Fund Operation Plan): "The Special Committee on Budget and Accounts shall hold the public hearing on a budget bill and a fund operation plan: Provided, That in the case of a supplementary budget bill or a modified fund operation plan, it may be omitted by a resolution of the Committee."

political parties followed suit and published 100 watch items. The voluntary participation of civil society organizations often led the agenda on transparency and participation in the budget-making process.

In response to the 1997 financial crisis, CSOs petitioned the National Assembly to enact the Special Law for Fiscal Soundness in 2000. To address the issues raised in the petition, a Special Committee on Fiscal Reform was organized within the National Assembly. After many public hearings and conferences, the National Fiscal Act was formulated and passed in 2006. This law is the cornerstone of new fiscal norms of transparency, accountability, and sustainability.

Sometimes, however, civil society sees the National Assembly as a problem rather than a solution. Politicians play a dual role of problem solving and problem making in budgetary transparency. Assembly representatives use many tactics such as log-rolling during the budget deliberation process. In particular, the final deliberation in the special subcommittee is not open to the public. Although full committee meetings are open to the public, the special subcommittee meetings make crucial deals about the final budget, giving rise to pork-barrel politics.

OTHER ACTORS.   Court rulings played a crucial role in promoting transparency and participation in Korea. In several cases, litigations proved to be a successful venue for change, as in the case of business expenses. Court rulings not only forced heads of local governments to release detailed information about their expenses, but also encouraged the central government to publish standards and guidelines for their use.

The role of the media was also critical in some instances, as NGOs were able to disseminate information to the public. For example, the *Gyung-Hyang Daily* featured articles on budget waste with the help of Citizens' Action Network throughout 2004. The symbiotic relationship was not limited to newer or smaller media outlets. Even the mainstream media took part. Virtually all mass media outlets report on the ten cases of waste that CABW announces each year.

International actors also played an important role in promoting various reforms for budget transparency. Reformers in Korea, both within and outside government, were able to get ideas and use examples from more advanced countries. The government studied and assessed models from other countries, such as the Organization for Economic Cooperation and Development's best practices for budget transparency, the New Zealand model of double-entry bookkeeping and accrual accounting, and the United Kingdom's top-down budgeting system. Civil society actors also benefited from close relationships with organizations in the United States, including the Center on Budget and Policy Priorities, the IBP, the CAGW, and the National Taxpayers Union.

Use of Budget Information

Enhanced budget transparency and increasing availability of budgetary documents facilitates the use of information by various stakeholders. Civil society organizations that have fought for budget transparency have actively used budget information to influence budgetary priorities and monitor waste. For National Assembly members, accessibility of budget information allows them to upgrade policy debates. The private sector also benefits from the use of budget information.

The Citizens' Coalition for Economic Justice successfully used budget information in a case involving the government's decision to construct a national cancer center. When the decision to build the 500-bed center was made in 1991, the Ministry of Health and Welfare estimated that construction would cost W41.9 billion (at the time, approximately $58 million). The budget grew over time, reaching more than W200 billion in 1999 when the center was finally completed, more than three and a half years behind schedule. The CCEJ compared the budgets of cancer wards at other university hospitals with the government's budget plan and found that the latter was excessive. The CCEJ presented its findings to the Board of Audit and Inspection, the supreme audit institution in Korea, and requested an audit. The BAI found that overlapping and unclear investments between the cancer center and a university hospital had caused inefficiency and budget waste.[12]

In 2005 debate arose about both the size and efficiency of government. Then liberal president Roh Moo-hyun tried to raise taxes and expand welfare expenditures. He emphasized that the ratio of total government expenditures to gross domestic product was only 28.1 percent, while that of an advanced country was usually 40 or 50 percent. However, some journalists opposed that logic. They calculated the ratio through the digital budget system and announced that the ratio was 37.8 percent.[13] The calculation of the size of government depended on whether public enterprises were included or not.

When the new conservative president Lee Myung-bak was elected in 2007, he pushed for tax cuts and fiscal expenditures to boost the economy. These measures were opposed by the liberal opposition party, which claimed that tax cuts would only help the rich. So a debate began on redistributive consequences of the proposed tax cuts, expenditures, and the fiscal deficit. All of the information was available through the digital system, and many experts and politicians participated in the debate. As a result of the debate, citizens learned about the policy

---

12. Ramkumar (2008, pp. 142–43).
13. This debate is well described and analyzed in Lee (2007, pp. 26–40).

positions of different parties and politicians. Government published that the fiscal deficit was W300 trillion, but, with the help of the double-booking system, the opposition party and some NGOs argued that the fiscal deficit was in fact W1,000 trillion.

As a consequence of its increased role in the budget process, the National Assembly established two important organizations. The National Assembly Budget Office (NABO) was founded in 2004, and the National Assembly Research Service (NARS) was founded in 2007, modeled on the Congressional Budget Office and the Congressional Research Service in the United States, respectively. They provide National Assembly members with systematic information related to the budget, which helps to strengthen the role of the National Assembly in the budget-making process. In particular, NABO publishes information on high-risk projects, project evaluation reports, and so on. Now, when members submit a bill, they are required to append cost estimates, which the NABO helps to compile. The cost estimation requirement has made the National Assembly pay more attention to the budget.

The use of budget information is increasing in the private sector as well. During the government-driven economic development period, the Korean government often resorted to a quasi-tax system, so-called "charges." But it was difficult to know how much burden this imposed on the private sector. In 2001 the basic Law for the Management of Non-Tax Charges was enacted, clarifying the conditions for using the charge system. The law also mandated annual evaluations of the charge system by private sector experts. As of 2006, there were 102 kinds of charges, and the total amount was W11 trillion. As this information was published, the private sector called for reform. Some in the business sector sued over some of the charges, arguing that they were illegal in light of the constitution, which states that there should be no taxes without laws. This budget information alerted citizens that the tax burden on businesses was much heavier than they had thought.

Effects of Budget Transparency and Participation

The increased budget transparency and participation have brought about positive changes in budgetary priorities, facilitated learning within government agencies, and contributed to reducing corruption.

Budgetary priority was given to national defense during the 1950s and the 1960s and to the economy during the 1970s and the 1980s. During the late 1990s, there was an apparent change in budget priorities. President Kim Dae-jung tried to expand the social welfare budget, although not to surpass the budget for economic development. Further efforts were made by President Roh Moo-hyun,

Figure 4-3. *Government Expenditure in Korea, by Sector, 1998–2008*

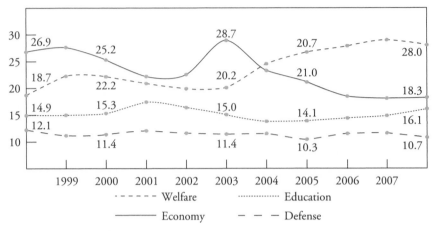

Source: MoSF (2009).

and the welfare budget surpassed the economic development budget during his presidency.

This kind of budgetary reallocation reflected demands from citizens and NGOs (figure 4-3). During the 1990s, many NGOs demanded an expansion of the welfare state. In particular, the demand for expanded social safety nets was accelerated after the financial crisis in 1997. Such a dramatic change was made possible by the Three plus One reforms. If the budget had been added up from the line ministry requests, such a dramatic change would not have been possible. When the dramatic increase in the ceiling for the social welfare budget was granted, many new programs were funded and existing ones were expanded. Many NGOs that advocated for social welfare could reinforce their activities, and the government reflected their voices with the support of the liberal president. The triangle of top-down system, National Fiscal Management Plan, and people's participation in the budgetary process helped to shift priorities in budget allocation.

The Three plus One reforms in Korea changed the budgetary process, requiring each ministry to develop its own decisionmaking logic. The K-PART (Korean program assessment rating tool) requires each ministry to offer detailed rationales for its budgetary programs and projects. As part of this process, each line ministry organizes self-evaluation committees that include outside experts and NGO activists. These committees offer government officials an opportunity to hear the concerns of civil society, creating a virtuous circle between transparency and participation and learning within government agencies.

Table 4-3. *Korea Institute of Public Administration Surveys on Perceptions and Experiences of Bribery in Korea, 2000–08*

Percent

Perception	2000	2001	2004	2005	2006	2007	2008
Extra payment is common[a]	68.8	62.4	60.6	56.2	50.4	58.8	56.5
Made extra payment to public officials	25.0	16.2	13.8	11.6	6.6	7. 4	4.8
Made extra payment to private business	n.a.	n.a.	7.0	7.4	7.2	6.4	3.9

Source: Jang (2008).

a. "Extra payment is common" denotes the percentage of respondents who chose 1, 2, or 3 from the answer choices of 1 to 6, where 1 represents "very common" and 6 represents "very rare."

n.a. = Not available

Over the last decade, enhanced transparency and participation have contributed to reducing corruption. As shown in table 4-4, the percentage of people who believe that "extra payments" are common when dealing with public officials declined from 69 percent in 2000 to 57 percent in 2008. The percentage of people who said they had bribed a public official during the last year fell from 25 percent in 2000 to 5 percent in 2008, according to surveys done by the Korea Institute of Public Administration.

Conclusions

A government budget can be seen as a "taxpayers' payment for services yet to be rendered." Seen this way, taxpayers are the principals, and government is their agent. Accordingly, some measures of accountability and performance are needed. During the authoritarian period in Korea, this relationship became distorted, and principals were not allowed to play an active role. Only after democratization in 1987 were taxpayers able to demand budget transparency and participation. With democratization came not only a change in political institutions, but also a proliferation of NGOs pushing for further reforms. Civil society became especially important in demanding and implementing reforms after the financial crisis in 1997. To meet the IMF's demand for more fiscal transparency, the newly elected Kim Dae-jung and his government initiated far-reaching reforms that went beyond the ones required by the IMF. President Roh Moo-hyun implemented further reforms, revising the basic fiscal law and introducing the Three plus One reforms. Behind all these reforms were persistent efforts by NGOs.

The relationship between good governance and better economic and social outcomes is widely acknowledged. Transparency is a key element of good governance. The budget is the single most important policy document of government, where policy objectives are reconciled and implemented in concrete terms. It should be comprehensive, encompassing all government revenue and expenditures, so that the necessary trade-offs between policy options can be assessed and fully accessible to the public and can be debated openly and with an adequate base of information.

The newly introduced systems of budget transparency and participation in Korea are expected to play a key role in promoting government accountability and effectiveness and to have positive economic and social consequences. However, institutions do not always perfectly align the interests of politicians with those of the constituents they serve, and some abuse still occurs. Fiscal democracy requires not only institutional reforms, but also reforms of the bureaucratic mind-set and culture. To fulfill the promise of transparency and participation, a virtuous circle is needed between institutions and culture.

In addition to the bureaucratic mind-set, Korea's institutions suffer from inevitable imperfections. A sudden exogenous shock can cause the system to weaken or fail. For example, the economic crisis in 2008 and 2009 weakened the economic situation in Korea. Additional funds to boost the economy were made available via a supplementary budget, which was not subject to careful scrutiny. The whole process was overwhelmed by haste. During the process, some sophisticated instruments, such as the preliminary feasibility studies, were omitted.

Transparency and participation can be compared to the trial and error of Sisyphus. To enhance transparency and participation, active and determined endeavors by citizens are imperative. In this sense, NGOs still have an important role to play in Korea.

References

IBP (International Budget Partnership). 2010. *The Open Budget Survey 2010*. Washington.

IMF (International Monetary Fund). 2001. "Report on the Observance of Standard and Codes (ROSC) Republic of Korea." Washington (www.imf.org/external/np/rose/kor/fiscal.htm).

Jang, Ji-won. 2008. *Hanguk Gonggong Bumuneui Bupae Siltae Chooi Bunseok [A Survey on the Trends of Public Sector Corruption in Korea]*. Seoul: Hanguk Haengjeong Yeonguwon (Korea Institute of Public Administration).

Lee, Wonhee. 2007. "Yesan Nangbi Daechu Bangan [Study on the System to Combat Budget Waste]." Report to the Ministry of Planning and Budget.

Mo, Jong-rin, and Barry Weingast. 2009. "Political Economy of Korea's Transition, 1961–2008." Draft.

MoSF (Ministry of Strategy and Finance). 2009. *Global Financial Crisis and Role of Korean Public Finance.* Seoul.

Ramkumar, Vivek. 2008. "Our Money, Our Responsibility: A Citizens' Guide to Monitoring Government Expenditures." Washington: IBP.

Schopf, James C. 2011. "Following the Money to Determine the Effects of Democracy on Corruption: The Case of Korea." *Journal of East Asian Studies* 11, no. 1: 1–40.

You, Jong-il. 2010. "Political Economy of Reforms in South Korea." Draft.

You, Jong-sung. 2012. "Transition from a Limited Access Order to an Open Access Order: The Case of South Korea." In *In the Shadow of Violence: Politics, Economics, and the Problems of Development,* edited by Douglas North, John Wallis, Steven Webb, and Barry Weingast. Cambridge University Press.

5

Budget Transparency and Accountability in Mexico: High Hopes, Low Performance

JOHN M. ACKERMAN

One would expect the emergence of democratic political competition in Mexico over the past decade to have had an immediate and irreversible impact on budget transparency and accountability.[1] Competition between different parties should lead to increased mutual oversight. In addition, the real possibility of losing political power at the next election should create strong incentives for government officials to reach out to citizens by involving and informing them better.

Nevertheless, progress has been extremely slow, and in some areas there are even signs of reversal. Mexico's Open Budget Index (OBI) scores are remarkably low, especially given the size of the country's economy and the relative strength of its government institutions. Mexico received a score of fifty in 2006, improved slightly to fifty-five in 2008, and then dropped to fifty-two in 2010.[2] The Latin American Index on Budget Transparency offers similar results. In that study, conducted in 2009, only 18 percent of those surveyed evaluated the government's

My most sincere thanks go to Ivan Benumea, law student at Mexico's Universidad Nacional Autónoma de México (UNAM), for his excellent research assistance. I would also like to thank Sanjeev Khagram, Paolo de Renzio, Archon Fung, Juan Pablo Guerrero, and the entire International Budget Partnership team as well as the authors of the other chapters in this volume for their important insights on previous drafts of this chapter.

1. Mexico's authoritarian state-party regime officially came to an end with the election of opposition candidate Vicente Fox to the presidency in 2000. This electoral victory ended seventy-one years of continuous rule by the Party of the Institutional Revolution (PRI). In the midterm elections of 1997, the PRI lost its majority control over the Chamber of Deputies, the "lower" house responsible for passing the budget, as well as over Mexico City, the country's political, economic, and demographic center. In addition, beginning in the 1980s the PRI slowly lost its hegemonic grip over the thirty-one state governments. In 2012, the PRI won back the presidency. It remains to be seen what impact this will have on budget transparency and accountability.

2. IBP (2010).

performance positively and only 5 percent thought that adequate channels existed for citizen participation.[3]

These low scores are also surprising because Mexico recently enacted a strong Access to Information Law that has been recognized as one of the model reforms in the world.[4] The country also has several strong civil society budget oversight groups that have used the law to obtain data on a wide variety of topics. But regardless of this apparently positive operating environment, Mexico continues to be only a mediocre performer with regard to transparency.

This chapter tries to explain the slow and irregular pace of change in Mexico. What reforms have been implemented, and how have they affected the budgetary and spending process? What political, institutional, and social factors might explain the uneven transformation of budget (and spending) accountability? What solutions might exist to the problem?

I begin by outlining the state of budget transparency in Mexico today and by tracing a timeline of the specific institutional and legal changes that have occurred during the fifteen-year period of political democratization. I then explore the underlying causes of and explanations for the current state of budget transparency in Mexico and briefly analyze the extent to which civil society has used budget information and the impact that this has had on government policies. I conclude with specific proposals on how to encourage positive change in the future.

The State of Budget Transparency in Mexico

The Mexican government complies with the basic level of budget information required to keep bureaucratic control over public spending. The executive budget proposal is well organized, with expenditures categorized by administrative, functional, and economic categories, although it also leaves a dangerously wide margin for discretionary spending. It also includes a detailed report on different sources of revenue, and there is basic comparability between each year's expenditures. There are no overtly "secret" spending categories. During the year, the executive dutifully complies with its monthly "in-year reports" on spending, and at the end of the fiscal year a relatively independent and well-funded Superior Federal Auditor (Auditoría Superior de la Federación, ASF) conducts a thorough review of spending. Mexico is far ahead of many of its neighbors such as Nicaragua, Honduras, and the Dominican Republic with regard to basic standards of budget transparency.[5]

3. Fundar (2009).
4. Ackerman (2007a).
5. Although Mexico is approximately at the same level as countries such as Guatemala and Costa Rica, which have much smaller economies and weaker states than Mexico.

Nevertheless, the transparency and accountability of the Mexican budgetary process suffers from enormous dark spots that allow for wide margins of discretion. These black holes exert a strong pull over the entire budgetary framework and significantly limit the extent to which civil society can effectively oversee, control, and evaluate compliance with the objectives of government programs.

In sum, the Mexican government generally complies with basic budgetary standards, but it has not yet begun to construct a truly open and democratic process that incorporates social actors as partners in the oversight and evaluation of government spending. In this section, we review each stage of the budgetary process with an eye to pointing out the specific strengths and weaknesses of the Mexican case.

Budget Formulation and Negotiation

The process of budget formulation and negotiation involves three actors: the executive, Congress, and civil society. Below I explore each one in turn.

EXECUTIVE BUDGET PROPOSAL. The executive budget proposal is drawn up with almost no congressional or civil society input and is missing crucial information that would facilitate oversight by external actors. The OBI gives Mexico's executive budget proposal a C rating and points out that it is particularly weak in the following areas:

—Lack of detailed information on previous years' revenues and spending in comparison with budgeted year,

—Significant problems with information on multiyear expenditures and revenue,

—Serious problems with reporting on "quasi-fiscal activities," "extra-budgetary funds," financial and nonfinancial assets held by the government, contingent liabilities, donor assistance, tax expenditures, and earmarked revenues,

—Insufficient nonfinancial data, such as the number of beneficiaries for expenditure programs, as well as lack of fully developed performance indicators,

—Missing crucial information on the composition of government debt and exactly how much debt is outstanding, and

—Incomplete explanation of how the proposed budget is linked to government's stated policy goals as well as deficient presentation of the impact of different macroeconomic assumptions (that is, sensitivity analysis) on the budget and on how policy proposals in the budget, as distinct from existing policies, affect expenditures and revenues.

The central problems are therefore comparability with other fiscal years, off-budget expenditures, performance indicators, and the effect of macroeconomic variables. This paints a picture of a budget that allows top public officials to exercise a large degree of discretion.

Table 5-1. *Percentage of Executive Budget Proposal Modified by Congress in Mexico, by Fiscal Year, 1998–2011*

Fiscal year	Percentage modified by Congress
1998	1.85
1999	2.84
2000	0.12
2001	2.55
2002	4.75
2003	2.55
2004	2.47
2005	6.25
2006	4.80
2007	3.97
2008	6.17
2009	6.97
2010	3.74
2011	2.43

Sources: Numbers for 1998–2003 refer exclusively to movements between spending categories (reassignments), calculated by Sour, Ortega, and San Sebastián (2003). Numbers for 2004–11 were calculated by the author based on formal reports provided by the Chamber of Deputies, including both reassignments and total change in size of budget between executive proposal and final budget. Alternative calculations, which come to the same conclusion with regard to reduced congressional strength, can be found in Pérez and Romero (2006), Sour and Munayer (2007), OECD (2009), and Fundar (2009).

CONGRESS. Even after ten years of democratic politics and an enormous increase in the power of Congress, the executive branch still plays an overwhelmingly dominant role in the process of design, negotiation, and spending of the budget. This is the case at the federal level, but even more so at the level of the thirty-one states and the Federal District. The percentage of the proposed federal budget that the federal Congress actually modifies each year is extremely small.

As shown in table 5-1, the general tendency is toward more active participation by Congress, beginning in 1997 when the ruling party, the Party of the Institutional Revolution (PRI), first lost its majority control over the Chamber of Deputies and especially since the formal democratic transition in 2000. Nevertheless, the percentage varies greatly from year to year and is not large overall (for example, 2.43 percent for the 2011 budget).

The OBI study points out that the Mexican legislature is particularly weak in overseeing, intervening in, and making more transparent the budgetary process. For example, Mexico receives a failing score (between zero and thirty-three out of 100) in the following areas: consultation between the executive and the legislature to determine budget priorities, testimony from the executive during legislative public hearings on budgets of central government administrative units, testimony from the public during legislative public hearings on the budgets of central government administrative units, availability of reports on legislative public hearings, legislative authority in law to amend the budget presented by the executive, legislative inputs when the executive shifts funds between administrative units, and time frame for the legislature to approve supplemental budgets.

The dominance of the executive is a paradox due to a few unique aspects of the Mexican budgeting process. First, up until a few years ago the president did not have the power to veto or even "return with comments" the budget passed by Congress, but was forced simply to publish it as passed. Even today, it is a very risky political move for the president to veto the budget, because doing so could easily lead to congressional deadlock and the failure to approve a final budget before the beginning of the fiscal year.

Second, there is no explicit rule as to what should happen if the budget is not passed before January 1. Technically, the failure of Congress to pass a budget shuts down the federal government until an agreement is reached. Theoretically, this gives Congress a powerful bargaining chip that should allow it to make significant changes to the federal budget and make the president pause before vetoing all or part of the budget and returning it to Congress.

Third, there is no formal limit on the type or number of modifications that Congress can make to the federal budget. Theoretically, Congress could change the entire budget, completely eliminate federal programs, and even create its own objectives and policies. It could ignore the budget presented by the executive and simply design its own, which it would then impose on the executive branch. In a Supreme Court decision regarding the presidential veto, the executive tried to get the justices to issue a formal decision with regard to the limits of congressional budget reassignment, but the court refused even to discuss the issue.[6]

Moving from the legal to the political realm, Congress is a key institution of the democratic transition and capable of embracing a wide range of perspectives. The Chamber of Deputies theoretically could use this legitimacy to get significantly involved in designing and changing the budget. Its position would be even stronger if it aligned itself with civil society and worked with groups and organizations to develop alternative budget proposals.

Nevertheless, Congress has been remarkably passive and ineffective since the ruling party lost its majority control over the Chamber of Deputies in 1997. It has never reassigned more than 7 percent of the national budget and never failed to pass the budget before January 1 or otherwise taken aggressive measures to threaten or gain leverage over the executive branch.

---

6. See the text of Controversia Constitucional 109/2004, Suprema Corte de Justicia de la Nación, Mexico (www.scjn.gob.mx).

CIVIL SOCIETY. The situation is even more problematic when it comes to the participation of civil society in the design and approval of the federal budget. Some special interests are well represented in Congress and make their presence felt, particularly during the discussion of fiscal policy. Particular sectors that feel they will be hurt by specific taxes—for instance, on cigarettes, alcohol, or luxury goods—normally have direct access to congressmen and can exercise a great deal of influence. The absence of clear rules on conflicts of interest or ethics for congressmen allows these relationships to flow freely.[7]

Nevertheless, civil society groups rarely, if ever, participate directly in budgetary decisions. During the process of discussing the budget, the Budget Commission holds dozens of public meetings to hear and analyze specific requests from federal government agencies as well from governors and other public officials. Each official argues in favor of and defends his or her pet projects. Social groups and nongovernmental organizations (NGOs) are sometimes also listened to if they protest or pressure enough, but their proposals are almost never taken into account.[8]

The Budget Commission does not make any proactive effort to involve common citizens or even NGOs directly in the process of budget review. It does not publish any information on the Internet about the key decisions that have to be made, about the criteria that will be used, or about the specific requests or demands that it has received. It does not publish or circulate a preliminary version of its formal proposal before sending it to the floor for a full vote or otherwise open itself up to public comment at any point in the process.

The negotiation within the Budget Commission takes place entirely behind closed doors, often with the direct participation of federal government envoys. Indeed, key negotiations often take place in federal government offices themselves. There is therefore a clear disconnect between the public "show" of openness through the public sessions of the Budget Commission and the actual process of budget reassignment.

Spending and Accounting

Once the budget is passed, important holes in the system of spending and accounting in the federal, state, and local governments work against full transparency in Mexico. The budget in the end is more of a "user's manual" or a "recipe book" than an "iron cage" for the federal government. The executive branch has a wide variety of ways in which it can unilaterally reassign funds and thereby overspend or underspend: (a) the discretionary power of the Secretariat of the

7. Cárdenas (2011).
8. See minutes of the meetings of the Budget Committee, Chamber of Deputies, Congress, September–November 2010, on file with the author.

Treasury (Secretaría de Hacienda y Crédito Público, SHCP), (b) government trusts and off-budget accounts, (c) institutional commitment and organizational compatibility with performance-based spending, and (d) procurement and government licensing.

First, the SHCP wields enormous power within the federal government. Although the budget always includes basic rules with regard to transfers between spending categories, the SHCP frequently skirts these rules and takes advantage of changing economic trends and legal technicalities to manipulate the use of the budget. For instance, the flow of tax revenues is not always regular and is often either larger or smaller than originally anticipated by Congress. The extremely volatile nature of oil income, which makes up almost a third of all government income, also plays an important role in opening up space for the power of the SHCP.

The executive branch issues reports each trimester about the current fiscal situation. But these reports do not include information down to the program level and do not need to be formally reviewed or approved by Congress. All government spending practices are eventually reviewed by the ASF, but its reports are not completed until long after the fiscal year has ended and cover only a small fraction of what is actually spent.

There are no cases of Congress or any other government actor directly intervening during the fiscal year to question or order the executive branch to change the use of specific budgetary funds. "Concomitant accountability" is almost entirely lacking.[9] When transfers do occur, they normally take money away from key social development areas that have larger budgets, such as education, health, housing, and social development.[10]

One typical example of discretionary overspending is in the area of government publicity and communications. The Mexican NGO Fundar reports that in 2009 spending in this category was 145 percent more than originally budgeted.[11] Congress had authorized a total of Mex$2,007,787,100 (approximately $200 million) and real spending reached Mex$4,702,013,400 (approximately $470 million). Overspending was high during 2009 because this was a midterm election year and the federal government evidently wanted to use government propaganda to influence voters in the election. Nevertheless, the tendency to overspend in this area was part of a long trend.

As shown in table 5-2, not only are there significant differences between the original budget (*presupuesto original*) and the formal amount spent (*presupuesto*

9. On the concept of concomitant accountability, see Ackerman (2005).
10. Pérez and Romero (2006).
11. www.las10faltantes.com/lasdiez.

Table 5-2. *Overspending in the Category of Publicity and Social Communication in Mexico, 2007–09*

pesos, thousands

Document	2007	2008	2009
Original budget	524,610.5	868,401.3	2,007,787.1
Amount spent			
Formal (public accounts)	1,444,603.5	3,010,795.9	4,702,013.4
Reported to Congress	4,099,337.0	5,473,476.5	5,371,418.5
Reported by the General Directorate of Publicity and Social Communications	3,150,393.0	4,279,667.0	4,617,357.6
Difference between the formal amount spent (public accounts) and the amount reported to Congress	2,654,733.5	2,462,680.6	669,405.1

Source: Fundar, based on reports from the SHCP.

ejercido, cuenta pública), but these numbers also do not match those in reports that other areas of government have presented to Congress.

The executive clearly has significant discretionary power, and there is little or nothing that Congress, or the common citizen, can do about it. The situation is even worse at the level of local government. A local NGO, the Instituto Mexicano para la Competitividad (IMCO), reports that during 2008 and 2009 states overspent 24 percent of their budgets on average, a total of Mex$687 billion.[12]

Second, a significant amount of government resources are never formally included in the "public account" and therefore are not formally budgeted or controlled by Congress, much less by society. Approximately Mex$267,075 billion (or $23 billion) is held in almost 600 government "trusts."[13] These trusts are funded in three ways. Some have their own source of income—for instance, the trusts that receive customs duties. Some are fed directly by the budget in order to create long-term funding for specific programs, normally in the area of education or social development. Some receive the surplus, if any, left at the end of the year, and the money is used either for future projects or sometimes for the salary of top public servants.

Once the money has entered a trust, new rules come into effect with regard to its use, since the trusts are technically "private" entities, even though their governing boards are normally controlled by public servants. In general, very little is

12. IMCO (2010b).
13. Numbers are for 2007. Sandoval (2007).

known about the spending practices of these entities. For instance, they systematically refuse to respond to requests for information, arguing that they are not government entities and therefore not legally obliged to hand over documents and information. The recent reforms of the federal oversight law gave the ASF explicit powers to audit government trusts, but this has yet to occur in practice. At the state level, only twenty of the thirty-one state budgets even include a list of the amounts contributed to government trusts.[14]

Third, there is a lack of institutional commitment to and organizational compatibility with performance-based spending. The federal government has dragged its feet in the practical implementation of performance reviews. Although the new Budget Law of 2006 required that a performance evaluation system (*sistema de evaluación al desempeño,* SED) be in place by 2008,[15] the government has issued a series of internal "agreements" allowing for gradual implementation of the system. By 2008, only two out of the eighteen general budget areas that fall under the system had even created performance indicators.[16]

In addition, the federal government has not modified its internal procedures and structures so as to transform the way in which the government carries out its duties. The impression is that the government has decided to comply with the new rules in form, but not in substance, a sort of "old wine, in new bottles" approach in which it imposes performance reviews on top of the same old hierarchical bureaucratic structures and practices. For instance, the external performance reviews conducted as part of the SED are generally deficient in quality.[17] In addition, the reviewers do not have sufficient independence or institutional protections to issue truly critical viewpoints. Each government agency is responsible for hiring its "own" external reviewers, which compromises the objectivity and quality of the reviews.

Other independently conducted external reviews reveal that the federal government has not made a successful transition toward performance-based management. A recent evaluation carried out by a local NGO (Gestión Social y Cooperación, GESOC) of more than 104 federal programs concluded that, on average, federal government programs receive a grade of 56.34 percent of compliance with the new mandate of performance-based management.[18] Four out of ten programs receive a failing score, below sixty, and only one program earns a score higher than ninety.

At the level of state governments, the situation is just as problematic. A recent study gave an average grade of 6.8 out of ten to performance indicators in the

14. IMCO (2010b).
15. See IMCO (2010b, sec. III) for a summary of the SED.
16. Colmenares Páramo (2010).
17. González (2008).
18. GESOC (2009).

thirty-one states and the Federal District. In general, the indicators themselves are of low quality, there is lack of connection between the different measurement parameters, and the indicators are not correlated with the overall formal statewide "development plan," which is published at the beginning of each administration.[19]

In addition, civil service reform has failed in numerous ways. On the one hand, the federal government has found ways to skirt the reform by creating new job categories that do not fall under the purview of the law. On the other hand, the Ministry of the Public Function (Secretaría de la Función Pública, SFP) imposed new rules in 2007 that significantly weakened procedural safeguards and allowed almost total discretion in deciding who receives promotions and fills empty posts. The situation is even worse at the state and municipal levels.

Fourth, one of the most important steps taken in the past ten years is the creation of Compranet, an Internet-based system for announcing and assigning government purchases.[20] This system introduces important safeguards, making the process much more transparent and auditable. Combining this system with the considerable amount of information that is also available through the Access to Information Law, society today has access to an enormous amount of information about government purchases that simply was not imaginable ten years ago.

Nevertheless, the high level of technical detail of government purchases makes it extremely difficult for normal citizens, or even sophisticated NGOs, to follow them and make a meaningful contribution toward accountability and the public interest. The government sometimes hires "social witnesses" as external experts to observe the procurement process, but this is very infrequent, and these witnesses lack independence since they are paid for by the government itself. Normal citizens and NGOs can directly observe some parts of the process, but this takes large amounts of time and is usually not worthwhile because the most important parts of the decision are in the end taken behind closed doors.

Another significant problem is the lack of competition in most of the important sectors of the economy. No matter how "transparent" the procurement process is, if there are only two or three possible providers, they have strong incentives to collude on prices and products. This opens the door to corruption and ineffectiveness.

Some areas of government have particularly important problems in this regard. For instance, the state oil company, Mexican Petroleum (PEMEX), operates under a special regime of transparency and accountability that allows it to set its own rules for procurement and subcontracting.[21] PEMEX is responsible for more than half of the procurement of infrastructure and a third of goods and services

19. ARegional S.A. de C.V. (2010).
20. www.compranet.gob.mx/.
21. Sandoval (2009).

of the federal government.[22] Nevertheless, it often uses its legal "autonomy" and its "corporate" nature to refuse requests for information and to prevent external audits.[23] The result is a generalized state of inefficiency and frequent corruption scandals.

With regard to licenses, the situation is even more problematic. Recently, the Secretariat of Communications has refused to provide the stenographic account of the session in which the Federal Communications Commission (Comision Federal de Telecomunicaciones) awarded a license for use of a valuable new digital bandwidth. Only two companies participated, and the government did not offer detailed reasons for why it chose one over the other.

Oversight

The OBI review points out that the "year-end" reports of the Mexican government are particularly deficient with regard to explaining how differences between the macroeconomic forecast and actual economic performance have had an impact on revenues, expenditures, and the performance of government programs. In addition, there are important problems with the strength and effectiveness of government and citizen oversight. Two broad problems are evident: (a) duplicity and lack of coordination and (b) impunity or absence of impact.

With regard to duplicity and lack of coordination, the Mexican government has no lack of oversight institutions. It has both a well-funded "internal" auditor or "comptroller" (the SFP), which is part of the president's cabinet, and a powerful "external" auditor (the ASF), which is formally part of the Chamber of Deputies. There is also an independent ombudsman's office: the National Human Rights Commission. With the new Access to Information Law, federal agencies now need to respond to frequent citizen requests for access to information about their activities. The Attorney General also has a special office responsible for investigating crimes committed by public servants.

In addition, each year, after the president issues his annual report on September 1, 2010, both chambers of Congress have the opportunity to meet with and question each member of the cabinet. A recent constitutional reform also allows Congress to pose explicit "parliamentary questions" to the executive, which the president is obliged to respond to within sixty days.

Within the executive itself, the SFP also competes and overlaps with the oversight directly performed by the SHCP. For instance, while the SHCP is in charge of coordinating the design and implementation of the SED, the SFP has a parallel program, the Special Program for Management Improvement (Programa Espe-

---

22. Fundar (2010).
23. Fundar (2010).

cial de Mejora de la Gestión), which is responsible for creating, evaluating, and using performance indicators.[24]

The central problem is, therefore, not lack of institutions, procedures, and programs, but lack of effectiveness and coordination. In general, federal public servants are overaudited, but underobserved.

The most disappointing aspect of Mexico's system of oversight and control is that the incredible amount of human and financial resources used to oversee and assure the quality of government programs in the end has very little impact. Impunity is the norm with regard to the investigation and prosecution of corruption. A recent performance audit carried out by the ASF revealed that less than 1 percent of the fines that the SFP formally issues are actually paid.[25] The vast majority of the cases end up stuck in or absolved in court. Each year the ASF issues a long list of violations and sanctions, but the SFP needs to follow up on most of these in order for them to take effect. This follow-up rarely occurs because the SFP has an evident conflict of interest: it is part of the same executive branch being questioned by the ASF. Criminal punishment is even less common. Although the SFP and the Attorney General frequently announce formal accusations against lower-level functionaries, top public servants are almost never accused, and even these "scapegoats" rarely end up behind bars.

Congress rarely, if ever, issues budgetary sanctions for bad performance. The Chamber of Deputies normally does not take into account the information provided by the ASF or the SED when deciding how to allocate funds.[26] Political criteria end up being much more powerful than technical criteria, as is generally the case with the process of budget negotiation discussed above.

Key Reform Moments

Before 1997, "budget transparency" was essentially nonexistent in Mexico. Both Congress and the judiciary were controlled directly by the president and did not make more than symbolic efforts to change the budget itself or oversee its use.[27] For instance, the Contaduría Mayor de Hacienda (Office of High Treasury Accounting, CMH), the institution responsible for overseeing the use of the budget on behalf of Congress before the creation of the ASF, equivalent to the Government Accounting Office in the United States, was famously ineffective, underfunded, and inactive. One of the clearest indicators of the lack of transparency

24. For a detailed description of this overlap, see Casar, Marván, and Puente (2010).
25. Ackerman and Sandoval (2009).
26. OECD (2009).
27. Wilkie (1967).

during this period was the existence of the now infamous "secret account" (*partida secreta*), which the president could use whenever and however he saw fit without having to report or explain these expenses to anyone. The generally accepted suspicion is that the president simply used this money for corruption and personal or political needs.[28]

The economic and financial crisis of 1994–95 led to an important push for greater transparency of some basic economic data, such as foreign currency reserves and foreign debt, since many observers attributed the crisis to a lack of transparency and an excess of discretionary spending.[29] Outgoing president Carlos Salinas (1988–94) inflated economic indicators and channeled government funds directly to the ruling party in order to assure his party's victory in the 1994 presidential elections. Both domestic and international investors therefore applied pressure on government to be more open in economic policymaking.

But 1997 was the crucial turning point because, during the midterm elections that year, for the first time the PRI lost its majority control over the Chamber of Deputies, the "lower" house responsible for passing the annual budget. All of a sudden the president needed the support of at least part of the opposition in order to get his budget passed. This led to an important sea change in the nature of political negotiation as well as some basic reforms that cleaned up the budgetary process. For instance, the "secret account" was immediately abolished. In addition, for the first time Congress was able to modify and reassign parts of the federal budget.[30]

The fifty-seventh Congress (1997–2000) also had a significant achievement in the area of budget oversight, transforming the CMH into the ASF and giving it expanded capacities and a significant level of constitutional autonomy and independence.[31] In 1999 Congress also granted full constitutional autonomy to the National Human Rights Commission.[32]

One of the most important factors that allowed Congress to become a central actor in national politics during this period, particularly with regard to the budgetary process, was the fact that the two most important opposition parties, the Party of the Democratic Revolution (PRD) on the left and the National Action Party (PAN) on the right, were able to construct a strategic majority alliance in Congress. If either of these parties or even a part of one of them had

28. Quesada (2006).

29. Pastor (1998).

30. For instance, in 1997 (1998 budget) key areas of social spending were increased by 22 percent and the value added tax was reduced from 15 to 12 percent. See Casar (2004).

31. Ackerman (2007b).

32. Ackerman (2007b).

allied with the PRI and the federal government, change would have been significantly limited.

For instance, at one crucial moment during the fifty-seventh Congress, PAN did decide to ally itself with the PRI in order to guarantee the total opacity of the highly questioned and corrupt bank bailout conducted by then-president Ernesto Zedillo in 1995.[33] Here the common social and economic interests of the PAN with the PRI were stronger than the common political interests of the PAN with the PRD. This was a major defeat for transparency and accountability and left a $6 billion debt that Mexican citizens are still paying back today.

With the presidential victory of Vicente Fox of the PAN in 2000, the political situation became even more dynamic. Although the PAN gained a significant presence in both chambers of Congress, it did not control the majority in either. Once again, it was necessary for the president to negotiate with other political parties if he wanted to get his budget passed. In addition, the PRI, as the most important opposition party, was suddenly eager to strengthen budget accountability and oversight of the federal government. In general, there was enormous social excitement about the arrival of democracy, which pressured both Congress and the executive branch to demonstrate that they were serious about bringing about change. It was in this context that the fifty-eighth Congress (2000–03) was able to pass a series of key reforms directly related to budget transparency.

First, in 2001 Congress enacted an entirely new Law of Superior Oversight, which gave flesh to the constitutional reform of 1999 that had created the ASF.[34] The new law gave the auditor significant new oversight powers. Although the ASF continued to be a part of Congress, the law established specific protections against congressional interference in its internal affairs. During the same year, Congress appointed a new auditor for a nine-year term, who proved to demonstrate significant independence and effectiveness.

Second, in 2002 Congress passed a revolutionary Access to Information Law. This law quickly became a model for other countries since it placed all federal institutions and agencies under its purview, formally established the "principle of maximum publicity," included strong procedural guarantees, prohibited exemptions in the case of "grave violations of fundamental rights," and created a specialized semiautonomous agency whose role is to assure enforcement.[35]

Third, in 2003 Congress created a new Civil Service Law that, for the first time in Mexico's history, sought to establish a permanent corps of middle-level public servants with expertise and independence from political pressures.

---

33. Sandoval (2011a).
34. Ackerman (2007b, p. 32).
35. Luna (2009) and Ackerman (2007a).

Although Mexico had some experience with civil service codes, most notably for its Foreign Service and the Federal Electoral Institute, the new law was supposed to transform the recruitment and promotion of public servants in the federal government.[36]

These three reforms created a new framework for accountability, particularly in the executive branch. At least on paper, very shortly after the achievement of political competition, Mexico had constructed a highly sophisticated three-prong legal mandate for the professionalization, oversight, and transparency of government spending.

Toward the end of the Fox administration, Congress passed another major piece of legislation that sought to reorient the budgeting and spending process toward performance. The Federal Budget and Treasury Responsibility Law, passed in 2006,[37] set up SED, a performance evaluation system within the executive that obliges programs to focus on results instead of only on cash flows and activities. The legislation required all government agencies to develop specific performance objectives, goals, and indicators as well as to contract "external reviews" for programs in order to evaluate their progress and impact. The changes also required Congress to take into account the results of performance reviews when examining budget proposals for the following year.

The reform also changed the dates for presenting and discussing the budget. Previously, the executive did not present the budget until mid-November, and Congress only had a few weeks to study, modify, and pass it before the winter recess. With the new rules, Congress gained precious time. Now the president needs to send his budget proposal to Congress during the first week of September, and the Chamber of Deputies has more than two months to review it before the deadline for passage (November 15 at the latest).

Another important development during the Fox administration was the Supreme Court decision in 2005 that, for the first time, allowed the president to veto the budget.[38] Before this, according to a strict interpretation of the constitutional text, the executive had no choice but simply to publish and enact the budget. He could not make any formal observations, much less return the budget to Congress. With the new plurality in Congress, such a situation could easily have led to increasing dominance of the legislature over the executive, for better or for worse. Nevertheless, in this historic case, the Supreme Court reinterpreted the constitution in such a way as to allow the president to veto and return specific

---

36. Guerrero (2003).

37. This law did not come into effect until the 2007 budget, when Fox had already handed over control of the federal government to his successor, Felipe Calderón, also from PAN.

38. Controversia Constitucional 109/2004.

parts of the budget to Congress. The Chamber of Deputies now has the option to change these elements or override them by a two-thirds vote.

During the administration of Felipe Calderón (2006–12), one of the most important reforms with regard to budget transparency was the constitutional reform passed in February 2007, which included a long list of constitutional guarantees with regard to transparency and access to information. These changes gave constitutional backing to Mexico's 2002 Freedom of Information Law and received unanimous support from all political parties. The reform aimed to improve compliance with the law, bring state and municipal governments up to federal standards, and open up both the judiciary and Congress to public scrutiny. At least on paper, Mexico now has one of the most solid access to information regimes in the world. Nevertheless, compliance with the reform has been problematic, and there is only limited evidence that access to information has transformed the corrupt and authoritarian ways of exercising power still prevalent in Mexico.[39]

Another major constitutional reform took place in 2008, which strengthened fiscal oversight and aimed to harmonize accounting practices between the municipal, state, and federal governments. One of the typical ways in which state and municipal governments have been able to avoid scrutiny has been, on the one hand, by exercising political control over auditors and, on the other hand, by using different and more ambiguous spending categories than the federal government.[40] This makes oversight more difficult and opens up important windows for moving funds in a discretionary manner. This constitutional reform sought to address both of these issues.

As a direct result of this constitutional reform, Congress passed, in 2008, a new General Law on Government Accounting, which applies to all levels of government. This law constituted a major step forward since it provides the base for harmonizing accountability between all levels of government. Nevertheless, the law does not apply to the budget itself, so state and municipal governments are still able to design their budgets in such a way as to hide important information.[41]

In 2009 Congress followed up by transforming the old Superior Oversight Law into the new Federal Oversight and Accountability Law.[42] This new law introduced some important improvements over the 2001 law. For instance, it gave more solid legal backing to performance reviews and required the ASF to follow up expeditiously on its recommendations. But it also has some worrisome aspects that may hamper the operation of the ASF and budget accountability in general. For instance,

---

39. Fox and others (2007).
40. Sour and Rosillo (2010).
41. IMCO (2010a).
42. Ackerman and Astudillo (2009).

it explicitly stated that government agencies cannot be punished or sanctioned for lack of compliance with performance reviews, eliminated the ASF's midyear report on federal spending, and kept the ASF's direct sanctioning capacities at a minimum.

Explanations

The Mexican case is highly paradoxical. The arrival of political competition has led to an avalanche of new laws and the development of a sophisticated institutional framework for the control and oversight of government revenue and expenditures. Nevertheless, in practice these laws and institutions have not been particularly effective in opening up budgets and spending to the public at-large.

It would be naïve to attribute the problems with budget transparency to a lack of knowledge, resources, or technological expertise. Mexico's top treasury officials are highly trained technocrats who are fully aware of international best practices in the area of budget transparency. The SHCP is also extremely well funded and has a large staff available to put together the annual budget.

The most likely explanation for the information deficit is that it is the result of a long history of bureaucratic opacity that has characterized the Mexican government for more than a century. The celebration of competitive elections has not led to a fundamental change in "bureaucratic culture," and top public officials continue to exercise as much discretion as possible in their management of public finances so as to be free to use the federal budget for patronage or other political or personal ends.

For instance, providing more detailed information on past-year spending practices or multiyear programs and performance indicators would give valuable weapons to opposition parties in their analysis of the federal budget. Also, full transparency on debt figures, tax expenditures, and other extra-budgetary funds would significantly limit the ability of the federal government to use these resources to cover political or other commitments. Finally, clear rules and predictions on the effects of macroeconomic conditions would significantly handcuff the government's ability to manipulate the use of excess oil revenues or compensate for a lack of income in this area.

The nature of government institutions, and the law itself, has always been contradictory in Mexico. The governing class has historically given great value to institutional development and defended the autonomy of the state. Throughout most of the twentieth century, political cadres did not normally come from the private sector, but were typically drawn from the professional class, social organizations, or academia.[43] Over time, a relatively stable political class grew up that

43. Camp (2002).

was intimately linked to the success and growth of government institutions as well as to the use and abuse of government budgets.[44] Thus the classic Mexican political adage: "To live outside of the budget is to live in error."[45]

Mexico has therefore inherited institutions that are technically "strong," insofar as they are powerful, well-funded, relatively autonomous, and generally respected by society. Nevertheless, the principal function of these institutions historically has not been to resolve social problems, stimulate economic development, or work in the public interest. To the contrary, it has been to favor particular interest groups, guarantee political stability, and promote the political careers of top bureaucrats.[46]

An indicator of the very real weakness of state institutions in Mexico is the fact that, to this day, the government only collects approximately 20 percent of gross domestic product in tax revenue.[47] This is due to three factors: dependence on oil revenues, the predominance of the informal sector, which employs almost a third of the labor force, and the incredible concentration of wealth and property ownership in a few hands.[48] Easy money from oil takes pressure off the need for fiscal reform. Both informal businesses and elite monopolists find it relatively easy to avoid the reach of the Treasury and free ride on the public services financed by the formal labor force and the working classes.

This situation permeates budget transparency in Mexico today. Although the government has a highly sophisticated institutional and legal structure for the control and oversight of revenues and expenditures, the degree of "flexibility" and lack of independent supervision are sufficient to assure a "healthy" level of discretion that allows government officials to use their positions not only to satisfy the needs of citizens but also to further their own political careers and personal interests. The predominance of the executive branch over Congress is also an inheritance of the tradition of centralized government power that held sway throughout the twentieth century under the authoritarian system.

The importance of oil revenues in Mexico is also an important factor. Easy access to money through the state oil company quickly accustoms public servants to the "joys" of discretionary spending. Indeed, countries highly dependent on oil

---

44. Sandoval (2011b).

45. In Spanish: "*Vivir fuera del presupuesto, es vivir en el error.*"

46. We therefore have a perfect example of what Guillermo O'Donnell has called the particularization of government institutions. O'Donnell (1973).

47. By far the lowest in all of the OECD (www.oecd.org/dataoecd/48/27/41498733.pdf).

48. For complete data on informality of the labor force see reports by Mexico's Instituto Nacional de Estadística y Geografía (INEGI). According to the OECD, Mexico ranks second in inequality among the thirty-four nations that form a part of the organization. The average income of the top 10 percent in Mexico in 2008 was twenty-six times higher than the average income of the bottom 10 percent. See OECD (2008).

revenues typically have serious problems with budget transparency. Compared with other oil-dependent countries, Mexico may actually be an overperformer, not an underperformer.

There are three reasons for the relative weakness of Congress in the budgetary negotiation and oversight process: (a) weak technical and professional capacities, (b) centralized decisionmaking, and (c) discretionary spending powers of the executive and centralization of tax revenues.

First, analysis of the budget requires large amounts of time, resources, and technical capacities. Before 1997, Congress was a rubber stamp and had no need to develop a sophisticated team of analysts and professionals capable of analyzing and reassigning the budget. In recent years, this has begun to change, and Congress has created specialized areas that support legislators when they participate in these decisions. Nevertheless, these areas are not particularly well funded, and appointments to them normally are not based on meritocratic recruitment but on political concerns.

Second, the discussion of the budget is managed almost exclusively by the Budget Commission in Congress. In particular, the president of this commission exercises powerful agenda-setting control. Evidence of this is the fact that, when the commission finally presents the budget to the floor, the discussion normally takes hours, as individual congressmen present specific reforms to the budget bill. Many legislators evidently feel that they were not taken into account in the commission's redesign of the original bill.

The larger problem is that individual representatives have very little power within Congress and normally respond to the dictates of the leader of their legislative group. For instance, the leaders of each group are in almost total control of the entire budget of Congress, and these resources are exercised in an entirely discretionary fashion, with almost no transparency or accountability safeguards. This centralization makes it relatively easy for the executive to negotiate and push for approval of its budget.

Finally, the executive can make a credible threat to punish the interests or constituents of any congressman or party that tries to alter the budget in an "unacceptable" way. The fact that 80 percent of tax revenue is collected by the federal government and 90 percent of the funds used by state and local governments are provided by the federal government puts the executive branch at a significant advantage vis-à-vis congress. Most congressmen have strong links to the corresponding state governments and are happy to exchange their vote for preferential or lenient treatment of their state governments by the federal government.[49]

49. Between 1989 and 2007, the thirty-one states and the Federal District governments went from spending 20 percent to spending 46 percent of the total budgetary spending in the country, becoming the

The combination of these three factors explains a large portion of why Congress has not exercised more independent power in negotiating and passing the federal budget since 1997.

With regard to civil society participation, one would expect congressmen to involve their constituents in the budgetary process in order to generate social trust and support for themselves and their party. This does not occur for various reasons:

—*Limited effective budget flexibility and responsiveness.* Mexico's budget is relatively small compared to the size of the country (only about 27 percent of gross national product), and approximately 85 percent of it is locked in each year. Therefore, Congress has a very limited margin within which to work and would have to disappoint the flood of specific and general requests and demands that would inundate Congress if the doors were truly opened up to society at-large.

—*Lack of attention and plurality in the media.* In Mexico, television is the principal source of news for approximately 90 percent of the population, and 95 percent of the television market is dominated by two large media companies, Televisa and TV Azteca. Citizens have little access to alternative news sources. These companies decide what is and is not relevant information for the public at-large. They do not encourage popular participation in the budget process and do not normally inform the public about the details of the negotiations. Most of the population, therefore, does not even know that it is being left out of the process. For this reason, the opacity of Congress does not have significant social costs.

—*Lack of strength and organization of civil society.* Although a handful of highly professionalized NGOs and civil society organizations try to make their voices heard each year, there is no coordinated effort by a broad-based coalition powerful enough to have an impact on the budget negotiation. The grassroots demands are normally reactive, responding to what the government has proposed, and highly particularistic, including requests for spending for individual projects or causes. Meanwhile, the professional NGOs normally lack the links to the grassroots and the media that would give them the political clout needed to have a significant impact.

—*Lack of transparency and formal oversight of the legislature.* In general, Congress does not comply with the basic rules of the Federal Transparency and Access to Public Government Information Law. Its archives are poorly organized, so even when access is formally granted, the information often is simply nonexistent. Access to committee work is also extremely deficient. The sessions are not publicly televised, and it is very difficult to access agendas and stenographic accounts

---

level of government with the largest share of spending. During this same time period, the states and the Federal District went from generating themselves 32 percent to generating 10 percent of their total income (IMCO 2010b).

of committee discussions. It is therefore very difficult for civil society groups to get involved in congressional activities.

Finally, one of the central reasons for the lack of coordination and the lack of impact of the system as a whole in Mexico is the fact that none of the institutions involved has real political and institutional autonomy. The SFP, the SED, and the Attorney General are all part of the executive branch and directly serve the president. Even the "external reviews" mandated by the SED are controlled directly by the agencies being evaluated. The Federal Institute for Access to Information (IFAI) has a bit more autonomy, but is highly vulnerable to pressures from the president.[50]

Although there is no problem with the executive having the tools to clean up its own house, a more external, objective view of the performance of the federal government is also needed. The ASF fulfills this role to some extent. Nevertheless, by legal design its reviews always come late, and its sanctioning powers are highly restricted. The new law does not require executive agencies to comply with the results of ASF performance reviews. In addition, the ASF is politically dependent on Congress. It is vulnerable to the changing winds of parliamentary politics and is under the constant watch of members of the Oversight Commission, which may or may not agree with an aggressive and independent auditing style.

At the state level, the situation is even worse. Although the constitution explicitly says that auditors in the states must receive appointments of at least seven years, most of them do not last for their entire term. A recent survey of forty-six state-level sitting and past auditors discovered that seventeen had lasted less than two years on the job.[51] Two had lasted less than a month.

Use and Impact of Budget Information

As a result of the opacity of the process of budget negotiation and expenditure, civil society has not played a significant role in the budgetary process in Mexico. Nevertheless, citizen groups have been able to gain access to crucial information on spending practices by using the relatively new and powerful Access to Information Law. In general, although society is kept at arm's-length from actual budgetary decisions, it can at least glance through the window at the workings of government and exert pressure from the outside. Nevertheless, government has begun to resist implementation of the new transparency law.

50. For instance, the IFAI recently refused to give citizens access to information on which public servants receive special "risk benefits," supposedly for their involvement in efforts to combat crime. Such categories are often used to cover up discretionary "benefits," which are distributed based more on political than on performance criteria. See Ackerman (2010).

51. IMCO (2010c, p. 13).

The number of requests for access to information has skyrocketed since the law first came into effect in 2003. From June 2003 until December 2009, the executive branch received 489,739 requests for access to information.[52] Of these, 117,597 were received in 2009 alone, almost twice as many as had been received only three years earlier in 2006.[53] Mexico ranks particularly high with regard to the response rate to citizen requests. A recent study conducted by the Open Society Institute found that Mexico has one of the lowest rates of "mute responses" in the world, with only 20 percent of requests not getting a formal response back from the government.[54] At the federal level the percentage of mute responses is even lower, around 7 percent. Independent NGOs, such as Fundar, have been particularly successful at using the laws to conduct close oversight of spending, for instance, in the area of agricultural subsidies or the use of government donations to nonprofit organizations.[55]

Nevertheless, both rank-and-file public servants and top officials in the federal government have put up significant resistance to full implementation of the new transparency, oversight, and performance evaluation laws. For instance, the transparency law has led to the dangerous practice of reducing the documentation of decisions and been very difficult to implement.[56] The new powers of the ASF have been challenged in court by the federal government and overturned in a series of historic decisions.[57] The federal government first dragged its feet on implementation of the Civil Service Law and then effectively killed it through a presidential decree issued in September of 2007.

Recently, the IFAI has come up against serious obstacles that limit its effectiveness. In a series of key cases, the federal government has openly challenged the authority of the IFAI and refused to hand over sensitive information that the IFAI has determined should be made public.

One key early case involved the request for documents used during the bank bailout of 1995. Here the IFAI required the Institute for the Protection of Banking and Savings (IPAB) to publicize the stenographic versions of the meetings in which it had decided exactly whom, how, and based on which criteria it would bail out after the 1995 financial crisis. In response, the IPAB handed over an extremely redacted version and then, perhaps even more worrisome, decided not to record stenographic versions of its meetings.

---

52. These numbers do not include requests submitted to Congress, the judiciary, autonomous agencies, or state and local governments.

53. IFAI (2010).

54. Open Society Justice Initiative (2006).

55. www.fundar.org.mx.

56. IFAI, CETA, and Probabilística (2007) and CIDE and COMAIP (2010, p. 120).

57. Ackerman (2007b, p. 32).

Another important case is the recent decision by the IFAI to require the National Tax Office to reveal detailed information about "fiscal credits" granted to large corporations. Here the Tax Administration Service refused to hand over the information and appealed directly to the courts, even though, legally, the decisions of the IFAI are final and cannot be appealed by the government agencies involved.[58]

The federal government has also been particularly resistant with regard to information related to public security, openly refusing to comply with a series of IFAI decisions related to the transparency of police investigators and law enforcement in general. In one famous case, the government even refused to provide information on the case of a citizen who was "disappeared" in the 1970s by government forces during the "dirty war" against regime dissidents. The IFAI had appealed to the special clause in the law that overrides all exceptions when "grave crimes against humanity" are involved. In addition, the Inter-American Court of Justice recently ruled on the topic. But the Attorney General still refused to provide information. The case will be decided soon by the Supreme Court.

Although presidents Fox and Calderón were in principle interested in modernizing and democratizing public administration, they apparently were not willing to roll up their sleeves to make sure that this occurred. While they supported passage of the new legislation, they did not put their political weight behind the new laws to make sure that they worked in practice.

With regard to citizen participation, federal and local governments are normally quick to call for "popular consultations" and set up "planning committees," "social comptrollers," or "social witnesses." Street and other spontaneous citizen protests are common and often have an impact.[59] Half of the thirty-two states have formal "citizen participation laws," which include plebiscites, referendums, and citizen initiatives.[60] In some locations, participatory budgets have been tried, for instance, in some boroughs of Mexico City (Tlalpán, Cuauhtémoc, and Iztalapala). In addition, a growing number of independent, professionalized NGOs have developed independent oversight projects.

Historically, the state-party regime was very interested in covering up its authoritarian nature by "consulting" with the people. Every six years, once the "official" presidential candidate was named, he would immediately travel around the country, listening to the proposals and ideas of citizens. Once he arrived in office, he would issue a public call to participate in developing the National Development Plan that would serve as the overall framework for his government's policies. In the end, he would ignore the consultations, and the National Development Plan would have little or no impact on public policies. This tradition of

58. Luna Pla and Rios Granados (2010).
59. Isunza and Hevia (2005).
60. Sandoval Ballesteros (2007) and Alarcón Olguín (2002).

simulating participation with the sole objective of boosting legitimacy instead of encouraging real oversight persists.

As a result of this inheritance, a series of specific problems hurt the effectiveness of the existing mechanisms:

—Most of the mechanisms used by government do not give citizens power over government policies; 67 percent of the formal mechanisms are strictly symbolic actions such as "suggestion boxes" or "providing information to users."[61]

—Most of the mechanisms are still not institutionalized in law, but depend on the goodwill of the government.

—There is a lack of coordination and articulation between different citizen participation initiatives. This is the case both with regard to government offices that encourage and invite participation and with regard to the citizen groups themselves.

—In general, few citizens participate in these initiatives. After decades of abuse and government trickery, citizens do not trust that their opinions will be taken into account and do not think that it is worthwhile to invest their time.

—Government-led citizen participation initiatives are often co-opted by the age-old practices of clientelism and corporativism, which have been dominant in Mexico for decades.

—In general, there is more emphasis on participatory schemes in the executive branch. The judiciary and the legislature do not receive the same attention from the public and do not reach out in the same way to the citizens.

In response to international pressures and proposals by local NGOs, the federal government has recently decided to issue a "citizen's budget" that seeks to explain the details of the budget process to common citizens.[62] The first version of this document leaves a great deal to be desired. It reads more like a propaganda pamphlet in favor of the federal government's policies than as an educational tool or as an instrument for strengthening citizen oversight of government spending. It therefore fits perfectly into the long tradition of simulated participation that has been typical of Mexican politics and institutions for decades.

Conclusions and Proposals

The best way to encourage greater budget transparency in Mexico is to attack the broader framework or "operating environment," which in practice disables the effectiveness of the numerous laws, procedures, and institutions that supposedly guarantee oversight and transparency. For instance, beyond the specific topic of

61. Isunza and Hevia (2005, p. 74).
62. The new citizen's budget is available at www.shcp.gob.mx/Documentos_recientes/pef_ciudadano_2010_060110.pdf.

budget transparency, reformers should tackle the larger issue of the transparency of Congress as a whole. Although both the Senate and the Chamber of Deputies comply with basic requirements as broad institutions, there is very little information on the activities of the commissions, the legislative groups, and the individual legislators in particular. In addition, historical information is extremely difficult to get due to a lack of systematic archives. This opacity allows individual congressmen to avoid public scrutiny and limits public participation in the budgetary process.

In addition, the present party system privileges loyalty to party leaders and government officials instead of to constituents. New legislation should open up political parties to public scrutiny and audits as well as democratize their internal decisionmaking process. This would reduce the authoritarian control of the party elite and the leaders of the legislative groups and force individual congressmen to reach out to the population at-large.

But perhaps the most important weak link in implementation of the new legal framework is related to the ineffectiveness of the civil service reform passed in 2002. Without a professional and independent cadre of bureaucrats, political and other criteria will always predominate over the honest and open delivery of goods and services to the population.

Another important reason why citizens do not participate more and politicians do not feel more beholden to citizens is that two television companies exercise almost total control over the public debate. The Internet, cable, and social networks have started to poke a small hole in this dominance, but this is by no means enough. Mexico needs to broaden the access to a wider diversity of opinions for the vast majority of citizens.

It also would be important to think about creating a new agency that centralizes and takes up many of the oversight functions presently distributed chaotically among different government agencies. If this agency were closely linked to citizen needs and interests, it could lead to major sea change in budget transparency and accountability. Possible models to learn from are in Ecuador and Taiwan.

Finally, the process of designing and negotiating the budget would benefit from a series of reforms, such as those proposed by Fundar.[63] Nevertheless, given the overall context described in this chapter, congressmen probably either will not commit themselves to following such procedures or will comply with them in name only.

In order for Mexico to take definitive steps toward budget transparency, more is needed than additional "political will" or technical fixes. The recent proposals issued by the Organization for Economic Cooperation and Development on the

---

63. See www.fundar.org.mx and for their budget transparency initiative, specifically http://fundar.org.mx/indicepresupuestoabierto2010/. See also Dávila and others (2004) and Pérez and Romero (2006).

topic imply more of the same.[64] Broader, more structural solutions are needed if Mexico is to live up to its potential as a leading democracy on the world stage.

References

Ackerman, John M. 2005. "Social Accountability for the Public Sector: A Conceptual Discussion." Washington: World Bank.

————. 2007a. "Mexico's Freedom of Information Law in Global Perspective." In *Mexico's Right-to-Know Reforms: Civil Society Perspectives*, edited by Jonathan Fox, Libby Haight, Helena Hofbauer, and Tania Sánchez, pp. 314–19. Washington: Woodrow Wilson Center for International Scholars.

————. 2007b. *Organismos autónomos y democracia: El caso de México*. Mexico City: Siglo XXI Editores.

————. 2010. "Transparencia traicionada." *Revista Proceso*, December 23 (www.proceso.com.mx/rv/modHome/detalleExclusiva/86668).

Ackerman, John, and César Astudillo, eds. 2009. *La autonomía constitucional de la Auditoría Superior de la Federación*. Mexico City: UNAM, Instituto de Investigaciones Jurídicas.

Ackerman, John M., and Irma Sandoval. 2009. "Fiscalización intraestatal y protección de programas sociales en México: Teoría, práctica y propuestas." In *Candados y contrapesos: La protección de los programas políticas y derechos sociales en México y América Latina,* edited by David Gómez-Álvarez. Guadalajara: Instituto Tecnológico de Estudios Superiores de Occidente, Programa de las Naciones Unidas para el Desarrollo (PNUD).

Alarcón Olguín, Victor. 2002. "Leyes de participación ciudadana en México: Un acercamiento comparado." In *Democracia y Formación Ciudadana*, edited by Judith Boxer and others. Colección Sinergia 2. México: IEDF.

ARegional S.A. de C.V. 2010. "Índice de transparencia y disponibilidad de la información fiscal de las entidades federativas 2010 (ITDIF2010)." Serie Rendición de Cuentas 29, no. 10 (www.aregional.com/mexico/?lang=es&PHPSESSID=73c7bv018o79918lq4342k82d5#).

Camp, Roderic. 2002. *Mexico's Mandarins: Crafting a Power-Elite for the 21st Century*. University of California Press.

Cárdenas, Jaime. 2011. "Parliamentary Incompatibilities and Conflicts of Interest in Mexico." In *Corruption and Transparency: States, Markets, and Society*, edited by Irma E. Sandoval. Washington: World Bank; Mexico City: UNAM, Instituto de Investigaciones Sociales.

Casar, María Amparo. 2004. "El proceso de negociación presupuestal en el primer gobierno de mayoría: Un estudio de Caso." *Impuestos y gasto público en México desde una perspectiva multidisciplinaria*, edited by Juan Pablo Guerrero, pp. 523–62. Mexico City: CIDE, Miguel Ángel Porrúa, and Cámara de Diputados.

Casar, María Amparo, Ignacio Marván, and Khemvirg Puente. 2010. "La rendición de cuentas y el poder legislativo." In *La estructura de la rendición de cuentas en México*, edited by Mauricio Merino, Sergio Ayllón, and Guillermo Cejudo, pp. 331–405. Mexico City: UNAM, Instituto de Investigaciones Jurídicas.

CIDE (Centro de Investigación y Docencia Económicas) and COMAIP (Conferencia Mexicana para el Acceso a la Información Pública). 2010. *Métrica de la transparencia*. Mexico (http://metricadetransparencia.cide.edu/metrica.html).

64. OECD (2009).

Colmenares Páramo, David. 2010. "Transparencia fiscal y gasto federalizado, colmenares páramo y asociados." Presentation at the Seminario Propuestas para una Efectiva Transparencia Presupuestaria, Instituto Federal de Acceso a la Información y Protección de Datos (IFAI) and the Instituto de Acceso a la Información Pública del Distrito Federal (InfoDF), March (www.ifai.org.mx/SeminarioPETP2010/downloads/DavidColmenares Paramo.pdf).

Dávila, David Estefan, and others. 2004. "Diagnóstico de negociación presupuestaria: Propuestas para fortalecer la transparencia y la rendición de cuentas." Serie Cuadernos del Seguimiento Ciudadano al Poder Legislativo en México. Mexico City: Fundar, Centro de Análisis e Investigación (www.fundar.org.mx/index.html/files/negociacion.pdf).

Fox, Jonathan, Libby Haight, Helena Hofbauer, and Tania Sánchez, eds. 2007. *Mexico's Right-to-Know Reforms: Civil Society Perspectives*. Washington: Woodrow Wilson Center for International Scholars; Mexico City: Fundar.

Fundar. 2009. "Índice latinoamericano de transparencia presupuestaria 2009." Mexico City (www.fundar.org.mx/fundar_1/site/files/iltpregional.pdf).

————. 2010. "PEMEX: Deficiencias estructurales para el control en la asignación de contratos." Mexico City: Fundar, Centro de Análisis e Investigación (www.las10faltantes.com/lasdiez/pemex/).

GESOC (Gestión Social y Cooperación A.C.). 2009. *Índice de desempeño de los programas federales (INDEP) evaluados en el ciclo 2008–2009*. Mexico City, October (www.gesoc.org.mx/docs/GSCP2009indepresumen.pdf).

González, Alejandro, ed. 2008. *¿Gobernar por resultados? Implicaciones de la política de evaluación del desempeño del gobierno mexicano*. Mexico City: GESOC (www.gesoc.org.mx/docs/GSCP2008Librogesoc.pdf).

Guerrero, Omar. 2003. *La ley de servicio profesional de carrera en la administración pública federal: Una apreciación administrativa*. Mexico City: UNAM, Instituto de Investigaciones Jurídicas.

IBP (International Budget Partnership). 2010. "Los presupuestos abiertos transforman vidas: Encuesta de presupuesto abierto 2010." Washington (www.internationalbudget.org/files/2010_Full_Report-Spanish.pdf).

IFAI (Federal Institute for Access to Information). 2010. *Informe de labores, 2009*. Mexico City (www.ifai.gob.mx).

IFAI, CETA (Centro Internacional de Estudios de Transparencia y Acceso a la Información), and Probabilística. 2007. "La cultura de los servidores públicos alrededor de los temas de transparencia y acceso a la información pública." PowerPoint presentation.

IMCO (Instituto Mexicano para la Competitividad). 2010a. *Índice de competitividad estatal 2010: La caja negra del gasto público*. Mexico City (http://imco.org.mx/indice_estatal_2010/secciones.html).

————. 2010b. "Presupuestos estatales: Opacidad que genera ineficiencia." In *Índice de competitividad estatal 2010: La caja negra del gasto público*. Mexico City (http://imco.org.mx/indice_estatal_2010/PDFS/Opacidad.pdf).

————. 2010c. "¿Quién vigila el gasto público? Las entidades de fiscalización superior en México." In *Índice de competitividad estatal 2010: La caja negra del gasto público*. Mexico City (http://imco.org.mx/indice_estatal_2010/PDFS/Quienvigila.pdf).

Isunza, Ernesto, and Felipe Hevia. 2005. *Relaciones sociedad civil-estado en México: Un ensayo de interpretación*. Background Paper. Mexico City: World Bank.

Luna, Issa. 2009. *El movimiento social de acceso a la información pública*. Mexico City: UNAM.

Luna Pla, Issa, and Gabriela Rios Granados. 2010. *Transparencia, acceso a la información tributaria y el secreto fiscal: Desafíos en México.* Mexico City: UNAM and IFAI.

Magaloni, Beatriz, and Alberto Diaz Cayeros. 1997. "Presidential Agenda Setting under Hegemonic Party Rule: Executive and Legislature in Mexico." Paper presented at the seventeenth World Congress of the International Political Science Association, Seoul, Korea.

Merino, Mauricio, Sergio Ayllón, and Guillermo Cejudo, eds. 2010. *La estructura de la rendición de cuentas en México.* Mexico City: UNAM, Instituto de Investigaciones Jurídicas.

O'Donnell, Guillermo. 1973. *Modernization and Bureaucratic Authoritarianism: Studies in South American Politics.* University of California, Institute of International Studies.

OECD (Organization for Economic Cooperation and Development). 2008. *Growing Unequal? Income Distribution and Poverty in OECD Countries.* Paris.

———. 2009. *Estudio de la OCDE sobre el proceso presupuestario en México.* Paris (www.oecd-bookshop.org/oecd/display.asp?K=5KSCM5C0L7TG&LANG=EN).

Open Society Justice Initiative. 2006. *Transparency and Silence.* New York: Open Society Institute.

Pastor, Manuel, Jr. 1998. "Pesos, Policies, and Predictions." In *The Post NAFTA Political Economy: Mexico and the Western Hemisphere*, edited by Carol Wise. Pennsylvania State University Press.

Pérez, Marian, and Jorge Romero. 2006. "Transparencia en el presupuesto público: Los desafíos de la rendición de cuentas." Mexico City: Fundar, Centro de Análisis e Investigación (www.fundar.org.mx/index.html/files/j834l58i845hik9.pdf).

Quesada, Sergio Aguayo. 2006. *La alianza cívica mexicana: Una izquierda en busca de identidad.* Mexico City: Colegio de México.

Sandoval, Irma Eréndira. 2007. *Rendición de cuentas y fideicomisos: El reto de la opacidad financiera.* Cultura de la Rendición de Cuentas 10. Mexico City: Auditoría Superior de la Federación, Cámara de Diputados.

———. 2009. "Combate de la corrupción estructural en PEMEX: Reflexiones sobre dos iniciativas de reforma a la Ley Orgánica de Petróleos Mexicanos." *Iztapalapa: Revista de Ciencias Sociales y Humanidades* 67, no. 30 (Julio-Diciembre): 77–100.

———. 2011a. *Dinámicas políticas de la liberalización financiera: Crisis, rentismo e 'intervencionismo' neoliberal.* Mexico City: Centro de Estudios Manuel Espinosa Yglesias.

———, ed. 2011b. *Corruption and Transparency: States, Markets, and Society.* Washington: World Bank; Mexico City: UNAM, Instituto de Investigaciones Sociales.

Sandoval Ballesteros, Netzai. 2007. "Leyes de participación ciudadana y democracia en las entidades federativas de México." Mexico City: UNAM, Facultad de Derecho.

Sour, Laura, and Laila Munayer. 2007. "Apertura política y el poder de la Cámara de Diputados durante la aprobación presupuestaria en México." Documento de Trabajo 192. Mexico City: CIDE (www.cide.edu/dts.php?pageNum_rsDTS=5&d=1).

Sour, Laura, Irma Ortega, and Sergio San Sebastián. 2003. "Política presupuestaria durante el gobierno de transición a la democracia en México 1997–2003." Working Paper. Mexico City: CIDE (www.presupuestoygastopublico.org/documentos/presupuesto/DT_142.pdf).

Sour, Laura, and Eunice Rosillo. 2010. "Evaluación de la estructura de la contabilidad gubernamental en los tres ámbitos de gobierno en México." In *La estructura de la rendición de cuentas en México*, edited by Mauricio Merino, Sergio Ayllón, and Guillermo Cejudo, pp. 287–329. Mexico City: UNAM, Instituto de Investigaciones Jurídicas.

Wilkie, James. 1967. *The Mexican Revolution: Federal Expenditure and Social Change since 1910.* University of California Press.

6

Guatemala: Limited Advances within Advancing Limits

AARON SCHNEIDER AND ANNABELLA ESPAÑA-NAJÉRA

The Guatemalan state mobilizes few resources, spends its meager revenues poorly, and provides only limited transparency and participation in budgeting. In raising barely more than 10 percent of gross domestic product (GDP) in revenues, the Guatemalan government secures only enough funding to cover basic functions, leaving the state vulnerable to crises, of which there are many of a natural, man-made, and purely political variety. The weak state administration is subsequently unable to protect itself from multiple, competing, and sometimes illicit actors who insert themselves into Guatemalan policymaking, complicating the budget process in ways that distort it from serving the public good. In sum, the state is unable to call on the resources of society to build capacity, is unable to use budgeting to direct public resources in an effective, efficient, and equitable manner, and can do little to stimulate growth or development. As a result, Guatemala remains in a vicious cycle of fiscal weakness, unaccountable budgets, and poor outcomes.

Parallel to this bleak scenario, however, the transparency of government accounts and their openness to public participation have improved notably. Guatemala scored the highest among Central American countries, at fifty out of 100, on the 2010 Open Budget Index (OBI) ranking, having climbed from a score of forty-six in 2006 and a brief fall to forty-five in 2008.[1] According to the terminology of the International Budget Partnership (IBP), which conducts the OBI survey, these scores "show that the government provides the public

---

1. Available at http://internationalbudget.org/what-we-do/open-budget-survey/rankings-key-findings/rankings/.

with some information on the central government's budget and financial activities during the course of the budget year." "Some" information is lower than "extensive" or "significant" but better than "minimal" or "scant or no" information. Conversations with policymakers and observers of Guatemalan budgeting identified major advances in the legal and institutional architecture of budgeting over the last two decades. Five markers of change stood out, including the 1992 Law of Government Contracts, the 1997 Organic Budget Law, the 1998 introduction of an information technology system for tracking government accounts (followed by the 2003 application of information technology to government purchases), the 2002 Law of the Comptroller, and the 2008 Information Access Law. Each of these changes was an important reform to the institutional incentives and constraints facing political actors during the budget process.

The simultaneous appearance of ongoing shortcomings in public finance alongside major moments of improvement presents a puzzle. How is it possible for a troubled country to take occasional legal and institutional steps to improve transparency? What was the immediate context of these changes, and are these moments of change aggregating to any kind of qualitative shift in budgeting? What have been the impacts of these changes, and what are their ongoing failures with regard to transparency and participation? Why have existing patterns of corruption and misuse of public funds persisted or returned despite these reforms, and why are they more prevalent in some areas of public activity than others?

This chapter seeks to provide a reasonable explanation for the apparent puzzle of Guatemalan budgeting: limited advances within advancing limits. Important legal and institutional steps to improve budgeting have opened potential opportunities for greater transparency and participation. However, actual practice has improved in only a limited way. There are major shortcomings in the implementation of legal and institutional changes, and powerful actors continue to find ways to subvert the process.

The results of the analysis suggest the need for a new approach to budget reform in Guatemala, as legal and institutional advances appear unable to alter the underlying structural conditions that limit actual practices of transparency and participation. This confirms the need for a broader political economy approach to budgeting in Guatemala (and elsewhere). Economic and political structures rooted in inequality and exclusion make weak complements for transparency and participation. Without a more cohesive coalition around an equitable and inclusive state, improvements to the legal and institutional architecture will do little to change the way powerful actors operate within Guatemalan budgeting.

Budgeting and Budget Transparency in Guatemala

The formal budget process in Guatemala follows a sequential process from formulation to approval, implementation, and evaluation.[2] At each stage, different actors have the opportunity and obligation to involve themselves in the budget process, and the rules and practices of these actors have important impacts on the amount of transparency and participation that enters the budget process.

This sequence is governed by the Organic Budget Law, passed in 1997, and guided by budgetary norms that are inserted into each annual budget. A host of constitutional and legal constraints fix the allocation for certain policy areas and institutions according to percentages of spending and receipts. For example, requirements earmark 10 percent of ordinary receipts and 1.5 percent of the value added tax for municipalities; 5 percent of ordinary receipts for the University of San Carlos; 1.5 percent of the value added tax for social spending, dedicated to food security, primary education, and security; and 1 percent of the value added tax for a social fund for rural investment.[3] In a 2005 study, Knight and Cabrera estimate that these earmarks sum up to almost 30 percent of the total budget.[4]

Together, these characteristics have produced some unusual characteristics of budgeting in Guatemala. In comparison to similar countries, Guatemala appears as a relative success story. As mentioned, in 2010, Guatemala scored fifty out of 100 on the Open Budget Index, improving on previous scores in particular because the government "now publishes a relatively comprehensive executive's budget proposal."[5] These scores place Guatemala at the top of the table for Central America, above the international average, and seventh in Latin America. The country's relatively strong score was due to adequate or good scores on the executive budget proposal, in-year reports, and audit reports.

This relatively positive review of Guatemalan budgeting stands in contrast, to some degree, to other evaluations of public finance management and state capacity. According to the World Bank Public Expenditure and Financial Accountability (PEFA) assessment, conducted in 2009 for the 2006–08 period, "The credibility of the budgetary figures of expenditures in the period analyzed was low."[6] With respect to the core dimensions of budgeting addressed here—transparency and participation—the PEFA surmised, "The budgetary information, in its diverse presentations, does not facilitate adequate monitoring of expenditures

---

2. The description of these formal structures is drawn from CIEN (2001) and OEA (2009).
3. CIEN (2001).
4. Knight and Cabrera (2005).
5. IBP (2010).
6. Blasco (2009, p. 4).

. . . and the procedures to transfer funds to municipalities did not facilitate the provision of reliable and timely information so as to be able to adequately formulate their budgets."[7] The review further observed with respect to accountability, "The systems of internal control and audit were effective in expenditure control. In general, the normative framework and control of the budget execution for the years 2006, 2007, and 2008 were ineffective in financial administration procedures."[8] Highlighting a problem that was picked up by the International Monetary Fund (IMF) and is discussed below, the PEFA noted, "Although prepared punctually and the presentation formalities to Congress and the Comptroller fulfilled in a timely manner, the financial statements of the central government reflected only the registered information and not the totality of the execution."[9]

Despite these fairly damning evaluations, the World Bank characterizes advances as focused on particular parts of government, especially within the executive branch: "Core aspects of the Executive—financial management systems, the budget process, tax administration, and procurement systems—as well as banking supervision attain moderate to robust ratings. Related, progress has been most substantial in the Executive—with improvements in financial management, procurement, tax administration, and budgeting—in addition to banking supervision and freedom of information."[10]

The normally reserved IMF came to relatively similar conclusions, citing areas of improvement and best practice, but noting in its *Report on the Observance of Standards and Codes: Fiscal Transparency Module*, "The decentralized and autonomous entities should form part of the regular budget process," a problem that has continued to this day. The IMF also found that quasi-fiscal activities are carried out by the state electricity company, the central bank, and the national mortgage bank, among other entities, and "there is no coordination between budgetary and extra-budgetary activities."[11]

In sum, the condition of budgeting in Guatemala presents unusual schizophrenia. Budgeting institutions and legal frameworks have evolved over the last decades, opening occasional opportunities for transparency and participation. Some of these are reflected in the relatively moderate and positive reviews of the IBP data. Unfortunately, these reforms and improvements have not fundamentally changed the way in which budgeting is actually practiced, and the country is left with parallel patterns of formal advances, ongoing shortcomings, and informal practices. Powerful economic and political actors continue to insert their

7. Blasco (2009, p. 5).
8. Blasco (2009, p. 5).
9. Blasco (2009, p. 6).
10. World Bank (2010).
11. IMF (2006, pp. 34–36).

preferences and capture for themselves a significant portion of public resources, occasionally operating through the formal rules of the budget process and occasionally distorting those rules to channel resources outside normal institutions. The World Bank and the IMF have been especially worried about these distortions, noting their potential to weaken not just budgeting but state finances more generally. To make sense of this pattern of limited advances within advancing limits, the next section explores watershed moments in recent years.

Transparency and Participation in Budgeting: Watershed Moments

In the last twenty years, significant advances have been made when it comes to budget transparency and participation. Interviews with observers and policymakers in Guatemalan budgeting identified five moments when transparency and participation were able to advance.

The first notable advance was the Law of Contracts, passed in 1992, which established norms and rules for the relationship between government and contractors implementing public programs. The law sought to decentralize and formalize certain relationships for contractors, following theories of principal-agent relationships in the public sector.[12] The law, proposed during the government of Jorge Serrano Elías, was consistent with his more general attempts to attack corruption by clarifying channels of bureaucratic responsibility and oversight. It would be regulated and implemented in subsequent governments, particularly the de León government that succeeded Serrano, with the support of international organizations and technocratic leadership within the Guatemalan bureaucracy.

The law establishes the Ministry of Finance as responsible for coordinating purchases, through its State Contracts and Acquisitions Normative Directorate. The law and its subsequent regulations require government to lay out its annual purchases and publish them for transparent information and public monitoring. In practice, most agencies lack an annual plan of purchases, and those plans that are presented remain general enough that public entities have ample room to assign expenses to a variety of products.[13]

Yet the unfortunate conditions of the transition from Serrano to de León limited the broader impact of the Law of Contracts. Serrano miscalculated popular support for his efforts and declared a self-coup by dissolving the Supreme Court and the Congress. This bid for power, justified as an attempt to root out corruption by consolidating administrative power, was opposed by other political actors and led to Serrano's resignation and ultimate replacement by the human rights

12. Mora (2009).
13. Acción Ciudadana and Fundación DESC (2006, p. 29).

ombudsman, Ramiro de León. The de León government enjoyed a degree of autonomy for having beaten back the attempted self-coup, and government technical staff, especially in the Ministry of Finance, used this autonomy to introduce regulations for different kinds of contracts, ministries, and levels of government. However, the lack of popular legitimacy for a government that assumed power without an election limited the degree to which these regulations could penetrate all areas, particularly the degree to which mechanisms of oversight and accountability were included in the rules for contracts. As Mora (2009) observes, "The law is imprecise in processes such as costing, requiring additional regulation for each bidding process. Nor are the criteria for evaluating goods and services well-defined, which leaves bidding and pricing extremely discretionary . . . Finally, in many cases the regulation of the law copies directly from the law itself, a practice that adds nothing to its application."[14]

The next major step forward came in 1997, shortly after the final Peace Agreement, with the Organic Budget Law. The Arzú government, freshly elected and having just shepherded through the final negotiations of the Peace Accords, enjoyed a rare moment of popular and legislative support. Backed by the business community and encouraged by international donors to seize the moment to push through additional reforms, the Organic Budget Law sought to provide order to the budgetary process. In particular, it fixed time periods and responsibilities for different branches of government, including the broad outlines and principles of budgeting.

Almost simultaneously, Arzú also pushed through the SIAF (*sistema integrado de administración financiera*), a financial administration system that computerized Guatemalan public finances and put them online. The rollout began slowly, and the system has not incorporated all levels of government or been maintained consistently, but it has significantly improved the previous placement of all financial information with the central bank, waiting for publication and dissemination through its mechanisms. Under SIAF, spending agencies can put their information directly into the system, bringing financial data to the public much faster.

The SIAF system, similar to automated systems introduced across Latin America, was greatly encouraged by international donors, especially the World Bank and the Inter-American Development Bank, which provided loans to finance its implementation. Under the next government, the Finance Ministry continued on this track, creating a website for transparency, including access to the SIAF system, and the system is now operational across all central government agencies and many decentralized entities, covering approximately 300 executive-level agencies, with website linkages to transparency portals.

---

14. Mora (2009, pp. 11–12).

Arzú's government pushed reform forward in the honeymoon of post–Peace Accord support, but the most difficult reforms, especially fiscal reforms linked to tax increases, were pushed to the end of the mandate. As the terms of remaining reforms became clear, Arzú allies increasingly abandoned his side, especially as it appeared that the right-wing populist Guatemalan Republican Front (FRG) party was likely to take over the presidency. The apprehension of the business sector particularly neutralized further reform efforts, and efforts to pass the Organic Budget Law stalled.

The next government, the Portillo administration, followed the electronic SIAF with an electronic system to track procurement called Guatecompras. The program publishes information on all purchases above Q 30,000 (quetzales), and it is now operating in central government agencies and some decentralized and municipal entities. Under the Berger government and the Colom administration, the amount of information that is available online has increased steadily, with the Ministry of Finance expanding the resources dedicated to supporting transparency and the amount of information readily available to the public.

These steps toward digitalization and informatization represent the generally shared consensus among the technocratic elite of all parties that greater transparency in public finances is useful. The amount of information and ease of access account for Guatemala's relatively high and improving scores on IBP evaluations. They also explain the relatively positive evaluations that the World Bank gives for improvements within the executive branch. However, the consensus behind increasing transparency has not always been sincere, and other priorities occasionally interfere with the consistent provision of online and up-to-date information. For example, the Portillo government initiated Guatecompras and a website for transparency only after a scandal forced the minister of finance, Weyman, to take steps to address accusations of corruption by his predecessor. Weyman himself was later tried for corruption, and the president he served, Portillo, was captured in an attempt to flee the country to avoid corruption charges that later fell apart in court in Guatemala.[15] In addition, when the pressure for greater transparency has been outweighed by political exigencies, governments have been perfectly willing to delay or shut down information on SIAF. The Berger administration used such shutdowns to complicate the transition to the current Colom government, and the Portillo government used them to fight repeated accusations of corruption.

Perhaps to counter the constant accusations of corruption, the Portillo administration took other steps to improve transparency, such as the Law of the Comp-

---

15. Portillo now faces extradition to the United States, where he is accused of laundering $70 million through U.S. banks.

troller passed in 2002. This law established mechanisms for oversight and sanction by the Comptroller General's office. The Comptroller General had existed in previous incarnations of the Guatemalan constitution and administration, but it lacked formal legislation to ensure its access to information and power to investigate and sanction. An automated system facilitates Comptroller audits during the fiscal year, and after the close of the year the Comptroller receives information on budget execution from the executive within three months. The Comptroller prepares an evaluation and report to the Congress within two months, with the power to investigate, request additional information, and initiate proceedings in cases of malfeasance. Yet the law remains ambiguous in certain areas, specifically with respect to allowable sanctions. A poorly defined career path for staff and the shortage of resources also pose serious problems for the functioning of the Comptroller's office. While the Comptroller has a fixed allocation in the budget, the resources provided and actually transferred have not been enough to sustain the institution, and the executive appears unwilling to provide additional resources to an entity that has occasionally been critical of the administration.[16] Furthermore, the appointment of individuals with personal and political ties to the executive has further weakened this entity.

The final legal and institutional advance was the Access to Information Law, passed in 2008. The law was among the clearest steps forward in transparency, matching international best practice, requiring state entities to make specific budget and salary information available to the public, and specifying the ways in which citizens can request information from government entities along with the amount of time entities have to respond to requests. The law had been in discussion in various forms, but had always stalled in Congress. The version that passed was borrowed in significant fashion from Mexican legislation, which at the time was making its way through a legislative committee.

By fortuitous circumstances, the proposal made its way quickly through Congress after languishing for years. The exact circumstances were less than propitious, however, as the proposal was seized in the midst of a scandal that seriously stained the Congress itself. In the midst of the financial crisis of 2008, the leaders of Congress had invested money from the congressional budget in the stock market. This practice had existed at least since the Portillo government, with the returns used by the congressional president and directorate to pad their budgets and distribute to allies. This time, however, the market crashed, eliminating the funds entirely; Congress lost Q 82 million overnight (approximately US$15 million). The congressional president was forced to step down, and members of Congress who had been complicit in the scheme sought to regain some semblance of

---

16. Reynoso Martínez (2008).

public trust. Transparency advocates in the Ministry of Finance, international organizations, and individual deputies seized the moment to push through the Access to Information Law, which passed with unanimous support.

Within the Colom administration, technocratic elites kept momentum moving on the Access to Information Law. Within the Finance Ministry, they created the Vice Ministry of Fiscal Transparency and Evaluation, established a participatory commission with specialized civil society organizations and donors, and established a Public Information Unit to handle requests for information.

The watershed moments described above marked significant steps forward in the potential for increased transparency and participation in Guatemalan budgeting. Yet each moment emerged in highly specific circumstances, and most reforms stopped short of their full potential. Instead, powerful interests and actors found ways to cut reforms short, and when reforms were implemented, they were eroded in intervening years until a subsequent crisis or opening made room for a new leap forward. Table 6-1 summarizes the circumstances of each advance, highlighting the political circumstances that opened spaces for technocratic and international supporters to advance reform and some of the reactions that limited their impact.

Shortcomings in Transparency and Participation in Budgeting

Despite the advances marked by watershed moments, the general pattern of budgeting in Guatemala includes significant weaknesses in transparency and participation. While the formal institutions and rules have advanced as a result of reforms, actual changes in behavior and impact have been limited. Three major shortcomings exist with regard to social funds, trust funds, and nongovernmental and international organizations. All three demonstrate a basic pattern in which funds are shifted off-budget or outside of the formal institutions that might preserve transparency and participation. Instead, shortcomings restore poorly monitored and narrow political processes for the allocation of resources, with predictable consequences for developmental impact and state capacity.

Social Funds

During the 1990s, international organizations, especially the U.S. Agency for International Development, the World Bank, and the Inter-American Development Bank, promoted social funds to accompany structural adjustment. Social policy was meant to soften the negative impact of the stabilization and liberalization goals of structural adjustment.[17] This meant minimizing the fiscal costs of

17. Bigio (1998).

Table 6-1. *Watershed Moments in Transparency and Participation in Guatemala*

Reform	Context	Reactions
Law of Contracts 1992	Serrano reform mandate	Serrano self-coup shortcuts reforms
Organic Budget Law 1997	International support in context of Peace Accords	Impending FRG election and departure of business allies limit advance
Information technology (SIAF 1997, Guatecompras 2001)	Technocratic elites join with international pressure under Arzú and Portillo	Some areas left outside electronic monitoring, shutdown for political reasons
Law of Comptroller 2002	Technocratic elite, international pressure in the context of Portillo administration corruption	Comptroller sanctioning power and internal administration kept weak
Access to Information Law 2008	Technocratic elites within the Colom administration join with transparency advocates in Congress and international supporters	Passed in the wake of congressional scandal, depends on technocratic autonomy in finance

Source: Authors.

social policy, for example, by targeting benefits and limiting their amounts. It also called for shifting social policy away from the state and away from the political process, reserving funds from privatization or international aid for social funds managed outside traditional budgetary and bureaucratic regulations. The strategy followed a general skepticism of government and sought to include participatory, decentralized mechanisms that would channel public money through private entities.[18]

In practice, social funds tended to proliferate and absorb general budgetary resources rather than resources from unusual sources of income. The funds, which lacked the same type of oversight and deliberation as other areas of expenditure, evolved into a convenient mechanism for obscuring public spending and promoting accumulation by well-connected interest groups and for securing political support. The total amount dedicated to social funds averaged around 10 percent of the budget, and each government made use of the funds to position favored candidates for future office. The Colom government initiated a new social fund dedicated to conditional cash transfers, called My Family Progresses, which quickly grew to be the third largest fund in amount. The fund was originally

18. Ruthrauff and Carlson (1997).

managed through the office of the first lady, who was to become the governing party candidate for the next presidential election, although public criticism forced the program into the Ministry of Education.

In total, social funds account for more than Q 5 billion (US$640 million), of which the largest are an education development social fund (PERC), a land grant fund, My Family Progresses conditional cash transfers, and a housing fund (see figure 6-1).

Trust Funds

The next major channels of alternative expenditure are trust funds, which are set up in various areas to hold deposits to be released over various time periods, occasionally extending various years. By placing the money in trust, Guatemalan governments avoid some of the planning limitations of annual fiscal expenditures that must be used within the fiscal year and theoretically facilitate execution while protecting funds from use for other priorities. In addition, by channeling low-interest deposits into the banking sector, the state may facilitate easier credit terms for those who do business with the trusts. Still, the proliferation of such funds, their use for expenditures that might easily fit within traditional ministries, and their liberal use of contracts with third-party providers suggest that trust funds have turned into vehicles for other purposes.

By placing funds into a trust, private and public banks receive an influx of capital for which they charge a commission and with which they increase their turnover and reserves, while the state earns a minimal return on its deposits. In addition, the regulations on the outlays of trust fund expenditures are more difficult to trace and less subject to traditional mechanisms of oversight and accountability. Those who provide materials or services to the state or receive soft loans may benefit beyond what was originally intended.

The funds themselves are authorized through the budget and recognized in the Organic Budget Law, but the only legal architecture governing them exists in a Commercial Code passed in 1970.[19] Since 1998, the Ministry of Finance has issued several ministerial agreements to orient their use and created a Department of Trust Funds within the Public Credit Directorate. Only in 2004 did Congress assign responsibility for overseeing movements in the trust funds to the Comptroller General's office.[20]

Examples of trust funds include a fund for the peace agreement and land payouts, FONAPAZ, and another for road and highway maintenance, COVAL. These are the two largest, at Q 6 billion each, followed by Q 4 billion for rural

19. Acción Ciudadano and Fundación DESC (2006, p. 36).
20. Decree 35-2004, Article 41.

Figure 6-1. *Social Funds in Guatemala, 1995–2010*[a]

quetzales, millions

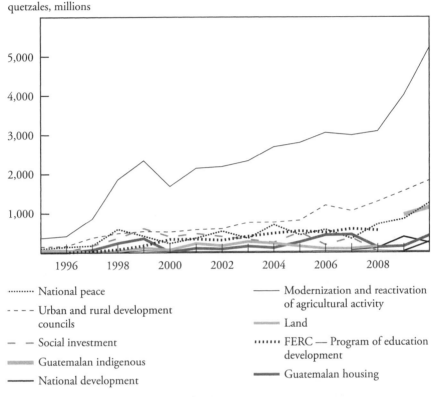

.... National peace

- - - - Urban and rural development
councils

— — Social investment

▬▬▬ Guatemalan indigenous

——— National development

——— Modernization and reactivation
of agricultural activity

▬▬▬ Land

▪▪▪▪▪▪▪ FERC — Program of education
development

▬▬▬ Guatemalan housing

Source: Data courtesy of ICEFI (www.icefi.org).
a. Until 2002, the rural and urban development councils were the Solidarity Fund for Community Development. The Fund for Social Investment was liquidated in 2007. The National Development Fund initiated activities in November 2007, and My Family Progresses included funds executed by the executive coordinator of the presidency until March 2009, when the Ministry of Education became responsible for managing the fund.

cooperative education, Q 1.8 billion for reforestation and preservation of water sources on public lands and in the countryside, Q 1.5 billion for subsidized housing, and almost Q 700 million for transportation in Guatemala City.[21] In certain years, outlays through trust funds are as high as 15 percent of the entire budget and 22 percent of the investment budget.

According to the Transparency International representative in Guatemala, "There can be two motivations to create a trust fund. One is that the bureaucrat wants to use the funds to deliberately realize corrupt transactions . . . Or that the

21. Ministerio de Finanzas Públicas (www.minfin.gob.gt/).

institution has the mandate to apply said funds to a specific program or to a specific target population . . . The trust fund is the guarantee that the funds will not be exposed to transfer to other priorities."[22] There have been scandals within the trust fund accounts, as in 2005 when the Guatemalan Housing Fund, with fourteen subfund accounts, transferred Q 266 million to a nongovernmental organization (NGO) with no experience in construction.

NGOs and International Organizations

Another area of dubious transparency and participation is in contracts with NGOs and international organizations. Sometimes, instead of executing projects directly, governments contract with these groups to undertake core functions, thereby evading some requirements of the Law of Government Contracts. The main justification for working through nongovernmental and international organizations is to pursue more effective and efficient execution of outlays without having to operate within cumbersome government bureaucracy. Trust funds, social funds, and line ministries all use this mechanism to facilitate their expenditure.

Yet oversight of these entities is weak. Some entities are created simply to execute an outlay, with no other capacity or function except to find a private sector entity that can be subcontracted to undertake the project. In such cases, the nongovernmental or international organization operates solely as a broker, securing the budget allocation, charging a commission, or simply holding onto the funds to earn interest while waiting to spend the money.

The political economy of such entities can operate through several possible mechanisms. The mechanism cited most consistently in interviews was Congress, generally through deputies on the Finance Committee. Deputies introduce amendments to specify the nongovernmental entity or type of entity that should receive an allocation, and they have been particularly adept at using the list of public works to channel resources. The list of public works, an appendix to the budget that outlines the jurisdiction and characteristics of multiple public works programs, can be used to channel spending to well-connected contractors and NGOs operating in narrow geographic bases, generally the bases of support for particular deputies.

Such contractors and NGOs can also submit their requests indirectly through the communal, municipal, and departmental development councils as well as directly through the relevant ministries, with the Ministry of Communications, Infrastructure, and Housing of particular importance in executing public works. Deputies then play the role of pressuring ministers to execute the projects, bring-

22. Acción Ciudadana and Fundación DESC (2006, p. 40).

ing potential recipients into Congress to embarrass ministries that have failed to execute a promised public work.[23]

The lack of oversight of these transfers and more generally in the execution of the budget becomes clear in isolated examples of corruption that are unraveled by civil society, the media, and occasional efforts by transparency advocates within the state itself. In 2010, for example, Congress and the Ministry of Health formed a Joint Technical Commission to examine the execution of public funds through NGOs.[24] According to Gladys Peñeda, a member of the commission, 49 percent of the NGOs receiving funds from the Ministry of Health were not meeting the terms of their agreements. The results of the commission were widely unpopular in Congress, where affected deputies—those who supported the delinquent NGOs—quickly mobilized to shut down the commission. The result was that, although the commission continues to exist within the Health Ministry, it is no longer operating in Congress and lacks the power to make surprise inspections or independently remove an NGO from the list of public fund recipients.[25] Moreover, no similar commission was created to explore the implementation of funds through NGOs operating through other ministries.

Guatemalan budgeting has also been clouded by the heavy presence of international organizations as executors of Guatemalan projects and programs. Such programs do not always provide transparency and participation to Guatemalan monitoring entities, although fully competent regulatory regimes may be operating within the international organization. In the event that suspicions arise about the use of funds, Guatemalan actors can do little to open accounts to scrutiny. To regulate how transfers to international organizations operate, Guatemalan budget authorities used the budgetary norms in 2010 to impose some conditions. Instead of lump-sum transfers, international organizations could receive tranches for 20 percent of their expenses, with subsequent payments on presentation of evidence of execution. Previously, international organizations had taken advantage of lump-sum transfers to earn interest on annual allocations and, in exchange, had looked favorably on the nominations of government appointees to staff positions within their organizations.

The use of nongovernmental and international organizations to execute projects and programs of the Guatemalan government clouds budget operations. In some cases, these mechanisms may facilitate expenditure and efficiency, but the lack of regulation and poor oversight provide opportunities for organizations

---

23. Interview, Carlos Barreda, formerly with the Vice Ministry of Transparency, June 14, 2011.

24. The commission was created in response to pressure from various NGOs that had been allocated funds through the list of public works but had never received the money from the ministry.

25. Interview, Gladys Peñeda, Joint Technical Commission, June 24, 2011.

operating through allies in Congress and the executive to direct public resources to private or unproductive ends.[26]

These areas of shortcoming suggest that watershed moments have had limited impact, with ongoing and significant ways in which funds are kept off-budget, rearranged once on-budget, and generally made difficult to monitor and hold to account. The resulting budgeting system deserves praise for the steps taken in a remarkably short period—Guatemala was, after all, the last country in the region to emerge from civil war and is now a leader in budget transparency indexes. Yet the shortcomings of the existing budget process suggest that much work remains to be done. As the following sections indicate, the shortcomings are more than temporary way stations on the route to better governance overall; rather, current Guatemalan budgeting reflects a more generalized state weakness. The determinants of watershed moments and the ongoing shortcomings indicate a budgeting regime that is purposefully weak to allow powerful actors to distort and dominate government decisions.

Factors Affecting Transparency and Participation in Budgeting

The previous sections have discussed, on the one hand, the watershed moments that expanded the potential for transparency and participation in budgeting and, on the other hand, the reality of limited advances and even reversal displayed by ongoing shortcomings. What can explain this apparent paradox of limited advances within advancing limits? This section explores some of the structural and institutional factors that make it likely that Guatemalan authorities will agree on occasional steps forward, even as they return more generally to the practice of undermining and weakening state institutions, especially in the area of transparency and participation. The core argument advanced here is that watershed moments are possible only in the context of episodic openings in Guatemalan politics. At these openings, technocratic elites and international actors insert an agenda for reform.

To make sense of this argument, it is necessary to understand the broader context of economic and political change in Guatemala. Guatemalan economic elites remain powerful and organized, with veto power over efforts to reform political

---

26. The critiques of the Center for International Human Rights (CIIDH) are more damning: "These irregularities indicate that annual allocations are dragged from one fiscal year to the next using administrative agreements, contracts with and reservation of trust funds for nongovernmental organizations and international organizations. The management of funds and implementation of public works through these mechanisms evade the Law of Purchases and Contracts, limit the oversight of the Comptroller General, and neutralize the action of control and oversight of the Congress. The use of funds through these schemes is the site of doubts and anomalies, as the money is not executed rapidly and has been discovered to have been deposited in banks to earn interest" (CIIDH 2008).

institutions, such as reforms to budget institutions. Yet elite groups remain divided among sectoral, familial, and regional divisions, even as new interests and sectors emerge and Guatemalan actors insert themselves in a globalized economy. These ongoing divisions prevent their unification behind a coherent plan for state reform, and they appear more willing to preserve a weak state than to allow any step forward that might favor one group or another. Elite fragmentation is complicated by a relatively weak civil society, able to advance demands for transparency and participation in budgeting, but wholly unable to extend beyond a narrow urban and middle-class presence.

A fragmented elite and a weak civil sector are borne out in the Guatemalan party system, as partisan organizations operate as temporary and personal vehicles for politicians with little social base. No party has retained the presidency in consecutive elections, and partisan representation in Congress changes frequently. From election to election, vote support fluctuates significantly, and even between elections, congressional representatives often switch parties in search of patronage resources or electoral advantage. As a result of this chaos in the party system, the political elites are no better suited than the economic elites to creating a consistent agenda in favor of budgetary reform. Instead, budgetary reform is possible only in the gaps, when a political opening makes it possible for technocratic and international actors to insert an agenda for reform. The paragraphs that follow describe these economic and political structures and what they mean for budgetary reform.

Like other countries in Central America, Guatemala experienced economic crisis, civil war, and regime change in the 1980s. An end to civil conflict came only in 1996, following a bloody and often brutal campaign that lasted two decades and left 200,000 people dead. The transition to democracy occurred in the midst of this heightened civil conflict, and political elites have been slow to adapt to democratic mechanisms of civil society activism, party organization, and electoral competition. This period coincided with a period of economic crisis, and economic elites began adapting their activities to a newly globalized pattern of international integration. Guatemalan budgeting was reorganized simultaneously with these economic and political changes, influenced by and influencing these changes, placing public finance at the heart of broader processes of regime change and economic transformation.

Economic and Social Structural Factors

The Guatemalan economy has been restructured as a result of civil war, changing patterns of demand in international markets, and the emergence of new dynamic sectors. These sectors have included assembly manufacturing for export, tourism, remittances, nontraditional agriculture, and natural resource extraction. They are particularly adapted to a reorganized international economy, in which firms, investments, and markets are more integrated, with Guatemalan producers benefiting from close proximity to the U.S. market. Growth picked up after the end of hostilities in the late 1990s and received new impetus with the boom in commodity prices in the 2000s.[27] Increasing integration with the international economy has produced a slight diversification of export products into new sectors, although traditional products and trading partners remain important.

Still, even in the context of greater international integration and moderate growth, relations of production in both new and traditional sectors have remained highly unequal and failed to make a dent in poverty. Data from the annual reports of the United Nations Development Programme paint a grim picture.[28] The share of people living in extreme poverty in Guatemala remains at 15.2 percent of the population, down from 15.7 percent in 2000, but still numbering almost 2 million people. Distribution remains among the worst in the world, with a Gini coefficient of .56, and inequalities on the basis of ethnicity and gender remain profound, with women earning only 38 percent of men's wages in the nonagriculture sector and indigenous children suffering twice the rates of malnutrition as nonindigenous children. In addition, Guatemala has become increasingly violent, returning to levels of homicide not seen since the civil war. As government pressure on drug cartels increases in Mexico, criminal gangs have increasingly seized territory in Guatemala, expelling residents from their lands, penetrating the justice system, and allying with powerful members of the political elite and the military.[29]

This pattern of development creates fragmentation within civil society at both the elite and civil society levels. Leading sectors remain divided between producers of newly emerging and traditional products, and civil society remains handcuffed by high levels of poverty, inequality, and exclusion. In the case of economic elites, they display an impressive capacity to coordinate their interests through powerful trade and sectoral associations, but also an equally impressive unwillingness to undertake a coherent partisan project or provide support to efforts to formalize and strengthen state institutions. Most prominent among private sector associations is the Coordinating Committee of Agricultural, Commercial, Industrial, and Financial Associations (CACIF), an entity encompassing chambers and associations for various sectors and supported by family and social bonds, as well as financial linkages that join leading firms across multiple sectors.[30] Despite dense networks of large-scale conglomerates in key sectors, the coordination provided by these networks is mobilized mostly in defensive fashion. Sectoral leaders

27. Agosín, Machado, and Nazal (2005).
28. UNDP (2009).
29. ICG (2010).
30. Cassaus Arzu (1995).

join together to block proposals and undercut efforts by sitting governments to make significant changes to institutions or legislation.

Instead of advancing a coherent political or economic project, economic elites prefer to retain state institutions permeable to the pressures and entreaties of well-connected and powerful interests. Individual business elites and sectoral leaders preserve their multiple and informal channels of access, operating in a fragmented and uncoordinated fashion to seek particularistic benefits from the state.[31] These defensive efforts materialize in staunch opposition to increasing revenues, while at the same time pursuing narrow benefits within the budget process.

Three patterns summarize the impact of these structural influences on budgeting. First, despite economic expansion and transformation, social relations remain highly exploitative, with continued inequality and poverty. Second, although new sectors have emerged, no economic sector has emerged as dominant, and leading economic actors appear satisfied with balancing their interests within trade associations and multiple formal and informal political vehicles, showing little desire to build state capacity in improvements such as transparency and participation in budgeting. Third, patterns of insertion of Guatemalan actors in the international economy are characterized by hard-to-tax sectors, privileged with multiple exemptions and incentives, and a general antagonism to state action that has starved the state of resources and constrained the fiscal revenues available in the budget.[32] This combination of structural factors consistently undermines budgeting in Guatemala, weakening mechanisms of transparency and participation even as some legal and institutional mechanisms advance.

There is growing pressure from the civil society to increase transparency and participation, but civil society actors remain weak. The civil war, which was particularly brutal and inordinately targeted at poor and indigenous citizens, seriously damaged organizational capacity among the people. Rates of civic participation and civil society organization, such as union membership, remain low in Guatemala, as are organizational density and trust.

In formal political institutions, some efforts to address the legacy of the war were written into the Peace Accords, such as a forum targeted to Mayan, union, peasant, and women's organizations, called the Civil Society Assembly. The Peace Accords also included specific pledges related to fiscal reform, with the March 1999 creation of the Preparatory Commission of the Fiscal Pact (CPPF), including academic, international, civil society, and private sector participation. This discussion produced the Collective of Social Organizations and a subsequent flowering of civil society organizations addressing fiscal issues.[33]

31. Segovia (2004).
32. ICEFI (2007).
33. Noriega, Alvarez, and Chocoj (2001).

Still, these organizations face important constraints on their efforts. They remain concentrated in the capital; they remain somewhat fragmented into particular areas of public policy of relevance to their constituencies (for example, women, indigenous, children, and human rights); and they have maintained varying degrees of independence from government, party, and private sector actors. As a result, civil society has been unable to act as a counterweight to private sector actors, who preserve access and influence through the continued informality that characterizes Guatemalan budgeting and the Guatemalan state.

To understand how these structural factors produce occasional advances in the midst of ongoing weakness in budgeting, it is instructive to look closer at how they played out during the negotiation of the Fiscal Pact toward the end of the Arzú presidency. The Arzú presidency was able to advance the Organic Budget Law in the honeymoon period after the Peace Accords, in 1997. The moment was one in which economic factions were neutralized, generally disconnected from the minutiae of reform, and eager to get on with the process of recovery. In this gap, the budget law was passed, advanced in particular by the technocratic elite within the bureaucracy and international actors associated with the peace process.

Once the reform was passed, however, the next order of business was a fiscal pact to raise the revenues that might make a new budget process meaningful. The Peace Agreement had included a pledge to raise revenues to 12 percent of GDP, and a series of roundtables were meant to bring together civil society and business sector elites in support of a fiscal pact. As CACIF perceived the impending victory of the FRG candidate for the presidency, it withdrew its support at the last minute, vetoing any increase in revenues and cutting short further discussion of budget reforms.[34] Civil society advocates lacked capacity to carry the reforms forward on their own, and technocratic and international actors were forced to wait until the next administration settled into place before advocating a deepening of fiscal efforts.

Party System

While a fragmented elite and a weak civil society are problematic for reform, they would not be so detrimental if political elites could develop a coherent program for governance. Unfortunately, the main legacy of the process of political liberalization that began in the mid-1980s and culminated with the Peace Accords is a party system that remains volatile, fragmented, and practically devoid of ideological content and greatly complicates policymaking.

Guatemala has had one of the highest rates of electoral volatility in Latin America. Between 1995 and 2007, Guatemala's average volatility was 48.7 per-

---

34. Knight and Cabrera (2005).

cent for the first round of presidential elections and 40.3 percent for legislative elections.[35] These numbers are just below those of some of the most volatile Andean countries, including those that have suffered traumatic collapses of the party system and democratic crises.[36] These high levels of electoral volatility contribute substantially to the dual budget-making process, creating a series of incentives for politicians to subvert the spirit of the law with regard to transparency and accountability.

High levels of electoral volatility create few incentives for party building, among either politicians or civil society. In Guatemala the political party is little more than an electoral label: parties are legally necessary to contest elections because they are the only organizations allowed to put forward candidates at the national level, but they are useful for little else. It is relatively easy to create a new party in Guatemala, and party labels are often considered to be "for sale," so that switching to a new electoral machine solves internal struggles for power since defections have no legislative or electoral cost. Parties fail to develop platforms, fail to retain members, and fail to sustain organizations either in the state or in society. This weakness has an important effect on the mortality and birth rate of parties. The party system is littered with examples of short-lived parties, including those that have secured, in their short history, important quotas of power.

The strong incentives to create new parties also result in a large party system, both during elections and in Congress. Between 1990 and 2007 Guatemala had some 5.82 parties. If we only include the post–Peace Accord period, 1999–2007, the average increases significantly to 7.23 parties, excluding the Arzú government, which was the last to have a legislative majority. This fragmentation of the system in conjunction with its fluidity has negative consequences for accountability. Voters must familiarize themselves with a host of new parties with every election, and each new mandate produces a large number of parties that are active in Congress and involved in the executive. Voters, civil society organizations, and subnational actors have difficulty knowing who is accountable for the policies implemented or where to make demands for greater transparency.

Weak political parties also mean that successful politicians are those who build a personal electoral following. In the Guatemalan Congress, numerous politicians have survived the death, or at the very least the decline, of their party, only to transfer their captured votes to another partisan vehicle. Such politicians switch party labels as they position themselves for an upcoming election, and their votes

35. The regional average for presidential elections was 17.4 percent for the 1980s and 27.2 percent for the 1990s (Roberts n.a.). At the legislative level, between 1989 and 2009, Latin America's average was 25.75 percent (Payne, Zovatto, and Mateo Diaz 2007).

36. Guatemala's volatility levels fall between Bolivia's 39.8 percent and Peru's 51.9 percent (legislative elections, 1993–2005 and 1990–2001, respectively). Mainwaring, Bejarano and Pizarro (2006).

are made especially important by an electoral system with proportional representation and closed party lists. Their large blocks of votes can carry them and other politicians into Congress, and they become coveted allies for any party list. While negotiations between these individuals and the party labels they lend their votes to are not public, the evidence of their payoff is in the legislative positions they secure: important commissions, such as the Congress Commission of Public Finance and Currency, allow them to secure public funds for their constituencies, further expanding their base of voters.[37]

Furthermore, because governments do not enjoy majorities in Congress, the executive has to cobble together a working majority to govern. As a result, deputies often switch parties at the beginning of a legislative year, especially after an election. Again, the negotiations that go on behind these party switches are not made public, but votes clearly are often exchanged for a distribution of goods, both congressional privileges and public works for the deputies' constituencies.

The weak parties and lack of governing coalitions reinforce a great deal of informality in the inner workings of Congress. This informality appears in the allocation of resources; for instance, it was long common knowledge that the Commission of Public Finance and Currency, composed of the important party and bloc leaders, held all of its important meetings outside of Congress, including those that drew up the list of public works. Thanks to outside pressure, from civil society, the media, and the international community, today the commission broadcasts its meetings live through the congressional webpage. While this does not guarantee that informal meetings no longer take place, it does constitute one step more toward greater accountability.

Guatemala's weak party system is also characterized by low levels of polarization. Parties do not distinguish themselves particularly on the basis of ideology or distinct positions on major policy and social cleavages, and high levels of volatility and alternation in power have not injected new or distinct policy positions into government. Low levels of polarization have existed since the beginning of the current period of democracy and have remained firmly in place long after the signing of the Peace Accords. Between 1995 and 2007 Guatemala has had, on average, a middle to low level of polarization of 3.39 out of a possible ten.[38] This is just below the regional average of 3.61 and far below the levels of the other two countries with a legacy of civil war in Central America, Nicaragua and El Salvador, with polarization levels of 6.86 and 6.72, respectively, for a similar time period. This low level

37. Less well-known individuals—those who do not have large electoral machines or who are seeking a candidacy for the first time—need to be able to contribute to the party's coffers, in addition to financing their own candidacy, if they want to be placed on the party's list.

38. This number is calculated with the Parliamentary Elites Survey, conducted by the Instituto Interuniversitario de Iberoamérica at the University of Salamanca, Spain.

of polarization is due to the fact that the vast majority of parties in the system, certainly those that have been able to secure a significant electoral base of support, fleeting as it might be, have been either centrist or conservative parties. The left has been almost completely absent from Guatemala's party system as a viable electoral choice. Centrist and right-wing parties, influenced as they are by their main campaign contributors among Guatemala's elite, have remained antagonistic or at least uncommitted to strengthening state institutions.

Guatemala's party system, with its weak parties, extreme fluidity, and lack of ideological polarization, sustains a chaotic and weakly institutionalized Congress. The leaders who can thrive in this congressional environment are those whose skill in manipulating informal practices secures a stream of benefits to their voter base and those they favor. Such actors have little incentive to increase the institutionalization of budgeting in Congress. As a result, opportunities for reform are rare, occurring only when a political opening neutralizes existing political factions.

Such a moment appeared in 2008 when the Access to Information Law was passed. As discussed above, the law passed in the midst of scandal, when congressional leaders had gambled with congressional funds and lost them in the stock market. The president of Congress had to step down from his post, and both the president's party and the main opposition faced widespread disapproval. In this unique moment, legislators with an accountability agenda could push for reforms. They were backed by civil society, media, and international actors, and they could choose from any of several transparency bills that had been languishing in committee for years.[39]

Still, no sooner had the moment passed than other legislators began working to preserve or restore the loopholes that allow business as usual. Some of the same legislators who had championed the accountability reforms returned to traditional practices in the Finance Committee of inserting amendments to target benefits and projects to their supporters and campaign backers.

Information and Impacts

Before concluding, it is worth reflecting on the possible long-term impact of limited advances within advancing limits. Guatemalan budgeting has made important strides since the early 1990s. These watershed moments have introduced transparency and participation into some areas of budgeting. Still, powerful actors have blocked further reform or preserved important areas of privilege, most importantly by keeping significant funds wholly off-budget or managed through otherwise unregulated or poorly monitored mechanisms.

39. Interview, Deputy Rosa Maria de Frade, June 25, 2011.

As a result, it makes sense to consider what the increase in information and simultaneous lack of increase in budgetary performance might produce. Citizens and advocacy groups are no longer in the dark, if they ever were, about the misuse of public funds. Scandal is a constant topic in the mass media, and exposing malfeasance in the management of public resources and power has become the specialty of organizations such as Acción Ciudadana and CIIDH. More considered analysis by think tanks such as the Centro de Investigaciones Económicos Nacionales (CIEN), the Asociación de Investigación y Estudios Sociales (ASIES), and the Instituto Centroamericano de Estudios Fiscales (ICEFI) is possible as a result of online availability of data and information, and technocrats within the Ministry of Finance appear committed to making an increasingly sophisticated and detailed amount of information available on the Internet.

However, increased access only exaggerates further the lack of improvement in significant areas of public finance. Public opinion surveys reveal a deep mistrust and overall malaise when it comes to citizen evaluations of government. According to Latinobarometro, only 28 percent of Guatemalans trust their government, and fewer than 15 percent trust political parties, Congress, the police, or customs officials.[40] This public skepticism is not without justification, as World Bank surveys of enterprises and business people find that firms lose 4 percent of their sales on security expenses or theft, small enterprises spend 4 percent of their sales in bribes to access public services, and 15 percent of entrepreneurs report frequent payment of bribes.[41]

Guatemalan budgeting has improved transparency and increased participation in occasional watershed moments over the last two decades. These advances publicize government finance, and a small segment of the nongovernmental and think tank world is making good use of available information. Still, the increased information has only highlighted the apparent paradox of Guatemalan budgeting: limited advances occur in the midst of ongoing weakness and occasional reversal.

Conclusions

Preceding pages have described the nature of budgeting in Guatemala. The country has made important strides in transparency, including the creation of a Vice Ministry of Transparency and new legislation requiring public access to information. The country has also introduced some institutional frameworks to encourage participation, such as local development councils. For a country recently

40. See Latinobarometro (www.latinobarometro.org/latino/LATDatos.jsp).
41. World Bank (2010).

emerging from civil war with chronic poverty and ongoing political instability, these advances are important.

Yet there are ongoing problems with budgeting in Guatemala. The country operates within a fiscal framework that is too narrow, with multiple mechanisms to ring-fence and obscure spending such as social funds, trust funds, and spending through third-party nongovernmental organizations and international organizations.

Together, the steps taken by committed members of the executive, pressed by members of Congress, and encouraged by actors in civil society have advanced the potential for more transparent and participative budgeting. The country is on a much more stable footing than it was a few years ago. Still, these advances have been limited by the general volatility and weakness of the political elite, as expressed in the party system, as well as by a social structure characterized by inequality, poverty, and exclusion, with dominant elites concerned mostly with blocking efforts to raise revenues rather than directing a coherent state-building agenda.

What are the prospects for the future in Guatemala? The newly elected leader, Otto Pérez Molina, won the presidency with a platform of law and order, drawing on his own past as a general in the army and director of military intelligence during the civil war. Pérez Molina won the presidency, but failed to win a majority in Congress, and his government will likely be as hamstrung as all previous governments. As a former military leader, Pérez Molina came to power advocating a state with greater capacity to attack organized crime, but he draws support from economic elites who are deeply suspicious of state power. The likely scenario is one of ongoing incapacity in general and ongoing constraints within budgeting. The incremental and limited advances in recent years may continue, but they will be as incomplete and as partial as ever.

References

Acción Ciudadana and Fundación DESC. 2006. *Poder discrecional y corrupción en Guatemala: Claves para ganar transparencia.* Guatemala City.

Agosín, Manuel, Roberto Machado, and Paulina Nazal. 2005. *Pequeñas economías, grandes desafíos.* Washington: Inter-American Development Bank.

Bigio, Anthony G., ed. 1998. *Social Funds and Reaching the Poor: Experiences and Future Directions.* Washington: World Bank.

Blasco, Antonio. 2009. *Performance Report on Public Expenditure and Financial Accountability (PEFA).* Washington: World Bank, Inter-American Development Bank, and the European Union.

Cassaus Arzu, Marta. 1995. *Linaje e racismo.* Costa Rica: Ed. Flacso.

CIEN (Centro de Investigaciones Económicos Nacionales). 2001. *Guía de aspectos presupuestarios y fiscales.* Guatemala City.

CIIDH (Centro Internacional de Investigaciones de Derechos Humanos). 2008. *Observatorio de gasto social.* Guatemala City.

IBP (International Budget Partnership). 2010. *The Open Budget Survey 2010.* Washington.

ICEFI (Instituto Centroamericano de Estudios Fiscales). 2007. *La política fiscal en la encrucijada: El caso de Guatemala.* Guatemala City.

ICG (International Crisis Group). 2010. "Guatemala: Squeezed between Crime and Impunity." Latin America Report 33. Washington: International Crisis Group.

IMF (International Monetary Fund). 2006. *Guatemala: Report on the Observance of Standards and Codes: Fiscal Transparency Module.* IMF Country Report 06/9. Washington.

Knight, Juan Alberto Fuentes, and Maynor Cabrera. 2005. *El pacto fiscal de Guatemala: Una oportunidad perdida.* Guatemala City: PNUD.

Mainwaring, Scott, Ana María Bejarano, and Eduardo Pizarro Leongómez. 2006. "The Crisis of Democratic Representation in the Andes: An Overview." In *The Crisis of Democratic Representation in the Andes,* edited by Scott Mainwaring, Ana María Bejarano, and Eduardo Pizarro Leongómez. Stanford University Press.

Mora, Marvin. 2009. *Estudio de la Ley de Contrataciones del Estado.* Guatemala City: Universidad San Carlos.

Noriega, Arnoldo, Enrique Alvarez, and Mario Chocoj. 2001. *Cuando la sociedad guatemalteca se encuentra: La negociación política del pacto fiscal.* Guatemala: Instituto de Estudios Políticos, Económicos y Sociales (IPES).

OEA (Organización de Estados Americanos). 2009. Guía práctica sobre análisis presupuestario. Guatemala City.

Payne, Mark J., Daniel Zovatto, and Mercedez Mateo Diaz. 2007. *Democracies in Development: Politics and Reform in Latin America,* rev. ed. Washington: David Rockefeller, Inter-American Development Bank.

Reynoso Martínez, Luis Fernando. 2008. *Estudio jurídico doctrinario de la Ley Orgánica de la Contraloría General de Cuentas.* Guatemala City: Universidad San Carlos.

Roberts, Kenneth M. n. a. "Party Systems and Electoral Volatility during Latin America's Transition to Economic Liberalism." Cornell University.

Ruthrauff, John, and Teresa Carlson. 1997. *Strategies for Guatemala: World Bank and Inter-American Development Bank Guide.* Washington: Center for Democratic Education.

Segovia, Alexander. 2004. *Modernización empresarial en Guatemala ¿Cambio real o nuevo discurso?* Guatemala: F & G Editores.

UNDP (United Nations Development Programme). 2009. *Human Development Report 2009: Overcoming Barriers; Human Mobility and Development.* New York: Palmgrave Macmillan.

World Bank. 2010. *Guatemala's CGAC Experience: Challenges, Achievements, and Opportunities.* Guatemala City: World Bank.

7

The Limits of Top-Down Reform: Budget Transparency in Tanzania

BARAK D. HOFFMAN

Budget transparency in Tanzania has improved greatly since the country transitioned to democracy in the early 1990s. Nevertheless, it remains a problem, especially in transforming greater openness into improved accountability. Tanzania's efforts to improve transparency have resulted mainly from the reforms that powerful presidents sitting on top of a fairly disciplined and hegemonic party implemented in return for foreign assistance. Political competition—manifested by rifts within the ruling party—also has been a source of greater openness, but it has played a far less significant role, especially in catalyzing institutional reforms in this area. Civil society, by and large, has not been a strong force for these changes.

Due to these factors, advances in transparency have occurred in a fairly systematic way, primarily through the creation of executive branch offices and agencies accountable to the president. Genuine institutional reform to increase the power of independent oversight bodies and Parliament and the development of a more forceful media and civil society have advanced far less. Because Parliament, civil society, and oversight agencies remain institutionally weak, they are generally unable to hold the executive branch accountable for its actions. Greater domestic demand for reform must occur to remedy these institutional weaknesses.

Three broad conclusions emerge from examining the politics of transparency in Tanzania. First, external pressure is not a substitute for internal demand. Because reforms in these areas have been the result mainly of foreign pressure, advances remain largely limited to executive discretion. Second, increased budget transparency has not led easily to greater accountability. For example, massive corruption scandals have erupted in Tanzania over the past two decades. An enormous amount of detail exists on the crimes committed and their perpetrators.

183

However, those at the center have not been held accountable and probably will not be in the near future. More broadly, while successive governments have created a relatively autonomous supreme audit institution (SAI), the National Audit Office (NAO), and other oversight agencies, they tend to lack significant enforcement power. Finally, opportunism, rather than sincere demands for reform, tends to link greater political competition with increased budget transparency in Tanzania. Thus improvements in financial openness as a result of political contestation have largely failed to produce substantive institutional reform in this area.

This chapter analyzes the politics of budget transparency in Tanzania, discussing the political context in which reforms to transparency occurred over the past two decades, examining the current level of transparency, and identifying the challenges to securing and advancing the reforms made. A final section provides concluding observations.

Political Trajectory

Since independence, Tanzania's political leaders have succeeded in creating a hegemonic and effective ruling party, the Chama Cha Mapinduzi (CCM), or Party of the Revolution.[1] The party's strength has been the principal source of and obstacle to reforms to improve budget transparency in Tanzania. This section discusses the political trajectory in Tanzania that has led to improvements in budget transparency. It also focuses on the contemporary influence of oversight mechanisms, specifically the powers of Parliament, the executive branch, autonomous agencies, and civil society.

Building the Party

Tanzania was a multiparty democracy at independence, but did not remain one for long. The Tanganyika African National Union (TANU) under the leadership of Julius Nyerere swept the country's first election in 1962, and the 1965 constitution created a one-party state. The 1977 constitution subordinated the role of the state to that of the party by placing the former under the jurisdiction of the latter.

To understand politics in Tanzania, one must begin with the CCM. Under Nyerere, the party became a mechanism of control and remains the only organization, including the government, with the capacity to exert power from the polit-

---

1. This analysis applies only to mainland Tanzania, not Zanzibar, the country's semiautonomous archipelago, except where specified. The CCM formed in 1977 in a merger between the mainland-based Tanganyika African National Union and the Zanzibar-based Afro-Shirazi Party, although the two had governed de facto as one party after Tanganyika and Zanzibar merged in 1964, following the Zanzibar revolution.

ical centers of Dar es Salaam and Dodoma to the remotest villages.[2] Nyerere built a hegemonic party, with accountability pointing upward to the president and the CCM Central Committee. Regional chairs were accountable to CCM leaders, district chairs reported to regional ones, ward chairs reported to district ones, and so on all the way down to ten-cell leaders in urban areas and village chairs in rural ones. Although touted by the CCM leadership as a means to ensure broad-based participation, it also served as an instrument of coercion: CCM leaders dispatched orders down the chain of command, and lower-level party officials reported upward to the president. Similarly, Nyerere centered power in the executive branch, relegating Parliament to the status of a debating chamber. Although its discussions were often lively, the body lacked substantive institutional political influence.

Transition to Democracy

The structures that Nyerere built survive to this day, albeit in a more attenuated form, because the CCM leadership preemptively transitioned to democracy, under the advice of Nyerere and in anticipation of strong domestic calls for it.[3] In the late 1980s, Nyerere understood that the demands for democratic transition sweeping Africa and other parts of the world would eventually come to Tanzania. He also realized that if Tanzania transitioned to democracy ahead of sustained domestic demand for it, the party could put in place rules and institutions that were highly favorable for the CCM to retain control long after Tanzania became a multiparty democracy. Due to weak internal demand for political reform, Tanzania's transition to democracy and the constitutional changes that guided it deliberately left an incomplete separation between the party and the state and did little to reduce the power of the executive branch.[4] Demands for greater transparency were neither a strong cause for nor a result of Tanzania's democratic transition.

Tanzania's transition to democracy did little to increase the formal power of Parliament or civil society.[5] While the legislature has become more assertive, due to rifts within the CCM and a forceful opposition, discussed in more detail below,

2. Tucker, Hoffman, and Mukandala (2010). Dodoma is the capital of Tanzania and Parliament meets there, while the State House and most government ministries operate out of Dar es Salaam.

3. Hoffman and Robinson (2009).

4. The effect of these blurred distinctions is most evident at the regional and district levels. As existed during the one-party era, the highest regional and district authorities—the regional commissioner and the district commissioner—are appointed directly by the president rather than elected. At the same time, the CCM constitution explicitly states that the regional and district commissioners are the party's representatives in the region and the district, respectively, thus obscuring where the party ends and the state begins.

5. Tucker, Hoffman, and Mukandala (2010).

institutional changes that provide Parliament with greater authority have not occurred.[6] Two decades after Tanzania's democratic transition, civil society remains a weak advocate for political reform.[7] According to Hyden and Mmuya (2008),

> Civil society is weak in Tanzania. Strong organizations representing the views of particular interest groups are few and far between. Only some of these are ready to take on a political role in the sense of voicing independent opinions in public. . . . The majority of these are primarily involved in delivery of services in social development contexts. Many would be what are called community-based organizations. These types of organizations generally do not take a political position but regard themselves as nonpolitical and involved in development.[8]

The blame is not civil society's alone. Rather, reflecting Tanzania's top-down transition to democracy, the government deliberately discourages civil society from engaging in advocacy by restricting the types of activities that nongovernmental organizations (NGOs) can undertake, casting a wide net on what it perceives to be prohibited political activity.[9] Recently, a few civil society organizations (CSOs) have begun to challenge these restrictions, in part, by employing greater access to government information as a mechanism for creating demand for more political accountability.

Rifts at the Top

The CCM's hegemony notwithstanding, internal rifts increasingly constitute a governance challenge within the party and the government because they reflect the former's weakening formal structures. These rifts have also been an indirect cause of greater transparency. Hyden and Mmuya (2008) have identified three main factions: (1) reformers, primarily younger members of Parliament (MPs), who realize that governance problems are threatening the party's control and reputation; (2) the old guard, composed of senior members, who believe that the party needs to protect its external image by solving problems quietly within the CCM; and (3) opportunists who have joined the party to secure privileged access to state resources. Others see the rifts in more prosaic terms, purely as the struggle for control of the party and the resources it commands and as the result of the weakness of Tanzania's current president, Jakaya Kikwete. Many see him as being keener to remain popular than to make difficult choices.[10]

---

6. Mukandala, Mushi, and Killian (2008) and Tucker, Hoffman, and Mukandala (2010).
7. Engel (2010), Hyden and Mmuya (2008), and Tucker, Hoffman, and Mukandala (2010).
8. Hyden and Mmuya (2008, p. 102).
9. Hyden and Mmuya (2008) and Tucker, Hoffman, and Mukandala (2010).
10. Mukandala, Mushi, and Killian (2008) and Tucker, Hoffman, and Mukandala (2010).

The practical consequence of these rifts is that they weaken internal governance of the party. Increases in transparency have been one consequence of the decline in ruling party discipline. This was most evident during Tanzania's ninth Parliament (2005–10), when Speaker Samwel Sitta, a member of a rival CCM faction to Prime Minister Edward Lowassa, revised Parliament's standing orders to allow it far greater capacity to oversee the executive branch.[11] These reforms included strengthening parliamentary committees, including creating a planning committee to discuss budget proposals and priorities; increasing the number of committees chaired by opposition MPs; empowering standing committees to organize public hearings to discuss bills and policy proposals; and introducing prime minister question-and-answer sessions.

Under Sitta, Parliament actively debated the budget far more than previous ones since Tanzania's transition to multiparty democracy. Although enhanced scrutiny began over issues of corruption (specifically the Richmond scandal),[12] investigations widened to many other areas during Sitta's terms as speaker. The vigorous budget debates that emerged in Tanzania's ninth Parliament have continued in its tenth one. Three prominent examples demonstrate these changes. First, during the debate over the 2011–12 budget, Parliament refused to pass the initial one that the executive branch submitted for the Ministry of Energy and Minerals as a rebuke over the country's ongoing electricity crisis, the failure of the budget to address the country's energy needs, and allegations that individuals in the ministry had attempted to bribe MPs to pass the budget.[13] Second, in August and September 2011, Parliament debated why some very large Tanzanian companies with close ties to the CCM were not on the list of the country's largest corporate taxpayers. Several MPs suggested that owners of these companies were able to secure favorable tax treatment because of their close ties to CCM individuals serving in the government.[14] Third, Parliament has been examining the generous compensation that senior political appointees and MPs receive.[15]

Nevertheless, while CCM rifts and a president with comparatively weak control over the party have been a source of transparency, these forces have failed to catalyze demand for substantive institutional reforms to ensure greater openness. Although Tanzania's Parliament now discusses the budget energetically, the only recent initiatives to increase its formal power over the budget have been Sitta's

11. Tucker, Hoffman, and Mukandala (2010).

12. The Richmond scandal involved the improper award of a contract to supply energy. Three ministers and an MP on the CCM Central Committee were implicated in it. It cost the government approximately $170 million, and Richmond failed to deliver the quantity of energy the contract demanded. Sitta's faction in the cabinet saw the scandal as an opportunity to bring down Lowassa.

13. Kisembo (2011).

14. "List of Taxpayers Ignites Debate," *Citizen*, August 29, 2011.

15. wa Kuhenga (2011).

revisions of Parliament's standing orders. Rather, the lively debates today tend to serve as a platform for disgruntled MPs to embarrass rivals in the executive branch and position themselves for the 2015 election.[16]

Rifts within the CCM have occurred numerous times in the past, and the party has been able to reform itself internally after each one. While it is far too early to tell whether this will happen again and even more speculative to believe that the party will fracture because of it, it is important to understand the context in which such rifts are occurring today.[17] First, as the CCM transforms from an ideological to a more pragmatic party, increasingly inhabited by people who view it as a vehicle for wealth accumulation, structures of internal discipline are necessarily weakening. Factions today largely form over efforts to gain access to state resources, not over ideology, as occurred in previous rifts. Second, structural changes, such as urbanization and growth of the private sector, are undermining many of the CCM's economic mechanisms of control that existed in the one-party era under a socialist economy. Third, the creation of political spaces outside of the CCM as a result of Tanzania's transition to democracy, such as private media, civil society, and opposition parties, while weak, nevertheless limits the extent of CCM's political control and has eroded its monopoly over flows of information and social organization.

Stirrings in Civil Society

Reflecting Tanzania's political realities, civil society can point to few achievements and exhibits little dynamism.[18] Civil society is not completely moribund, however, and over the past few years some organizations have begun to challenge the CCM more forcefully. Perhaps their greatest accomplishment to date has been the result of the efforts of Haki Elimu to hold the Mkapa administration accountable for its promises on primary education. In 2005 the organization placed several radio and television advertisements criticizing the government for not living up to its commitments in this area. The government, specifically Minister of Education Joseph Mungai, denounced Haki Elimu and banned it from undertaking studies or publishing information on the education sector for eighteen months, arguing that the ads violated guidelines prohibiting NGOs from engaging in political activity. The government's overreaction caused a huge outcry in civil society and the media, and it eventually backed down.

The episode was a clear success, as the ads that Haki Elimu currently runs are even more critical of the government. It also opened space for other NGOs, such as Sikika, Twaweza, and Policy Forum, to criticize the government. However, the

16. Kaijage (2011).
17. James (2011) and Hyden and Mmuya (2008).
18. Engel (2010), Hyden and Mmuya (2008), and Tucker, Hoffman, and Mukandala (2010).

lesson to take from the NGO's ban is that what caused the government to allow civil society to be more assertive was not necessarily Haki Elimu's actions, but the government's overreaction to them. Had the Mkapa administration acted with more restraint, it probably would not have needed to cede the ground it did. In addition, while the government is more accepting of criticism from civil society today than it was in the past, its tolerance operates through lax enforcement of laws regulating the operations of CSOs, not changes to them.

Following Haki Elimu's example, several CSOs are attempting to employ budget transparency as part of their program activities. For example, Research on Poverty Alleviation, perhaps the most influential think tank in Tanzania, places budget data and audit findings at the national, regional, and district levels on its website. Policy Forum publishes periodic reviews of government performance, including governance, service delivery, and budget implementation. Uwazi operates across a range of sectors, such as education, health, and water. In part, it works to disseminate information in ways that ordinary people can grasp easily. The organization also seeks to empower people by conveying the message that families and communities have the ability to solve problems and the right to demand greater accountability. Moreover, it operates a budget portal on its website to monitor progress in budget implementation and respond to audit findings. Furthermore, the organization has initiated several follow-the-money campaigns. Sikika performs a function similar to that of Haki Elimu in health and documents wasteful government spending. Finally, Twaweza, an NGO that attempts to catalyze bottom-up pressure for reform and a financial supporter of Uwazi, is undertaking a rigorous evaluation of the impact of greater information on citizen action.

The operations of these organizations are impressive and may catalyze further efforts. However, they operate mainly in Dar es Salaam, and it is difficult to gauge the impact of their work. Nor have their actions led to legal reform, even in the laws that severely circumscribe their ability to criticize the government. In addition, NGOs often see each other as competitors for scarce resources and hence fail to cooperate as a means of leveraging their influence.

Weak Pressure from the Private Sector and Society

Structural factors, specifically economic and social ones, have not been a strong source of demand for reforms to transparency. This section attempts to explain why social cleavages have failed to emerge as interest groups seeking this outcome, with the qualification that it is typically more difficult to explain why an action did not occur than to explain why it did.

Since Tanzania's transition to capitalism, domestic economic forces, either the emergence of private sector interest groups or pressures emanating from widening inequality, have failed to catalyze demands for greater transparency or political reform more broadly. Tanzania's largely crony form of capitalism likely explains why private sector interest groups have not formed to press the government for greater financial transparency. Politicians and politically well-connected elites with privileged access to state resources constitute much of the private sector in Tanzania. For this reason, actors in it have not emerged as a coherent interest group pressing for greater transparency. In Tanzania, many of the largest business people either are members of CCM or have close ties to it. In addition, the government is one of the largest consumers of the products the private sector creates. In particular, state contracts and distorted regulatory structures, at both the local and national levels, are a particularly crucial element of Tanzania's political economy.[19] Given the incomplete separation between the party and the state, much of the private sector sees cooperation with the CCM, not opposition to it, as the most efficacious mechanism for generating profits. The CCM encourages these links because the party needs campaign finance and because allocating economic resources through ties to the party is an effective means of exercising political control of the private sector.

Tanzania's widening income equality also has failed to catalyze interest groups fighting to rectify the fact that the benefits of Tanzania's recent economic gains have flowed largely to a small number of well-connected elites. Although it is difficult to say why this has not occurred, two possibilities exist. First, while inequality is growing in Tanzania, it is still moderate, especially in comparison to its peers.[20] Second, because patronage networks dominate access to jobs and financial resources, individual incentives exist among ambitious Tanzanians not to challenge the system, but to become part of it.

Unlike many of Tanzania's neighbors, social forces—principally ethnic ones—also have failed to catalyze demand for political reform. While the absence of deep ethnic tensions has been a source of stability in Tanzania, it also has not been a source of political pressure. Although it is difficult to predict with certainty how greater ethnic frictions would affect politics in Tanzania, evidence from Zanzibar suggests that they would not create a propitious political environment for enhanced transparency. Ethnic rifts in Zanzibar between the Arab and African populations on the islands run deep. Due to these tensions, CCM control has been far less secure and more repressive on Zanzibar than on the mainland. Recent political compromise to address the archipelago's ethnic tensions, specifically the

---

19. Providing state contracts and other forms of favorable economic treatment for select firms and individuals in return for campaign contributions and party support more generally is arguably the core of Tanzania's political economy.

20. For example, Tanzania's Gini coefficient, 34.6, is the lowest in East Africa. Burundi's is 42.4, Kenya's is 42.5, Rwanda's is 46.8, and Uganda's is 45.7.

power-sharing agreement in 2010 between the CCM and the Civic United Front (CUF), did not introduce more transparency into the government of Zanzibar.[21]

External Sources of Reforms to Increase Transparency

If domestic demands for greater transparency in Tanzania have generally been weak and not resulted in significant institutional reforms, what has been the impetus for the range of policies the government has implemented to improve financial openness over the past two decades? For the most part, the impetus has been donor pressure.[22] This section discusses the influence that donors have exerted over reforms that the government has enacted to increase transparency.

In the early 1990s, after two decades of economic stagnation, CCM leaders concluded that central planning and socialism had become a failed economic policy. They decided to undertake reforms to create a more capitalist economy and reduce the country's debt.[23] After several failed attempts to design their own economic reform programs, the government turned to bilateral donors and international financial institutions for assistance.[24]

The origins of Tanzania's reforms lie in the problems that emerged during its economic transition to capitalism in the early 1990s. Soon after the country began to undertake reforms to create a market economy under a series of donor-designed structural adjustment programs, corruption exploded during the term of Tanzania's second president, Ali Hassan Mwinyi (1985–95). In retrospect, this should not have come as a surprise for two reasons. First, Tanzania's economic transition followed a path of liberalization without regulation.[25] This combination permitted well-placed public servants and political leaders to benefit enormously from privatization of government properties and enterprises because they could undervalue the assets and determine who could buy them. Second, corruption was emerging as a problem even before the onset of economic reforms, as

21. The CCM-CUF rift dates roughly back to Omani rule of the archipelago in the nineteenth century. During this period, Arab settlers on the islands began importing large numbers of slaves from the mainland to work on plantations in Zanzibar. Britain made the archipelago a protectorate in 1890, and Zanzibar became independent in 1963. At that time, Britain handed power back to the sultanate, the Arab ruling family in power when Britain took control. Soon after independence, the Zanzibar revolution, led by the primarily African Afro-Shirazi Party, overthrew the sultan. In 1964 Tanganyika and Zanzibar formed a political union, the United Republic of Tanzania, yet Zanzibar retained significant autonomy over its internal affairs. In 1977 the Afro-Shirazi Party formally merged with the CCM. The CUF traces its lineage to opposition to CCM rule (but not necessarily support for the sultanate). Zanzibari of Arab descent tend to support the CUF, while the CCM's supporters are predominantly African.

22. Mukandala, Mushi, and Killian (2008) and Tucker, Hoffman, and Mukandala (2010).

23. In the early 1990s, Tanzania's external debt was close to 160 percent of gross domestic product, and external debt service was 40 percent of exports.

24. Harrison (2001) and Stein (1991).

25. Hyden and Mmuya (2008) and Tucker, Hoffman, and Mukandala (2010).

the structural deficiencies created by the command economy, such as shortages of basic commodities and disincentives to sell to state-run agricultural bodies, caused citizens to circumvent the system.[26] Tanzania's transition to capitalism rapidly accelerated these nascent trends.[27]

As the extent of corruption became more evident (especially with release of the Warioba report in 1996),[28] donors demanded that the government put in place structures to ensure more transparency and accountability in the budget and its regulation over the economy. Successive governments have acquiesced in these demands, but generally in only a pro forma manner.[29] Thus over the past two decades a vast array of relatively ineffective oversight and regulatory agencies have emerged in Tanzania, such as the Prevention and Control of Corruption Bureau (PCCB), the Public Procurement Regulatory Authority (PPRA), and the National Audit Office.[30]

Perhaps the clearest evidence of the impact of external pressure on budget transparency is the number of laws that donors have demanded that the government implement in order to receive financial assistance. The most significant action the government has taken to improve transparency, the 2001 Public Finance Act, was a requirement for Tanzania to receive debt relief under the Enhanced Heavily Indebted Poor Countries (HIPC) Initiative.[31] The act required the government to make budget data publicly available and considerably strengthened the authority and autonomy of the NAO. Full implementation of an integrated financial management system and employment of a medium-term expenditure framework for budget planning were other HIPC conditions.[32] In addition, as conditions for continued budget support, donors required Parliament to pass the 2008 Public Audit Act to enhance the NAO's power and independence, to initiate several anticorruption programs, and to improve public financial management.[33] More broadly, nearly all of Tanzania's major reform pro-

---

26. Hyden and Mmuya (2008).

27. Tripp (1997).

28. Warioba (1996).

29. Hyden and Mmuya (2008) and Tucker, Hoffman, and Mukandala (2010).

30. The PCCB serves four functions: train government agencies on detecting and preventing corruption; advise the public on ways of preventing corruption; cooperate with international organizations in preventing corruption; and investigate and, subject to dictates from the Directorate of Public Prosecutions, prosecute individuals suspected of corruption. The PPRA mandate covers five areas: ensure fair and competitive procurement standards; harmonize procurement processes across government ministries, departments, and agencies; set procurement standards; monitor compliance with procurement procedures; and improve procurement capacity. The NAO is "the appointed statutory auditor of revenue and expenditure of all ministries, departments of the government, public authorities, and other bodies or authorities which receive funds from the Consolidated Fund." See http://www.nao.go.tz/aboutus.php.

31. IMF and IDA (2001).

32. IMF and IDA (2001).

33. URT (2008).

grams in financial management, such as the Public Sector Reform Program, the Local Government Reform Program, and the Public Financial Management Reform Program receive substantial donor support, and progress in implementing them are conditions for it.[34]

The agencies and programs the government has created as a result of these demands have an enormous amount of potential to increase budget transparency, and this has occurred in several areas. For example, due to changes resulting from the Public Finance Act, aggregate budget data are accessible, timely, and reasonably accurate. Despite these efforts, transparency in general, and its impact on accountability more specifically, remains a problem and seems to have deteriorated over the past few years. Creating agencies and reform programs has been far from sufficient for ensuring their effective operation. Specifically, increased access to financial information has failed to catalyze greater pressure on the government to improve its performance. The rest of this section attempts to explain why investing large sums of money and effort into increasing budget transparency has achieved only limited success in catalyzing greater accountability in Tanzania.

Design Flaws

Why have top-down reforms that the powerful executive branch in Tanzania has designed and implemented not improved accountability? Numerous studies suggest that capacity constraints constitute the main challenge to improving the effectiveness of these programs and agencies. Nevertheless, this superficial explanation, while partially true, is misleading, as a more thorough political economy analysis suggests intentional design flaws are also part of the problem.[35]

Numerous examples of these flaws exist. Perhaps the most prominent is that the autonomous and semiautonomous agencies the government has created to

34. The broad purpose of the Public Sector Reform Program is to improve transparency, accountability, and resource management in service delivery. The program contains five core elements: improve performance by decentralizing and expanding key ministries, departments, and agencies; facilitate private sector participation in service delivery by privatizing and contracting out noncritical services; introduce results-orientated management; modernize information and communication systems, including an integrated computerized human resources management system; and design a meritocratic civil service. The overarching objective of the Local Government Reform Program is to facilitate administrative, fiscal, and political decentralization in Tanzania. It also seeks to improve service delivery at the local level, create more effective local government, and encourage public participation in local government. The Public Financial Management Reform Program is Tanzania's main program for improving public financial management. Its ultimate objective is to obtain more effective and efficient allocation of resources to achieve more equitable and better service delivery.

35. Hyden and Mmuya (2008), Mukandala, Mushi, and Killian (2008), and Tucker, Hoffman, and Mukandala (2010). The most obvious example is the glaring lack of resources allocated to the Directorate of Public Prosecutions, the only government agency with the capacity to prosecute, compared with the generous funding allocated to investigative agencies such as the PCCB and the PPRA (see Tucker, Hoffman, and Mukandala 2010).

improve its capacity to regulate the economy lack enforcement power and many, like the PCCB and the PPRA, are politically compromised because they fall under the office of the president. These agencies can investigate wrongdoing, but only the Directorate of Public Prosecutions under the Attorney General has the power to prosecute. The Directorate of Public Prosecutions is severely underresourced, and the attorneys working in it receive only a small fraction of the income they could earn in the private sector. Similarly, the NAO has significant autonomy but lacks enforcement capacity. In addition, the Business Registrations and Licensing Authority (BRELA) refuses to release information on the owners, directors, and major shareholders of Tanzania's corporations, making it difficult to trace the links between politicians and the private sector. Finally, the Local Government Reform Program and the Public Financial Management Reform Program have been ongoing for more than a decade, yet most local governments still have inadequate financial management systems. In the 2009–10 NAO report on local government authorities, for example, less than half had received an unqualified audit, and the NAO reported that, in general, the performance of local government authorities was deteriorating (NAO 2010).

These shortcomings notwithstanding, placing agencies responsible for oversight and prosecution in the executive branch is common in presidential systems. Enforcement of their responsibilities often derives from legislatures that typically possess the power to subpoena government officials, and perhaps remove them from office, if they fail to do their jobs effectively. Most of Tanzania's MPs lack these incentives. In addition to the CCM's dominance, all of Tanzania's ministers and deputy ministers must come from Parliament. Since executive branch appointees possess greater power and earn more money than MPs, many of them seek such appointments, and loyalty, not opposition, to the president has tended to be the more efficacious route to obtaining these coveted positions. Not only MPs who concurrently serve in the executive branch, but also those who aspire to these positions lack the incentive to provide government oversight. In addition, the president has strong influence over the appointment of approximately eighty-five MPs.[36] Thus close to half of Tanzania's 357-member Parliament typically are either serving in executive branch positions or are indirect presidential appointees. For these reasons, Parliament does not place pressure on autonomous and semi-autonomous agencies or on the Attorney General to enforce the law.

---

36. Ten are direct presidential appointments, and the balance comprises women the party elects. The president exercises significant power over the latter because to date all of Tanzania's presidents have concurrently served as leaders of the CCM. The exact number of women the party can appoint varies from election to election, as the constitution allocates 102 seats for women, and parties get to appoint them in relation to their share of the seats they hold in Parliament.

The argument that capacity constraints cause these entities to perform their job ineffectively is difficult to accept. The executive branch—the branch of government that has implemented the numerous reforms making budget information more transparent, such as releasing budget proposals and implementation, progress, and audit reports to the public—is the same branch that has designed programs to ensure accountability for the use of these funds, yet the former operates far more effectively than the latter.[37] It is difficult to believe that capacity constraints as opposed to intentional design flaws are the reason why some offices and agencies operate far more effectively than others. BRELA is a clear example. The agency possesses the information that could clarify the links between politicians and the private sector. It needs little capacity to release this information to the public yet resists demands to do so. To understand why capacity constraints alone fail to explain why Tanzania's reform programs have fallen short of donor expectations requires seeing the problem through the lens of a big picture. Only then can we ascertain the appropriate details and contextualize the significance of them.

Placing Transparency in Its Proper Political Context

The CCM has managed to undertake tremendous political and economic reforms over the past two decades without losing political and economic control of the country.[38] As recently as two decades ago, Tanzania was a one-party state, with no meaningful distinction between the civil service and the party bureaucracy and a government presiding over a command economy. Today, Tanzania is a multiparty democracy with a distinction (albeit at times blurred) between the party bureaucracy and the civil service, and the economy is in private hands. Yet CCM leaders remain at the very top of all of these structures. They preside over two vast bureaucracies—the party and the civil service—and most of the country's leading business people are either members of the CCM or have close ties to them. To be able to execute such far-reaching political and economic reforms without losing control of either realm can only happen through strategic planning and strong capacity.

We thus need to treat with skepticism the claim that capacity constraints and unforeseen pathologies in institutional design are the principal reasons why

37. Tanzania's most recent public expenditure and financial accountability assessment starkly makes this point. According to URT (2010, p. 4), "Tanzania has a good record of overall budget performance. . . . However, the processes of the PFM [public financial management] system face a number of shortcomings . . . In general, accounting, recording, and reporting remain weak. . . . Internal audit is poor. . . . There is little available information on the delivery of resources to service delivery units."

38. Hoffman and Robinson (2009), Hyden and Mmuya (2008), Mukandala, Mushi, and Killian (2008), and Tucker, Hoffman, and Mukandala (2010).

Tanzania's oversight authorities fail to perform their functions. Due to the CCM's clear ability to secure its priorities, even if institutional failures were not deliberate, the government could easily rectify them.[39] Many of the weaknesses in financial transparency identified here appear to be deliberate features of institutional design.[40]

For these reasons, examining data from periodic public expenditure reviews, monitoring progress in implementing financial management systems, such as the integrated financial management system, or scouring the audit reports of the Comptroller of Accounts and Auditor General is unlikely to find evidence of commitments to reform.[41] The middle- and lower-level civil servants in charge of these areas are not the obstacles to greater transparency and accountability in Tanzania. Rather, the chief problem stems from the top. An entrenched political and economic oligarchy is deeply content with the status quo, as they are the prime beneficiaries of it. It is hard to imagine reform coming to Tanzania from the civil servants who are accountable, ultimately, to this elite, especially since many of them hold their jobs through clientelistic relationships with more powerful individuals in the government or the CCM. Similarly, it is also difficult to believe that the transparency resulting from rifts within the ruling party will be a source of genuine reform in the near future. Leaders of the CCM's disgruntled factions have employed transparency primarily as a weapon to bring down rivals. While it is possible that opportunistic motives could lead to genuine reform, evidence for this does not yet exist.

Top-down economic and political reforms, rifts within the CCM, and increasingly assertive—yet still comparatively weak—opposition parties, media outlets, and civil society organizations all account for part of the increase in transparency that has occurred in Tanzania over the past two decades. Yet, for the most part, greater transparency has not led to improved accountability. While information is problematic in Tanzania, especially at the local level (for example, whether a school has received the capitation grants that cover school fees), focusing on these aspects of Tanzania's governance challenges misses the larger picture.[42] Survey data show that Tanzanians are well aware of the country's transparency problems.[43] Tanzanians possess sufficient information to understand the government's shortcomings. Tanzania's challenge is not transparency. It is accountability.

---

39. The argument that rifts within the CCM prevent the government from instituting these changes is difficult to sustain because many of these reform programs began under Kikwete's predecessor, Benjamin Mkapa, who held a firm grip over the party.

40. See Hyden and Mmuya (2008) and Tucker, Hoffman, and Mukandala (2010).

41. Hyden and Mmuya (2008).

42. Hyden and Mmuya (2008).

43. See, for example, PCCB (2009).

While greater internal demand for accountability is almost certainly necessary for reforms in this area to occur, it is nevertheless not clear how the party would respond to such calls. In particular, the party possesses and has employed two other mechanisms for addressing the pressure for political reform: patronage and repression.

State of Budget Transparency

This section analyzes the current state of budget transparency in Tanzania. The first part examines quantitative measures of budget openness. It shows that, while the data reasonably reflect the problems in Tanzania, they fail to demonstrate adequately its principal problems. The second part provides this political economy analysis in more detail.

Data

This section compares financial transparency in Tanzania according to two quantitative measures. It begins with data from the Open Budget Index (OBI) and then turns to Global Integrity Scorecard ratings.

OPEN BUDGET INDEX DATA. Table 7-1 examines trends in the OBI ratings from 2006 to 2010. For the 2010 index, Tanzania received an unimpressive forty-five out of 100. The data also show no clear trend over time. Tanzania's performance fell from forty-eight in 2006 to thirty-six in 2008, before rising in 2010. One shortcoming of examining aggregate OBI data over time is that the 2006 results are not completely comparable to the 2008 and 2010 ones because the 2006 overall score does not include a citizen's budget or in-year reports, unlike subsequent ones.

Tanzania's score improved from 2008 to 2010 due to the weighting of the index. Its score on the enacted budget fell from sixty-seven to zero, and its mark on the audit report fell from sixty-seven to forty-nine.[44] By contrast, its score on the executive budget proposal rose from forty-one to fifty-six. Because OBI weights the executive budget proposal much heavier than the other two components of the index, Tanzania's overall score rose, even though two components of the index fell and only one increased.

We now analyze OBI data in greater detail by examining information on the quality of budget estimates, the strength of the legislature and the NAO, and additional critical information for budget transparency. The OBI covers twelve measures of the quality of budget estimates. As shown in table 7-2, Tanzania generally scores quite well along this dimension, and there were few changes in this area

44. It is not entirely clear why Tanzania's score on the audit report fell between 2008 and 2010 because the score rose on the subcomponents of that entry.

Table 7-1. *Open Budget Index Results for Tanzania, 2006, 2008, and 2010*

Document	Availability, 2010	Comprehensiveness		
		2006	*2008*	*2010*
Pre-budget statement	Produced, not published	C	E	E
Executive's budget proposal	Published	C	C	C
Enacted budget	Produced, not published	...	B	E
Citizen's budget	Not produced	...	E	E
In-year reports	Published	B	B	B
Midyear review	Not produced	E	E	E
Year-end report	Not produced	E	E	E
Audit report	Published	C	B	C
Overall performance		48	36	45

Source: International Budget Partnership.
... = Not applicable.

between 2006 and 2010. These results are not surprising, as they occurred largely in areas under control of the executive branch. Perhaps most striking about these data are the differences between the very good scores on sources of revenue and general expenditures (including budget classification and program budgets) and the very poor ones on quasi-fiscal expenditures (for example, indirect subsidies or approval of expenditures outside the budget process), extent of classified expenditure, and extra-budgetary funds (for example, state pension funds). These findings suggest either that budget transparency reforms have yet to reach several areas of government fiscal activity or that the government has reacted to greater trans-

Table 7-2. *Open Budget Index Data for Quality of Budget Estimates in Tanzania, 2006, 2008, and 2010*

Category	2006	2008	2010
Budget classification by administrative unit	A	A	A
Budget classification by function	A	C	B
Economic classification of budget	A	A	A
Individual program budget	A	A	A
Sources of tax revenue	A	B	A
Sources of nontax revenue	B	B	A
Extra-budgetary funds	D	D	D
Intergovernmental transfers	C	C	B
Transfers to public corporations	C	D	B
Quasi-fiscal activities	D	D	D
Extent of classified expenditure	D	D	D

Source: International Budget Partnership.

Table 7-3. *Open Budget Index of Legislative Strength in Tanzania,*
2006, 2008, and 2010

Indicator	2006	2008	2010
Legislature's receipt of budget	C	C	C
General committee hearings	D	B	D
Specific committee hearings with government	D	C	D
Specific committee hearings with public	D	C	D
Release of reports of hearings	D	D	D
Breadth of information legislature receives	D	B	B
Legislature's legal ability to amend budget	D	D	D
Comprehensiveness of information legislature approves	B	B	D

Source: International Budget Partnership.

parency in some parts of the budget, in part, by shifting expenditures away from its publicly visible parts to less observable areas.

OBI data on legislative strength in the budget process demonstrate the institutional weakness of the legislature. Tanzania receives barely above a D in this area—the lowest grade on the OBI index—and its score has deteriorated since 2006 in two areas: general budget hearings and comprehensiveness of the information the legislature receives (table 7-3). That Tanzania's score fell in this area between 2006 and 2010 is somewhat surprising given that Samwel Sitta, perhaps the most outspoken speaker of Parliament since Tanzania's transition to democracy, led Parliament during this period.[45]

Data on the strength of the National Audit Office are consistent with recent trends in Tanzania (table 7-4). In particular, it is evident that the 2008 National Audit Act significantly increased the NAO's independence, as reflected in rising grades for the ability of the NAO to undertake audits, including in the security sector, and its greater budget autonomy. The data also show that the NAO still possesses institutional shortcomings, as the scores in enforcement capacity—executive report on addressing audit findings and progress tracking reports—remain weak.

Finally, data on Tanzanians' access to critical budget information reify that Tanzania's top-down reform process has fallen short on genuine democratic reform in many areas (table 7-5). As with the power of the legislature, Tanzania

45. The change in the grade on general committee hearings appears to be a result of a revision in OBI's methodology, as OBI researchers revised their perception about whether Parliament held public hearings between 2008 and 2010. The 2008 results on this question suggest that, even though Parliament does not publicize budget hearings, they are public. The 2010 responses imply that the reviewers placed more weight on poor knowledge of these hearings and low attendance at them than whether the hearings were formally open to the public. The score on the comprehensiveness of the information on the budget approved by the legislature fell, by contrast, because the government posted the information on the Internet in 2008, but not in 2010.

Table 7-4. *Open Budget Index of Strength of the Supreme Audit Institution (SAI) in Tanzania, 2006, 2008, and 2010*

Indicator	2006	2008	2010
Timing of audit release	C	B	B
Autonomy of SAI head	B	B	B
Ability of SAI to undertake audits	C	B	A
Budget autonomy of SAI	D	D	B
Ability of SAI to audit security sector	...	D	A
SAI public outreach	...	B	D
Legislative scrutiny of audits	A	A	A
Executive report on addressing audit findings	D	D	D
SAI or legislature progress tracking report	D	D	D
Legislature review of security sector audits	D	D	B

Source: International Budget Partnership.
... = Not applicable.

scores barely above a D in these categories. In particular, Tanzania does not have a right to information law, and public access to government program expenditures and progress is very weak.

Overall, OBI data are highly consistent with Tanzania's trajectory of top-down reform. Tanzania performs well in areas under the control of the executive branch, such as the release of budget information. At the same time, citizen access to information and legislative power are weak, and the NAO has independence, but lacks enforcement powers.

GLOBAL INTEGRITY SCORECARD DATA. Overall, data from the 2006 and 2010 Global Integrity Scorecard relating to transparency suggest that little has changed in Tanzania over the two time periods, as the aggregate score increased

Table 7-5. *Open Budget Index for Additional Key Information in Tanzania, 2006, 2008, and 2010*

Type of information	2006	2008	2010
Public budget summary	B	B	B
Citizen's budget	D	D	D
Nontechnical budget definitions	C	D	D
Right to information in law	D	D	D
Public access to program expenditures	D	D	D
Public access to program progress	D	D	D

Source: International Budget Partnership.

Table 7-6. *Global Integrity Scorecard Data for Tanzania, 2006 and 2010*

Indicator	2006	2010
Legal right to information	33	0
Effective right to information	5	13
Legislative input into the budget	25	25
Citizen access to budget process	33	50
Legislative oversight of public funds in law	100	100
Effectiveness of legislative oversight of public funds	38	50
Effectiveness of public procurement process	83	75
Citizen access to public procurement process	83	100
Effectiveness of privatization process	75	67
Citizen access to privatization process	69	80
Supreme audit institution in law	100	100
Effectiveness of supreme audit institution	56	72
Citizen access to SAI reports	67	100

Source: Global Integrity.

slightly, from fifty-nine to sixty-four (table 7-6).[46] However, these differences understate Tanzania's improvements in this period, according to Global Integrity's measures. The main reason for this is that the largest decline, from thirty-three to zero in the legal right to information, overstates this fall, as the higher score in 2006 was the result of an access to information bill that the Kikwete administration was intending to introduce in Parliament. It fell to zero in 2010 because this never occurred. Tanzania's score improved significantly in several areas, most prominently citizen access to the budget process and SAI reports, the effectiveness of the SAI, and legislative effectiveness in budget oversight. Overall, OBI and Global Integrity data are reasonably consistent, especially regarding poor citizen access to information, the legislature's inability to affect the budget, and increasing audit effectiveness.

The data from each of these measures generally correspond to perceptions about the status of financial transparency in Tanzania today. The difficulty lies in interpreting what the data imply about the process of improving performance in this area. If the most efficacious reform process constitutes incremental changes in the capacity of government agencies, these data would be helpful. However, if these data reflect broader political forces, not simply weak capacity in the areas they assess, working to improve these indicators directly is an unlikely route to greater openness. To ascertain the nature of these constraints requires contextualizing the data in a more comparative political analysis of reform in Tanzania. This

46. See www.globalintegrity.org/report.

understanding is also necessary in order to determine how opportunities for greater reforms might emerge.

Politics of Reform in Tanzania

Munck and Leff (1997) argue, "The mode of transition affects the form of post-transitional regime and politics through its influence on the pattern of elite competition, on the institutional rules crafted during the transition, and on key actors' acceptance or rejection of the new rules of the game."[47] This is very evident in Tanzania. Its democratic transition did not produce a clean slate on which new forms of government could form.[48] Rather, political legacies and transition paths affected both the trajectory and the results of reform.

Tanzania's transition toward democracy corresponds to what Munck and Leff term "transition from above," a ruling power that initiates a transition in the context of weak opposition so that it can establish rules favorable to its retention of political control. Reforms to increase transparency in Tanzania provide substantial evidence to substantiate this process, as they emerged largely in response to external demands on the country's powerful executive in the context of a firmly entrenched hegemonic party. The result was the creation of a series of programs and agencies to implement reforms that contain structural deficiencies to ensure that they do not upset the ruling party's control. The most crucial flaw is that Parliament lacks the incentive or capacity to provide effective oversight. Increased openness has also resulted from rifts within the ruling party. However, because these individuals have employed transparency as a mechanism to gain power within the CCM, not replace the party or reduce the influence of the executive branch, their efforts have not resulted in institutional changes in this area.

In Tanzania, the overwhelming majority of reforms have come from inside the government at the highest levels. Presidents Mwinyi, Mkapa, and Kikwete have all made calculated bets about how much institutional change they need to achieve (or to be perceived as achieving) to address the concerns of their mainly external critics and ensure that donors continue to provide the country with significant amounts of foreign aid.[49] What all three administrations have learned is that they can undertake what seem to be substantive improvements in governance without sacrificing political control due to the CCM's entrenchment and the government's ability to engineer ineffective reforms. Thus Tanzania's gains in finan-

47. Munck and Leff (1997, p. 345).
48. Tucker, Hoffman, and Mukandala (2010).
49. Hyden and Mmuya (2008), Mukandala, Mushi, and Killian (2008), and Tucker, Hoffman, and Mukandala (2010).

cial transparency over the past two decades have done little to improve political accountability, as the CCM strategically embraces reforms in such a way as to ensure that they do not achieve this result.

For these reasons, working directly to improve quantitative indicators on budget transparency does not appear to be the most efficacious method for improving the impact of financial openness on political accountability. For the latter to occur most likely requires catalyzing greater demand for it.

Consolidating and Advancing on Gains

This section discusses what must occur in Tanzania to consolidate the gains in transparency it has made and to secure further progress in this area, especially in transforming greater openness into improved accountability, and what could set back these efforts. Khemani (2007) argues that transparency alone is unable to lead to greater government accountability. Rather, she maintains that, for this to occur, more openness must coincide with changes in the incentives for politicians to act. An active media and civil society are important components of this political structure. However, the most effective one is creating powerful oversight bodies, such as a legislature or independent agencies with the capacity to hold government accountable for its actions, working alongside media outlets and CSOs that share this objective.

The main obstacle to reform in Tanzania is the stubborn satisfaction with the status quo among the CCM's leaders. The CCM's structures ensure that politics in Tanzania is highly institutionalized, and the party's leadership has countenanced nearly all of the reforms to increase transparency that have occurred there. Not surprising, as this chapter has explained, they have failed to catalyze greater accountability in any meaningful (that is, institutionalized) sense. Rather, the CCM's leaders have managed to ensure that the structures they created to give the appearance of greater accountability have failed to perform their function effectively.[50] Dislodging the status quo will be difficult.

The depth of the CCM's entrenchment presents an enormous challenge to breaking the status quo in Tanzania. To date, the party has won with overwhelming majorities in all of the country's multiparty elections, without having to resort to overt intimidation and vote rigging, except in some specific parliamentary constituencies.[51] Whether the party would engage in such practices is difficult to

---

50. Hyden and Mmuya (2008), Mukandala, Mushi, and Killian (2008), Tucker, Hoffman, and Mukandala (2010).

51. Hoffman and Robinson (2009) and Tucker, Hoffman, and Mukandala (2010). This refers only to mainland Tanzania, not Zanzibar.

know, but the levers it has to ensure that its hegemony falls well short of overt intimidation and fraud are quite clear. Not only is the government the country's largest employer, but many Tanzanians work for companies that are owned by members of the CCM or allied with them. These individuals often face pressure to support the CCM.[52] Moreover, the country's largest domestically owned media houses are also under the control of CCM members.[53] Thus large parts of the private sector, the media, and the country's formal sector workforce, both public and private, have an interest in seeing the CCM remain in power. While the opposition party Chama Cha Demokrasia na Mandaleo (CHADEMA)[54] did unexpectedly well in the 2008 election, this occurred in the context of a president perceived to be weak and in the absence of widespread intimidation. For these reasons, the CCM's power seems secure for the near future.

One possible route to shaking this status quo would be the unlikely event of a split within the CCM. The factions that have grown in the party since the 2005 election have deepened and show no signs of healing soon. Yet even in the unlikely case that the party would split, it is far from certain that this would improve transparency and accountability in Tanzania, at least in the short run, as the fights within the various CCM factions that have formed over the past few years have been over access to power rather than issues of governance. More broadly, the CCM has ruled Tanzania since independence, and it is very difficult to make any predictions about the impact of a CCM split on governance in Tanzania.

A reasonable, but unlikely, scenario for greater reforms to transparency is an alliance between frustrated CCM MPs, opposition ones, and a more forceful civil society. The evidence to support the emergence of such a coalition in the near future does not exist. Parliament is a doubtful place for a coalition of reformers to emerge in the near future. While CCM MPs joined forces with the opposition over the Richmond scandal, cooperation to hold the executive branch more accountable in other areas has rarely occurred and has not achieved institutional reform. Moreover, the opposition's share of seats in Parliament—just over 25 percent—is not sufficiently large to force reforms against the CCM's interest. Although it is possible that popular opposition MPs, such as Zitto Kabwe and Wilbrod Slaa, could ally with frustrated CCM MPs, such as January Makamba, such a coalition does not appear likely any time soon. Civil society is unlikely to

---

52. Hoffman and Robinson (2009) and Tucker, Hoffman, and Mukandala (2010).

53. Kenya's Nation Group also publishes several newspapers in Tanzania. The Nation Group believed that foreign ownership would allow it to provide more critical coverage of events in Tanzania because it would be free from the political pressure encountered by domestically owned publications. This proved not to be the case because the paper's local reporters did not believe the Nation Group's owners could offer this shield.

54. Swahili for Party for Democracy and Development.

mount a serious challenge to the status quo in the near term, although the efforts of the CSOs documented here are attempting to catalyze it.

Could the CCM reform itself? This is certainly possible, especially if party elders and younger reformers come together to weaken the power of the party's more opportunistic members. However, the current trajectory is not encouraging, given that governance indicators have been weakening in Tanzania over the past few years. Whether this reveals a growing sense of impunity among CCM's leaders or is only evidence of Kikwete's weak party leadership is not clear. Reflecting these governance shortcomings, the CCM suffered a setback in 2010, and several CCM MPs lost their seats to members of opposition parties. Fear of losing power might make these changes possible, although a more disciplined CCM would have many other channels for regaining control, such as patronage and repression.

An even more ambitious—and less plausible—source of reform would be constitutional changes to reduce the power imbalance between the executive and legislative branches. Reducing the executive branch's capacity to appoint MPs and to select ministers and deputy ministers from Parliament is necessary for providing Parliament with the ability and incentive to perform effective oversight of the executive branch. Nevertheless, such a change is unlikely at the moment.

What role, if any, can donors play to advance reforms to transparency? This is a difficult question to answer. While they have been the primary force for the top-down reforms that various governments have implemented over the past two decades, these changes have fallen far short of transforming transparency into demands for accountability. In particular, the small number of CSOs working in this area, such as Haki Elimu, Research on Poverty Alleviation, Sikika, and Uwazi, encounter immense challenges. Support for these groups is worthwhile and almost certainly necessary to ensure that transparency leads to greater accountability, even if such an outcome does not seem imminent.

By contrast, working with Parliament is far more difficult. During the investigations over Richmond, for example, many donors expressed strong support for the MPs, including those in the CCM, who were at the forefront of exposing the scandal. President Kikwete rebuked these organizations for taking sides in internal CCM fights. Since Parliament's oversight of the executive branch often exists in the context of wider battles within the CCM, it is not an area where donors can easily play a supportive role.

Conclusion

Tanzania has undertaken genuine improvements in financial transparency over the past two decades. Budget data are far more available and credible than they were in the past. Enterprising politicians, members of civil society, and the media are using it to hold politicians and government officials more accountable for their actions than in the past. These changes notwithstanding, what citizens have also learned is that transparency does not easily lead to accountability.

Tanzania needs institutional reform—and much more domestic demand for it—to create more effective oversight. The most difficult challenge to achieving this outcome is that the CCM's leaders are content with the status quo. While rifts within the CCM and growing assertiveness in the media, opposition parties, and civil society are bringing a greater level of transparency than hitherto existed, the ruling party remains firmly in control, and it is far from evident whether a stronger or weaker CCM would be a more propitious circumstance for greater accountability. On the one hand, faced with weakening control, fear of losing power could be an effective means of exercising discipline. At the same time, the CCM could choose to employ levers other than these reforms, most notably patronage and repression, to reassert its authority. For greater institutional reform to occur in Tanzania, demands for transparency must occur from within the country, as decades of donor-led reform have not achieved this outcome.

References

Engel, Hermine. 2010. "Seizing and Stretching Participatory Space: Civil Society Participation in Tanzania's Policy Process." Power of Civil Society Working Paper 1. The Hague: Hivos and the International Institute of Social Studies.

Harrison, Graham. 2001. "Post-Conditionality Politics and Administrative Reform: Reflections on the Cases of Uganda and Tanzania." *Development and Change* 32, no. 4: 657–79.

Hoffman, Barak, and Lindsay Robinson. 2009. "Tanzania's Missing Opposition." *Journal of Democracy* 20, no. 4: 123–36.

Hyden, Göran, and Max Mmuya. 2008. *Power and Policy Slippage in Tanzania: Discussing National Ownership of Development.* Sida Studies 21. Stockholm: Swedish Agency for International Development.

IMF (International Monetary Fund) and IDA (International Development Agency). 2001. "Tanzania: Completion Point Document for the Enhanced Heavily Indebted Poor Countries Initiative." Washington.

James, Bernard. 2011. "Stage Set for Final Face-Off." *Citizen,* October 15.

Kaijage, Florian. 2011. "Shaky Government or the 2015 Politics?" *Guardian* [Tanzania], August 21.

Khemani, Stuti. 2007. "Can Information Campaigns Overcome Political Obstacles to Serving the Poor?" In *The Politics of Service Delivery in Democracies,* edited by Shantayanan Devarajan and Ingrid Widlund. Stockholm: Sweden Ministry of Foreign Affairs.

Kisembo, Patrick. 2011. "Power Crisis: Miracle in Three Weeks?" *Guardian* [Tanzania], July 19.

Mukandala, Rwekaza, Samuel Mushi, and Bernadetta Killian. 2008. "The Political Economy of Tanzania: A Policy Note." Dar es Salaam: World Bank.

Munck, Gerardo, and Carol Leff. 1997. "Modes of Transition and Democratization: South America and Eastern Europe in Comparative Perspective." *Comparative Politics* 29, no. 3: 343–62.

NAO (National Audit Office). 2010. *Annual General Report of the Controller and Auditor General: On the Financial Statements of Local Government Authorities.* Dar es Salaam.

PCCB (Prevention and Control of Corruption Bureau). 2009. "National Governance and Corruption Survey." Dar es Salaam.

Stein, Howard. 1991. "Economic Policy and the IMF in Tanzania: Conditionality, Conflict, and Convergence." In *The IMF and Tanzania*, edited by Horace Campbell and Howard Stein. Harare: SAPES.

Tripp, Aili. 1997. *Changing the Rules: The Politics of Liberalization and the Urban Informal Economy in Tanzania.* University of California Press.

Tucker, Stevens, Barak Hoffman, and Rwekaza Mukandala. 2010 *Democracy and Governance Assessment of Tanzania.* Washington: USAID.

URT (United Republic of Tanzania). 2008. *General Budget Support Annual Review: 2008 Final Report.* Dar es Salaam.

———. 2010. *2009 Public Financial Management Performance Report on Mainland Tanzania.* Dar es Salaam: Public Financial Management Working Group Tanzania.

wa Kuhenga, Makwaia. 2011. "'Posho! Posho! Posho!' Is This the Real Issue in Tanzania?" *Citizen,* July 4.

Warioba, Joseph. 1996. *The Report of the Presidential Commission of Inquiry against Corruption.* Dar es Salaam: United Republic of Tanzania.

8

The Diversification of State Power: Vietnam's Alternative Path toward Budget Transparency, Accountability, and Participation

JONATHAN WARREN AND HUONG NGUYEN

In the past two decades Vietnam has been transitioning from a centralized, Soviet-oriented, planned economy into a decentralized, state-directed market economy with deepening ties to East Asian and North Atlantic countries. This tectonic shift has led to reconsideration, if not revision, of virtually every facet of government policy and practice, including those related to the budget. Standards and ideals of accounting practices, budget-making processes, and oversight, which most contemporary North Atlantic and Pacific societies define as ideal, have gradually been adopted in Vietnam. This process has been neither one of shock—as was encouraged by North Atlantic advisers in the wake of the Soviet Union's collapse—nor one of emulation. Rather reform has been a steady, step-by-step experimental process tailored to local particularities. Because of the new ideals of modernity adopted in 1986, commonly referred to as Doi Moi or "Renovation," reforms have enjoyed high-level political backing. Indeed successive government and party leaders have instigated and backed constitutional, legislative, and policy initiatives with varying degrees of prodding and encouragement from the general public, businesses, international organizations, and other branches of government, such as the National Assembly, State Audit Vietnam (SAV), and the Vietnamese Fatherland Front (VFF).

As a consequence of these changes and dynamics, Vietnam has contributed to the larger global trend of the 1990s in which governments began enhancing and deepening budget transparency, accountability, and participation. Just over one decade ago, the entire budget in Vietnam was deemed a state secret. Presently in-year and enacted budgets are published on government websites. Moreover, institutional mechanisms of oversight have been strengthened, and there is greater opportunity for public input. One of the principal comptrollers, the National Assembly, has become increasingly bold in challenging the Politburo. Deputies call government ministers to testify before the National Assembly, frequently press them to explain the performance of their ministries, and periodically reject government proposals. These and other developments have led various transnational organizations, such as the World Bank and Asian Development Bank, to conclude that substantial improvements in the budgeting system have been made.[1]

The fact that there have been improvements does not mean that budget transparency and participation are good or even fair in Vietnam. Vietnam is still very much in transition, with an overall level of transparency that most consider to be poor. In 2010, for instance, it received an Open Budget Index (OBI) score of fourteen. This was an advance from 2006, when it scored three, but it still placed Vietnam lower than any other country in Southeast Asia. Summarizing Vietnam's score, the International Budget Partnership (IBP), which produces the OBI score, notes, "The government provides the public with scant information on the central government's budget and financial activities. This makes it virtually impossible for citizens to hold the government accountable for its management of the public's money."[2] Perhaps even more troublesome, the government entities directly responsible for budgetary oversight—namely, SAV, the National Assembly, and the VFF—are also constrained by information gaps. For example, certain revenue streams, especially revenues from crude oil and land, are underreported. Some areas of the budget, most glaringly the Politburo's expenses and expenditures, are exempt from audit examinations. The discrepancies between the budgeted and the actual outcomes for expenditures and revenues are not provided in year-end or audit reports. Finally, capital and recurrent expenditures are not disaggregated but instead are integrated into a single budget.

Despite these and other ongoing challenges and weaknesses, progress has been made and is likely to continue for the foreseeable future. From the vantage of the transparency literature, such steps forward are surprising, if not puzzling. Few of the social and institutional conditions exist that are theorized as being key to advancing transparency. In *The Right to Know*, for instance, Ann Florini observes that "all" of the seventy countries that adopted disclosure laws and policies by 2006 were "pressed by the spread of democratic norms, the increasing strength of civil society organizations, and the rise of an increasingly independent media."[3] On all of these metrics, however, Vietnam lags. Some democratic reforms have

1. See ADB (2009) and World Bank and Government of Vietnam (2008).
2. IBP (2010, p. 1).
3. Florini (2007, p. 8).

been made, in that elections are held for the National Assembly. Yet candidates are vetted by the Vietnamese Fatherland Front and, with a few exceptions, must be members of the Communist Party of Vietnam (CPV). Civil society, measured in terms of volunteer organizations or nongovernmental organizations, is weak. And even though freedom of the press has expanded, the content is still tightly controlled by the CPV. Moreover, the heads of the party and government, such as the Politburo, are considered largely beyond reproach.[4]

The Political Economy of Transparency

If the typical factors—namely, democratic reforms, a bustling civil society, or a robust press—have not been behind the development of greater levels of transparency in Vietnam, then what has been responsible for the changes?

During the first ten years after 1975, when the Democratic Republic of Vietnam (which in 1976 became the Socialist Republic of Vietnam) defeated the U.S.-backed Republic of Vietnam army, reunified the country, and consolidated power, the country was in dire economic straits. Largely isolated from the world, the economy was so weak that at least 70 percent of the population lived at or below the poverty line, and Vietnam was a net importer of basic staples such as rice. Not surprising, there was growing unease with the direction of the country. Perhaps of equal importance, the Soviet Union, which had been a key ally, source of aid, and model of modernity, was undergoing a deep crisis. In this context, the CPV decided to break with many of the modernization goals and ideals articulated by a Stalinist-Leninist framework. This watershed moment for Vietnam was Doi Moi. Increasingly the middle- and high-income countries of East Asia and the North Atlantic were looked to as a source of ideas about how to restructure the economic and political spheres.

In subsequent years, Vietnam changed from a relatively isolated, planned economy to a state-led, mixed economy that is well integrated in global markets. A series of important legislative and policy initiatives have sought to bring Vietnam more in line with the so-called "best practices" of government, including budget-

---

4. Vietnam is a one-party state headed by the CPV. The National Party Congress is the highest body of the CPV and meets every five years. The Party Congress (498 members) elects the Central Committee (160 members), which in turn selects the Politburo (fourteen members), the Secretariat (eight members), and the general secretary, who is in charge of the Politburo and Secretariat. The Politburo sets policies, and the Secretariat is responsible for their implementation. The general secretary, president, prime minister, and chairman of the National Assembly are all members of the Politburo. The government consists of the prime minister, three deputy prime ministers, ministers, and heads of organizations of ministerial rank. The government is accountable to the National Assembly and reports both to the National Assembly and to the president. Members of the National Assembly are elected through national elections held every five years.

ary ones. A new constitution was adopted in 1992. This was followed by the Law on the Organization of the Government (1992), Public Administrative Reform Master Plan, 2001–2010, more commonly referred to as Project 30 (2001), State Budget Law (2002), State Audit Law (2003), Anticorruption Law (2005), and Law on Cadres and Civil Servants (2009). Moreover, and perhaps most significant, Vietnam joined the World Trade Organization in 2007.

In addition to the adoption of a new compass of modernity, transparency has been furthered by the normative order. Vietnam is unique in that a revolutionary nationalism prevailed in the twentieth century. Many Vietnamese, if not most, rallied to the Viet Minh because of its promise to deliver national liberation and reunification, land and greater equality for the peasantry, and societal advancement. These expectations and ambitions continued to influence government policies in subsequent years. For example, the fiscal decentralization process in Vietnam favors rural and poorer sectors. Provinces with higher poverty headcount ratios receive larger per capita fiscal transfers from the central government.[5] And as mandated by State Budget Law (2002), equalization transfers are given to all provinces based on the poverty rate and whether the province is in a less economically advantageous location.

In an analogous way the moral economy has affected government policies related to budget transparency and participation. Most Vietnamese would likely prefer democratic reforms and greater freedom of expression. In general, these concerns pale in comparison to the desires for economic growth and a reduction in corruption. Over the past thirty years, Vietnam's economy has been expanding rapidly, an average of 7 percent a year, to the point that it is on the cusp of becoming a middle-income economy. The poverty rate has dipped below 20 percent, and the country is one of the world's biggest exporters of commodities such as rice and coffee. Consequently, there is a general level of satisfaction with the government's handling of the economy.

The same cannot be said about graft. As various surveys have shown, misuse of public resources raises the most public indignation.[6] The degree of government corruption is, of course, largely unknown. Economists we interviewed at the World Bank insisted that government graft is significantly less severe in Vietnam than in many other parts of the world. One noted that in Vietnam, in contrast to East Africa where he had worked previously, projects for which monies were allocated have been completed. Although the scale of corruption is unclear, the widespread discontent with it is not. In addition to the survey data noted above, many

5. ADB (2009).

6. See General Statistics Office of Vietnam, "Results of the Survey for Household Living Standards 2008" (www.gso.gov.vn/default_en.aspx?tabid=491).

commented to us in formal interviews that one of the main reasons they had supported the government's decision to join the World Trade Organization was the hope that membership would help to clean up government and coax it into becoming more merit based. And in informal conversations, complaints about government corruption were commonplace. In these settings, the anger was palatable, bordering on rage.

The government's sensitivity to this issue was on display as early as 1996 with the sentencing of those held responsible for corruption within the state-owned enterprise, Tamexco. Most of upper management was sentenced to either life sentences or death. Many believed that the central government did not want to hand down such harsh punishments, especially since the practices for which the officials were convicted were and are so common, such as lending to indebted companies, operating multiple books, and selling shares in the names of relatives. However, "As the case started to attract attention . . . a point of no return had been reached . . . and the Politburo felt a need to make an example out of [them]."[7] This illustrates how even in an institutional context in which the public has few formal mechanisms for registering discontent, let alone the electoral ability to remove government leaders from power, popular sentiment is still consequential. Further evidence of this is the spate of anticorruption laws and policies that have been enacted in the subsequent fifteen years, such as the Anticorruption Law passed in 2005, which called for a broad range of procedures to enhance budget transparency, accountability, and participation as a tool for reducing government malfeasance. Some of the key measures included a requirement to make public and transparent most government activities and sectors; the use of bank accounts to pay salaries and execute other state budget transactions; the mandatory declaration of the income of government officials, especially those in higher positions of authority; an increase in internal oversight through inspections, audits, investigations, adjudications, and parliamentary supervision; encouragement of whistle-blowing by civil servants; and the promotion of a larger role for civil society organizations (CSOs), the media, businesses, and ordinary citizens in reporting and denouncing corruption.

In sum, much like James Horsely reports in China, the CPV "seems to recognize that in order to maintain its legitimacy and address the complex issues of governance amid rapid development," corruption must be curbed.[8] Its "leaders understand that a modernizing [Vietnam] requires a government that is efficient, law-abiding, and relatively open."[9] Furthermore, they appreciate that their credibility, if not political survival, is at stake. And so it is largely with these objectives

7. Gainsborough (2010, p. 68).
8. Horsely (2007, p. 58).
9. Horsely (2007).

and concerns in mind that the CPV and the Vietnamese government have embraced budget transparency, accountability, and participation.

State Retreat?

The reforms that have followed in the wake of Doi Moi have often been interpreted in the West through the lens of neoliberalism and thus misread as evidence of state retreat.[10] In certain respects, the state has indeed been downsized. For instance, a for-profit private sector has been ceded space in the economic realm. State-owned enterprises have been equitized and allowed to make production decisions and oversee their financial well-being.[11] More room has been granted to CSOs; as of 2008 there were 400 legally registered associations (up from 100 in 1990). Finally, key social services, such as health care and education, have been extended the authority to perform and finance their functions independently. On balance, however, the government has grown rather than shrunk. This is especially true in its so-called gate-keeping functions. The number of public sector employees responsible for carrying out inspections, issuing licenses, and overseeing access to resources regulated by the state has increased steadily.[12]

If the state has not retreated, then it certainly has been reshaped. One of the biggest changes has been the devolution of power, which has shifted authority from the central government to the provincial, commune, and district levels. In 1996 provincial governments were assigned 100 percent of some taxes—namely, those on land, housing, natural resources, and various fees and charges—and were allowed to share other taxes, such as value added, remittance, enterprise, and personal income taxes, with the central government. Districts and communes were similarly assigned some revenues, albeit relatively minor ones such as the trade license and slaughter tax, various other fees and charges, and "people's contributions." They also were permitted to receive a percentage of provincial revenues. In 2002, with passage of a new State Budget Law, the system of equalization transfers from the central to the provincial level was advanced further and provincial governments were allowed to borrow for infrastructure projects. Perhaps most significant, the share of expenditures decided at the subnational level reached almost half of total public expenditure.

10. See Landerman (2009).

11. This issue is more complex than it may appear on the surface. For example, Martin Gainsborough finds that, even though formally independent, the directors of equitized companies "continued to report to a wide range of state authorities on a regular basis . . . In addition, nearly all companies now had a representative from the provincial department of finance . . . representing the state interest in the company. The representative (and sometimes representatives) usually sat on the company's internal audit board" (Gainsborough 2010, pp. 102–04).

12. See Gainsborough (2010).

Another major change in governance, and likely the most consequential for the question of transparency, has been the diversification of powers at the central level of government. In addition to the historical division of power within the upper echelons of government between the president, prime minister, Politburo, and general secretary of the CPV, other spheres or branches of government have been elaborated and strengthened. First, the judicial branch has been granted greater levels of independence. Judges have more autonomy to rule according to provisions of the law rather than internal instructions or guidance set forth by the CPV. Second, an independent auditing branch, the SAV, was created in 1994 and given responsibility for auditing all agencies and organizations using state monies. As of 2005, it reports to the Standing Committee of the National Assembly rather than the Politburo. Various civil service institutions, such as the Ministry of Finance, Ministry of Justice, and State Treasury, have been given greater power to carry out their responsibilities. The National Assembly, Vietnam's legislative branch, has been authorized to approve budgets and can cast votes of confidence on government policies. Finally, the VFF increasingly plays a role similar to that of civil society organizations. An umbrella organization of so-called mass movements, the VFF is charged with supervising the activities of the government. Endorsement by the VFF is generally required to be a candidate for election to the National Assembly.

Thus the Vietnamese state has undergone not liberalization but rather a broadening and diversification of institutions within the parameters of a one-party state. This process has moved Vietnam in the direction of greater separation and balance of power. As we detail below, this division of labor within the central government, combined with the agreed principles of transparency set forth by the CPV, has allowed for the advancement of budget transparency, accountability, and participation. One sector or faction of government is less able to skirt agreed norms in order to advance particularistic interests because more effective mechanisms of oversight and control have been institutionalized thanks to the branching out, rather than retreat, of state power.

Points of Resistance to Budget Transparency

To reiterate, the move toward a government that is more participatory, transparent, and accountable enjoys broad support in Vietnam. There is "an unusually high degree of consensus on the direction of reform throughout the public sector."[13] The value of being better able to track and manage the flow of resources is clear not only to those leading the effort, such as the Ministry of Finance and State Treasury, but also to those implementing the reforms in the various in-line

13. ADB (2009, p. 20).

ministries and local governments and those undertaking newfound roles of oversight, such as the National Assembly, the SAV, and the VFF.

Where disputes have emerged is with regard to the pace of change. The business community, international organizations, and the general public believe that the pace is far too slow. Budget transparency, accountability, and participation are considered wise policy objectives that should be implemented as quickly as possible. From the perspective of at least some government officials, however, the calculus is more complicated. In general, these officials want to continue with the reforms, which they believe are crucial to modernizing Vietnam and achieving the development goals of building Vietnam into a middle- to high-income economy.[14] They also understand that the public concern with corruption must be addressed. The credibility of the CPV, and therefore their own legitimacy, is wrapped up with anticorruption reforms that include advancing transparency. However, they want to control or modify the reforms so that their reputations are not jeopardized and revenue streams are not completely shut off.

One hallmark of the government reforms since Doi Moi has been not the privatization of state entities, but rather their commercialization. This has effectively "turned bureaucrats into state entrepreneurs."[15] State officials have been able to profiteer by providing "private entrepreneurs with access to state-held means of production (land, factories, etc.), access to contracts that the state-owned enterprises were in a better position to win as a result of their state-endowed assets, and bureaucratic advantages in navigating the selective bureaucratic intervention of a state groping to devise control mechanisms in the uncharted territory of a market economy."[16] Thaveeporn Vasavakul (2008) notes other forms of state entrepreneurship. One can profit through grease or speed money, the privatization of state property, and the selling of state power. Not coincidentally, then, there is often a strong association in contemporary Vietnam between public office and money making. And since many, if not most, of these modes of state entrepreneurship are of questionable legality, transparency threatens not only these revenue streams but also the careers of some officials. This, then, accounts for much of the resistance to the implementation of transparency laws and policies, which has slowed, but not halted, reforms.

The Mechanisms of Transparency

In *Full Disclosure,* Fung, Graham, and Weil (2007) note that transparency systems often fail because they impose "costs on a small group of information disclosers

14. Kwakwa and Anderson (2011).
15. Nguyen-vo (2009, p. 11).
16. Nguyen-vo (2009, p. 12).

in the hopes of generating benefits for a large and dispersed class of information users. Since the stakes are higher for the potential disclosers, they dominate the political processes that shape transparency systems over time."[17] In Vietnam this has not happened. Even though the particularistic concerns and motives of government officials affect the pace of change, these "disclosers" have not been able to undermine or thwart the broader trend toward greater levels of transparency and participation. In this section, we outline the reasons why the forces for transparency have had the upper hand.

Prefigurative Practices

As noted, a great deal of political power has shifted from the central to the provincial, district, and commune levels.[18] Also mentioned, almost 50 percent of taxes are collected and managed at the nonfederal levels. As a means for introducing oversight over these revenue streams, the Grassroots Democracy Law was passed in 1998 and then strengthened in 2003 and 2007. Four major rights were granted: the rights to decide, supervise, be informed, and consulted. The law asserts the importance of publicizing information and calls on the active participation of citizenry in making decisions. More than a decade later, however, the results are limited. Although the principles of greater participation and more access to information are clear, the mechanisms for participatory planning and for information provision are opaque. The biggest problem, however, is that most major fiscal decisions are made at the provincial and not the commune level. Thus there is a "misalignment of accountability with the new arrangements."[19] Nonetheless, this law introduced practices and expectations that could spread to other levels of government.

Increased Access to Information

Despite the fact that the general public continues to receive inadequate information about budget matters, steps have been taken to improve this situation. For example, the government currently discloses online (in both Vietnamese and English) annual budget documentation, in-year budget execution reports, summaries of state audit reports, and contract information. Actual expenditures at the central, provincial, and district levels are divulged, and the country's quarterly estimated budget execution reports are posted on the Ministry of Finance website within a month of the end of the quarter. The collection and use of contributions made by individuals and organizations must also be publicized, as well as several aspects of the finances of state-owned enterprises.

17. Fung, Graham, and Weil (2007, p. 106).
18. Prefigurative practices are practices that are nascent and yet to be normalized or generalized.
19. ADB (2009, p. v).

On another front, the National Assembly has been conducting live televised discussions of state budget deliberations since 1994. These broadcasts enjoy high viewer ratings. This information is facilitating oversight of the budget processes by social organizations and unions, employees, and the general public. Moreover, there is anecdotal evidence that it is affecting the outcomes of National Assembly elections: members who prove themselves more willing to question government figures and pose more pointed questions enjoy more favorable support in elections.

Finally, a growing amount of government data, especially survey data, is being compiled and has influenced government reform, including budget-related practices. Despite ongoing methodological concerns, this shift has been labeled "an important milestone for Vietnam."[20] In the 2008 Vietnam Household Living Standards Survey (VHLSS), a new governance module was attached to the biannual census and administered to more than 9,000 households across Vietnam.[21] The questions focused on citizen satisfaction with government services, participation in policymaking, and access to information. Another important source of data is the Provincial Competitiveness Index (PCI), which is based on results from an annual survey conducted by the Vietnam Competitiveness Initiative and the Vietnam Chamber of Commerce and Industry. As noted in ADB (2009), "The PCI is widely acknowledged to have been a positive influence on the competitive spirit of the provinces, all of whom would like to see themselves ranked higher year after year. It is also a somewhat unique source of data on the institutional environment facing firms. With over 7,000 firms participating in this survey in 2008, the annual PCI survey offers a valuable cross section of firms' views," which indirectly inform and therefore affect the policies and practices of the central government.[22]

Capacity Building

State Audit Vietnam has improved its approach to financial and compliance audits. Also performance audits have been incorporated in the regular audits of the SAV. The number of auditors in SAV is still not commensurate with the task. To help to fill the gap, SAV has been allowed to contract private sector auditors since 2003. In addition, it is entitled to 2 percent of the actual amount discovered by the SAV and collected for the state budget, providing both the means and greater incentives for vigorous auditing.

Civil service reform has been advanced as a way to improve the quality of services provided by the SAV and other government entities. Attempts to specify and

---

20. ADB (2009, p. 7).

21. General Statistics Office of Vietnam, "Results of the Survey for Household Living Standards 2008" (www.gso.gov.vn/default_en.aspx?tabid=491).

22. ADB (2009, p. 7).

evaluate the tasks of managers better as well as to create a system that is more meritocratic have been promoted as a means of attracting and retaining high-quality workers. Still, much work is needed to improve the quality of civil servants, such as focusing more on rewarding positive performance and good decisionmaking. The current system is skewed toward punishing mistakes, which creates an institutional culture that is too risk averse and hampered by the incessant need to get authorization from one's superior. The Asian Development Bank has argued that reforming this accountability system is one of the toughest challenges that Vietnam will face as it advances toward becoming a middle-income country.[23]

Finally, the general system of accounting standards has improved. An updated and improved chart of accounts has been developed, which has resulted in more consistency of classification of revenues and expenditures in budgeting and accounting. A road map for public sector accounting standards has been issued, which, if implemented, would provide a more standardized basis for preparing government financial statements. Furthermore, TAMIS, an integrated computerized financial management system, was rolled out in 2009. All of these steps have enhanced the ability of civil servants to improve cash flow, arrears, and expenditure management and controls.

State Diversification

Capacity building, increased access to information, and prefigurative practices have all contributed to the advance of transparency. However, the institutional diversification of the state is the one change that has allowed these gains to be leveraged into a virtuous cycle. As the Vietnamese government has evolved during the past few decades, different branches of government have been developed or given more authority. The maturation of these differentiated spheres within the central government has resulted in an increasing separation and balance of powers. The three most significant institutions, at least for transparency, are the National Assembly, the Supreme Audit Vietnam, and the Vietnamese Fatherland Front.

The 1992 constitution established the National Assembly as a body fully independent from the executive. In addition to approving the allocation of the budget among various sectors, programs, and provinces, the National Assembly has the right to cast votes of confidence and monitor anticorruption. There are constraints on who can be a candidate for the National Assembly (for example, more than 90 percent are members of the CPV), but it is otherwise a democratic body. And there is a high degree of participation in the elections. Most important, the National Assembly now has an external oversight role. One important caveat, however, is that its power has been limited by the formation of a Standing Com-

23. ADB (2009, p. 4).

mittee that has been granted all decisionmaking powers when the National Assembly is not in session, which is often the case.[24]

Originally established in 1994, State Audit Vietnam was transformed in 2005 into an independent institution reporting to the National Assembly and is now responsible for auditing all agencies and organizations using state monies and property. It no longer reports to the Politburo but instead reports directly to the Standing Committee in order to assist its budget oversight activities. The SAV routinely finds substantial amounts of misused public funds. Yet the impact of its findings is muted by the fact that it lacks the authority to penalize those found to have engaged in corruption, which curtails its ability to compel the government to act on its reports.[25]

Lastly, the Vietnamese Fatherland Front has come to play an increasingly important, albeit indirect, role in the budget process. Established in 1977, this voluntary government organization is encouraged to supervise many of the activities of the government. Anchored in mass participation and popular associations, the VFF is constitutionally recognized as the voice of the people. It has a particularly significant role in elections. Almost all candidates are nominated by (and members of) the VFF, with only a few "self-nominated" candidates avoiding the VFF's veto. As the official voice of the people and the organization that endorses candidates to the National Assembly, the VFF has taken a predominant role in bringing popular concerns to the National Assembly. It collects opinions, petitions, and grievances through surveys and consultations with its network of mass organizations. These are reported every year at the opening of the National Assembly. In the 2009 opening, the VFF was allowed the keynote role. One of the issues in the foreground was corruption and waste. The VFF petitioned the government "to speed up the public administration reform, to strengthen and promote openness and transparency in order to stop and roll back corruption and waste, especially in the fields of land administration, investments, capital construction, and use of public assets. Voters also petition the National Assembly to strengthen and to enhance effectiveness of its oversight in this regard."[26]

Thus the diversification of state power has increasingly meant that some individuals and organizations within the central government benefit from transparency norms and information and therefore have an immediate interest in consolidating gains and advocating for further improvements in disclosure systems. These actors can and often do use transparency policies for career advancement, institution building, or interagency competition. Most government officials undoubtedly value anticorruption policies as positive for Vietnamese society.

24. de Renzio, Gomez, and Sheppard (2009, p. 64).
25. de Renzio, Gomez, and Sheppard (2009).
26. Central Committee of the VFF (2009).

However, in addition to the commitments to these principles, government offi-cials can seize these agreed norms and values, at strategic moments, to carve out or protect resources and political space for themselves and the institutions for which they work and with which they identify. This evolving set of intermediaries within the central government has, in recent years, created a relatively fertile ter-rain for mechanisms and dynamics to emerge that help to protect transparency policies from degenerating and allow them to "gain accuracy, scope, and use over time, becoming . . . sustainable."[27] That is, transparency policies are nurtured, emboldened, and elaborated, at least in part, because they serve as effective tools of institutional and career competition. This sort of constructive rivalry and pol-itics is only viable in an institutional context in which the bureaucracy is suffi-ciently diversified so that a critical mass of relatively autonomous agencies and organizations coexists.

Government Performance

Moving from an overall score of three to fourteen in the past four years is not likely to affect government performance in a profound way—at least in any way that is readily or easily detectable. This said, some evidence of progress was the decision by the National Assembly not to authorize the construction of a high-speed rail system between Ha Noi and Ho Chi Minh City. This major infra-structure project, proposed by the Politburo and endorsed by the prime minister as well as the World Bank, was rejected by the National Assembly in the summer of 2010 on budgetary grounds. The National Assembly is not merely a rubber stamp of the desires of the party leadership, and, in practice, there is a higher degree of scrutiny of major decisions about the national treasure.

In general, the biggest perceptible changes in government performance in recent years have had little to do with budget transparency. Instead, they are the result of state streamlining and downsizing. One example of this is the program for one-stop shops. The idea is that citizens can go to one place to deal with administrative tasks such as notarizing documents and registering land and busi-nesses. The first one-stop shop was piloted in 1996 in Ho Chi Minh City and was made compulsory in 2007 for all departments and procedures at the local levels and scaled up to the central level. The 2007 regulations allowed and encouraged the introduction of "interlinkage" one-stop shop initiatives, which connect dif-ferent administrative levels and sectors, further simplifying procedures for citizens and enterprises. According to the Asian Development Bank, "By most accounts,

27. Fung, Graham, and Weil (2007, p. 106).

the one-stop shops are successful. For citizens and firms, the prospect of long lines and unanswered questions are less of a concern than they had been in the past. In the Binh Thuan and Kien Giang examples, the time for business start-ups reduced from twenty-six days to fifteen days and from fifteen days to five days, respectively."[28]

Another major change has been in the administration of certain public services, especially health and education: 100 percent of public health services at the central level and 88 percent at the local levels were granted autonomy under both the 2002 and 2006 regulations. There have been several positive effects: administrative costs have been reduced, managers have become more dynamic and entrepreneurial, organizational structures have been enhanced, and human resources have been used more efficiently. The quality of recruitment and appointment of key personnel has also improved, and competition among health service providers for quality and customer service has increased. All of this is reflected in recent survey research (the 2008 VHLSS), which finds that the vast majority of households think that health and education services have improved since 2006.[29] The biggest negative is that devolution has led to high out-of-pocket costs for residents due primarily to corruption in the form of unofficial payments or "gifts" that doctors, nurses, and administrators in hospitals increasingly expect.

If there is little concrete to report with regard to the effects of budget transparency on government performance, there clearly is a tremendous amount of momentum behind enhancing transparency, oversight, and participation. In 2008 the Ministry of Finance said that the SAV would focus on the following tasks: standardize audits; make audit documents simpler, more user-friendly, and more practical; annually select, commend, and reward gold-quality audits to honor excellent, brave, devoted, and creative auditors; make activities of audits transparent and public; better ensure the independence of auditors; strengthen the professional ethics of auditors; and attempt to upgrade and adopt the most advanced technologies and audit methods. In 2009 the government adopted the National Anticorruption Strategy 2020, which explicitly recognized the role of openness and transparency in reducing corruption and included an action plan, complete with timetables for legislative action. Vietnam Innovation Day 2009 picked as its theme "More Accountability and Transparency, Less Corruption," and associations, mass organizations, and the private sector submitted 150 proposals with innovative ideas for reducing corruption. In June 2010 Vietnam ratified the United Nations Convention against Corruption. And the government is

28. ADB (2009, p. 55).

29. General Statistics Office of Vietnam, "Results of the Survey for Household Living Standards 2008" (www.gso.gov.vn/default_en.aspx?tabid=491).

expected to adopt a new decree on the oversight of administrative procedures, which, among other things, will help to ensure the systematic and continuous application of the principles of efficiency, transparency, and consultation in the development of new administrative procedures and the revision of existing ones.

Conclusions

The move toward greater levels of transparency in Vietnam was initiated by the economic and paradigmatic crisis that the CPV confronted in the mid-1980s. In response to this predicament, the party rejected many of the tenants and policies of Soviet-style communism, but did not make a complete break. Vietnam is still a one-party state with the CPV at the helm. Moreover, the party leadership continues to define recent economic reforms as "socialist-led market developments." In practice, however, Vietnam has increasingly looked to the liberal and social democratic political economies of the North Atlantic and East Asia as a source of ideas for reform. Coupled with the CPV's appreciation that political stability and its legitimacy hinge on reducing government corruption, this has generated nearly universal support for transparency policies and initiatives throughout Vietnam.

General commitments to transparency norms alone, however, often do not result in improvements in budget practices. In Vietnam the principal mechanism that has converted such goals into sustainable practices has been the increasing diversification of the central government. The creation and elaboration of different institutional spheres within the central government has helped to create a virtuous cycle. The fact that there are intermediary entities such as the National Assembly, the State Audit Vietnam, and the Vietnamese Fatherland Front, with increasing degrees of autonomy and institutional interests of their own—not to mention sincere convictions that transparency is an important goal—has set in motion a sustainable transparency system. These organizations have helped to ensure that gains are consolidated and built upon.

Vietnam thus represents an anomaly within the transparency literature, which posits the centrality of a free press, democratic polity, and robust civil society. Little of this exists in Vietnam, and yet progress continues to be made. Consequently, this case study should prompt a reevaluation and nuancing of the causal models of budget transparency. It illustrates that a wider repertoire of strategies is available for advancing budget transparency, accountability, and participation than has commonly been assumed. This insight should prove valuable for those working with governments keen on improving transparency but resistant to other sorts of reforms, such as creating a more open press or a competitive political system. In the coming years, Vietnam should continue to contribute to the transparency literature by allowing us to observe precisely how transparent a government can become absent the ingredients that have been assumed to be so essential to achieving such an outcome.

References

ADB (Asian Development Bank). 2009. *Vietnam Development Report 2010: Modern Institutions*. Joint Donor Report to the Vietnam Consultative Group Meeting, Ha Noi, December 3–4. Ha Noi: Vietnam Development Information Center.

Central Committee of the VFF (Vietnam Fatherland Front). 2009. "Report: Synthesis of Opinions and Petitions of Voters and the People." Delivered at the fifth session of the twelfth National Assembly, Ha Noi, May 19.

de Renzio, Paolo, Pamela Gomez, and James Sheppard. 2009. *Budget Transparency and Development in Resource-Dependent Countries*. Oxford: Blackwell Publishing and UNESCO.

Florini, Ann, ed. 2007. *The Right to Know: Transparency for an Open World*. Columbia University Press.

Fung, Archon, Mary Graham, and David Weil. 2007. *Full Disclosure: The Perils and Promise of Transparency*. New York: Cambridge University Press.

Gainsborough, Martin. 2010. *Vietnam: Rethinking the State*. London: Zed Books.

Horsely, Jamie P. 2007. "Toward a More Open China?" In *The Right to Know: Transparency for an Open World*, edited by Ann Florini. Columbia University Press.

IBP (International Budget Partnership). 2010. *The Open Budget Survey 2010*. Washington.

Kwakwa, Victoria, and Jim Anderson. 2011. "New Year's Resolution: Shine a Light to Reduce Corruption in Vietnam." *Thanh Nien*, December 31.

Landerman, Scott. 2009. *Tours of Vietnam: War, Travel Guides, and Memory*. Duke University Press.

Nguyen-Vo, Thu-Houng. 2009. *The Ironies of Freedom: Sex, Culture, and Neoliberal Governance in Vietnam*. University of Washington Press.

Vasavakul, Thaveeporn. 2008. "Recrafting State Identity: Corruption and Anti-Corruption in Doi Moi Vietnam from a Comparative Perspective." Paper presented to "Rethinking the Vietnamese State: Implications for Vietnam and the Region," Vietnam Workshop, August 21–22, City University of Hong Kong.

World Bank and Government of Vietnam. 2008. "Vietnam Country Financial Accountability Assessment." Washington: World Bank, Financial Management Unit, Central Operational Services Unit, Vietnam Country Management Unit, East Asia Pacific Region.

9

Capturing Movement at the Margins: Senegal's Efforts at Budget Transparency Reform

LINDA BECK, E. H. SEYDOU NOUROU TOURE, AND ALIOU FAYE

African countries do not score well on budget transparency, according to the Open Budget Index (OBI) ratings for 2010. Their poor performance may be attributed to a combination of factors identified in the OBI report, including a significant level of aid dependency, economic underdevelopment, and a lack of or weakness in democratic institutions. Yet even within Africa, there is wide variation in OBI scores, from top-ranking South Africa, whose score of ninety-two out of 100 surpassed that of all other countries surveyed, including long-established Western democracies, to the lowest-ranking countries of Chad, Equatorial Guinea, and São Tomé and Príncipe, which each received a score of zero for their complete lack of public access to budget information.

A closer look at the OBI scores reveals that Anglophone African countries, not only the South African outlier, have fared significantly better than their Francophone counterparts, while Lusophone Africa has a mixed record. With the notable exceptions of Mali and Morocco, whose respective scores of thirty-five and twenty-eight indicate a "minimal" level of budget information, Africa's former French and Belgian colonies characteristically provide "scant to no information" to their citizens. While these Francophone countries are joined by Nigeria on the bottom rung of the OBI scale, most of the continent's former British colonies provide at least "some" budget information, with ratings ranging from forty-one to sixty points. A reasonable explanation for this clustering could be that postcolonial Africa continues to be influenced by its diverse colonial legacies. This argument, however, requires a half-century of path dependence from the colonial state as opposed to any contemporary modeling, as France and the United Kingdom received identical OBI scores of 87 percent in both 2008 and 2010 based on the provision of "extensive" budget information by their governments.[1]

To assess alternative explanations for the relatively poor performance of Africa's Francophone countries, this chapter focuses on Senegal, one of the six former French African colonies that received a score of five or lower in 2010.[2] While Senegal's OBI score of three reflects a continuing need for budget reform, we maintain that the lack of transparency and limited popular participation in the Senegalese budget process is less a reflection of its colonial legacy than of the current socioeconomic and political contexts in which it operates. By contrasting Senegal with Mali, its better-performing neighbor, we demonstrate that African countries with limited economic resources can nevertheless enhance their budget transparency and participation by liberalizing their political institutions and increasing the engagement of non-state actors in budget processes.[3]

Budget Transparency and Participation in Senegal

Despite a general increase in OBI scores worldwide, Senegal's 2010 survey shows no improvement from its negligible score of three out of 100 in 2008.[4] This rating indicates that the government of Senegal provides the public with very limited information on the central government's budget. Only three of the eight budget documents identified by the OBI as critical to an open process are published (the enacted budget, in-year reports, and the audit report), although all eight documents are produced by the government, with the exception of the citizen's budget. Moreover, Senegal's two major oversight bodies—the legislature and the supreme audit institution—are weak, lacking the resources and capacity to exercise their powers either to amend the executive's budget proposal or to monitor budget execution. As a result, the OBI report maintains that it is "virtually impossible for citizens to hold the government accountable for its management of the public's money."[5] Senegal's negligible score suggests that there has been little to no improvement in budget transparency and participation since the early years of its highly centralized authoritarian state (1963–80), despite more than two decades of political, economic, and juridical reform. To

1. In the first OBI survey, France received the highest score of 89 percent, followed closely by the United Kingdom with 88 percent. IBP (2007).

2. These were Burkina Faso (five), Niger and Senegal (three), Cameroon (two), Algeria (one), and Chad (zero).

3. The OBI and research for this chapter were conducted before the Malian coup in 2012. It will be informative to observe how the change in Mali's regime will influence its budget transparency.

4. Senegal was not one of the countries included in the initial 2006 surveys.

5. OBI (2011).

assess the accuracy of Senegal's stagnant scores on the OBI, we review the country's historical lack of budget transparency and participation and recent efforts at budget reform.

A Tradition of Executive Dominance in the Postindependence Period

At the time of independence in 1960, Senegal's legal system, including its fiscal laws, was modeled after the French colonial state with its emphasis on *mise-en-valeur* (development), which required significant state involvement in the economy and a Jacobin-style centralized state with a dual executive that quickly became a form of hyper-presidentialism similar to the French political system under Charles de Gaulle.

Under the charismatic leadership of President Leopold Sedar Senghor, Senegal's ruling Socialist Party (PS), its highly compliant National Assembly, and the various councils, commissions, and committees created to advise the government all served as channels for disseminating information from above rather than as a basis for dialogue and debate. Other than a handful of trusted advisers, the role of these institutions in the budget process amounted to little more than a rubber stamp on presidential initiatives. After a political showdown in the early 1960s that eliminated the post of prime minister, Senegal adopted its first fiscal codes that concentrated power in the hands of the president and his minister of finance.[6]

In the new Senegalese state, popular participation was constrained by various political and socioeconomic factors, including economic plans that were more declarative than participatory and low levels of literacy among Senegal's largely rural population.[7] Budget transparency was also limited by Senegal's lack of economic development and revenue resources and frequent external shocks, such as the French withdrawal of subsidies for Senegal's peanut cash crop in 1965, the oil crisis in the 1970s, and recurrent droughts. This led to mounting budget deficits and government reliance on extra-budgetary assistance from international donors, especially France, to meet its obligations. In the face of mounting financial problems, Senegal adopted a new organic law in July 1975 giving the executive branch even greater financial prerogatives to the detriment of Parliament's role in the budget process.[8]

The instability of Senegal's political economy resulted in a series of political and economic reforms, beginning with the progressive return to a multiparty

6. Mamadou Ndiaye (2010).
7. Republic of Senegal (1963).
8. Biram Ndiaye (2010).

system (1978–80) and the negotiation of Senegal's first structural adjustment program (SAP, 1979–80). The parties to SAP negotiations, however, were limited to the government and the Bretton Woods institutions in conjunction with other international donors that pronounced the goals and conditions of the SAP to the Senegalese public. While the donors' periodic reviews included representatives of various business organizations and workers' unions, Senegal was signing programs with donors without consultation with, let alone support from, the population.[9]

Meanwhile, critics of SAP complained that Senegal was submitting to the dictates of international financial institutions. Mounting political pressure and the violence following the 1988 reelection of Senghor's designated successor, Abdou Diouf, contributed to the government's decision to cease compliance with the SAP, resulting in its suspension (1989–93) and the deterioration of Senegal's relations with the international donor community.

Increased Participation in Economic Policy

After the contentious 1993 presidential elections, the newly reelected Diouf administration formulated an emergency plan intended to respond to popular protests against declining economic conditions and to avoid international pressure for devaluation of the currency.[10] More than prior government initiatives, non-state actors, specifically business leaders and academics, were invited to participate in formulation of the 1993 emergency plan. Throughout most of the 1990s, dialogue with non-state actors was confined largely to the private sector, although an independent media and civil society organizations (CSOs) had developed with political liberalization in the 1980s. The incorporation of civil society actors—in particular, nongovernmental organizations (NGOs), community-based organizations, and various types of federations and coalitions of societal actors—into forums for dialogue, debate, and negotiation on public policy only came about with the introduction of the Poverty Reduction Strategy Paper (PRSP) process in 1999. A precondition for debt relief and concessional financing by the World Bank and the International Monetary Fund (IMF), the PRSP lays out the country's macroeconomic, structural, and social policies and programs to promote growth and reduce poverty, as well as the related need for external financing. Prepared every three years, one of the core principles of the

---

9. Berg (1990).

10. Senegal has a shared currency, the franc of the African Financial Community (fCFA), with six other former French colonies in West Africa and more recently Guinea-Bissau. The fCFA was pegged to the French franc until 1999, when the euro was created by the Economic and Monetary Community of the European Union.

PRSP approach is that the process should be "partnership-oriented," involving the participation of all stakeholders, including CSOs.

The participation of civil society in economic policy debates was reinforced by the establishment of partnership agreements between African, Caribbean, and Pacific countries and the European Community, more commonly referred to as the Cotonou Agreement. Like the PRSP process, the Cotonou Agreement recognizes the importance of consultation with non-state actors, although the "contracting parties" in this case are the two sets of state actors from the African, Caribbean, and Pacific countries and the European Union.

While various international and government stakeholders assert that the involvement of civil society actors in these forums, particularly the PRSP, implicitly assures their inclusion in the budget process, this does not replace informed popular participation in the budget process, which remains essentially limited to commentaries in the media responding to government pronouncements and leaked information. As even international donors such as the European Union recognize, the PRSP is disconnected from the budget, with a tendency to be more like a document for donors than for the Senegalese state.

Nevertheless, over the last decade, significant legal and institutional reforms have enhanced the transparency of the budget process and legislative participation in the formulation, approval, and oversight of the government budget. Although Senegal's poor performance on the OBI indicates the limited nature of these improvements and the need for further reforms to ensure budget transparency and participation, it may also indicate a need to revise the OBI criteria and methodology to capture the impact of reforms on budget openness.

Efforts to Reform Senegal's Budget Process

Over the last decade, Senegal has undertaken dramatic revisions of its constitutional and legal framework regulating the budget process, with a heavy emphasis on increasing transparency and participation at least with regard to the legislature. While some of these changes reflect political developments within the country, much of the impetus for these reforms has come from beyond Senegal's borders. In addition to pressure from the donor community, the West African Economic and Monetary Union (WAEMU) has played a critical role in promoting budget reforms in Senegal and other member states.

As both a currency and a customs union created on the eve of the 1994 devaluation of the Franc CFA, one of the objectives of WAEMU is to harmonize legislation by member states, particularly regarding fiscal policies. Before their adoptation into Senegalese law, directives from the WAEMU's Council of Ministers are not legally binding, although they have fundamentally influenced the economic and fiscal policies of member states wishing to safeguard the value of the common currency and its link to the euro.[11] This includes recent constitutional and legislative reforms undertaken by Senegal to enhance the role of Parliament in all three stages of the budget process: formulation, approval, and oversight.

Budget Formulation: Introduction of Parliamentary Budget Orientation Debates

Members of Parliament (MPs) as well as ordinary citizens and CSOs have been relatively uninvolved in the drafting of Senegal's government budgets. This task has been fulfilled by the executive branch, which primarily consults with international donors and arbitrates among competing ministerial demands for budget allocations.

In 1998, however, President Diouf introduced an annual "budget orientation debate." Each spring, in addition to extensive negotiation with the various ministries, the Ministry of Economy and Finance (MEF) solicits comments from Parliament on the five major strategic axes of the draft budget: modernization of the state, infrastructure, social services, development programs, and private sector enhancement. The minister of finance submits an initial budget orientation document to the Finance Commission of the National Assembly, which deliberates on the proposal and then reports back to the National Assembly, where it is debated in a plenary session.

The debate, which lasts fifteen days, affords MPs an opportunity to voice their concerns and differences regarding the proposed budget strategies; however, its impact on the final budget proposal is limited at best. According to S. M. Thiam, an opposition leader who served as vice president of the National Assembly's Commission on the Economy, Finance, Planning, and Cooperation from 1998 to 2001,

> The formulation of the budget is an affair for the technocrats of the MEF. It is not a participatory process. [The creation of] the budget orientation debate was an achievement for the National Assembly, but it takes place under conditions that do not permit parliamentary representatives to influence budget decisions. [For example,] there is an inequality in the resources at the disposal of the Parliament and the Government . . . [which] should present a background document to guide the debate . . . [In addition,] the fifteen days given to the deputies is insufficient.

11. European influence over the policies and directives of the WAEMU extends beyond the currency link, as the European Union has provided extensive financial aid to the WAEMU since its inception. See "Histoire de l'UEMOA" (www.uemoa.int/uemoa/historique.htm).

Similar critiques have been echoed by members of the president's own ruling party. During the FY2011 budget debate, a deputy from the Parti Démocratique Sénégalais (PDS) complained that "year after year" the government of Senegal has presented the same documents, despite complaints by MPs that "the cost of the state must be reduced, that agencies that have become nebulous have to be eliminated."[12] The specific issues that he and other MPs raised had no impact on the final budget proposal.

In contrast to parliamentary debates, budget negotiations with the various ministries are more lengthy, vigorous, and influential. Over the course of several months, the MEF holds budget conferences with each ministry. These negotiations center around not only the MEF's proposed budget allocations (*enveloppes sectorielles*) but also the performance reports produced by each ministry. Based on these negotiations, the MEF presents a revised budget to the prime minister, who then presents an "arbitrated budget" to the Council of Ministers. The Council of Ministers, however, will not adopt a budget unless it is to the president's liking. Thus, as one MEF official stated, "The president is the final arbitrator" in the budget formulation process.

Unlike the ministries, Parliament does not provide alternative proposals for higher funding or defunding of particular programs or sectors. The MPs do not have sufficient human or material resources to provide an alternative cost-benefit analysis of the executive's proposed budget. There is no Parliamentary Budget Office to help MPs, many of whom are illiterate, to interpret complex budget information or to compile alternative budget strategies and formulas.

The disparity between the extensive ministerial budget conferences and the limited parliamentary budget orientation debates reflects the focus of budget formulation on the arbitration of interministerial demands for resources rather than the input of Parliament on behalf of their constituents, let alone direct popular participation. The MEF pre-budget statement is not disseminated to the public, although highlights are reported in the press along with parliamentary deliberations, in contrast to other countries with similarly low OBI scores. While such informal distribution should not substitute for official dissemination to assure more complete and equitable access to budget information, the OBI methodology does not recognize the contribution that informal distribution makes to budget transparency, which would differentiate Senegal from other low-scoring countries.

Budget Approval: Constitutional and Legal Reforms of Parliament's Role

After the historic election of opposition leader Abdoulaye Wade in 2000, Senegal ratified a new constitution in 2001 that retained Senegal's presidential sys-

---

12. Biram Ndiaye (2010).

tem, despite Wade's electoral promise to establish a parliamentary system with greater checks on presidential power. While most of the articles in the new constitution outline the extensive powers of the president, Parliament does enjoy explicit constitutional powers related to its approval of government budgets. Under Article 68 of the 2001 constitution, the executive branch is required to submit a budget proposal to Parliament by the beginning of its ordinary session each fall. Parliament then has up to sixty days to deliberate. If the president does not present a budget proposal in sufficient time for Parliament to consider the bill in its ordinary session, the session is automatically extended until a Finance Law is adopted.

In addition, under Article 82 Parliament has the right to amend the state budget proposed by the executive. However, no budget amendment may either decrease state revenue or increase public expenditure unless the amendment includes a provision that "effectively eliminates or reduces an expense or creates or increases revenue." While ostensibly included to control deficit spending, Senegalese stakeholders see this provision as effectively preventing MPs from exercising their parliamentary prerogative to amend the budget, presumably because they lack the capacity to produce such complex financial adjustments.

Following ratification of the 2001 constitution, a revision of the Organic Finance Law governing government budgets introduced several provisions designed to reinforce Parliament's capacity to deliberate on the executive's budget proposal. For example, budget transparency was enhanced by including public debt as an ordinary expenditure in the budget rather than burying it in an annex. In addition, the format of the budget was simplified, with a clear division into two parts, revenues and expenditures, along with the inclusion of a three-year budgetary plan under a medium-term expenditure framework that permits legislators to assess the direction of Senegal's fiscal policy.

Nevertheless, in the absence of a budget summary, the complexity, density, and technical nature of the budget continues to limit the capacity of Parliament to serve as a check on the executive's dominant role in the budget formulation process. This is compounded by Parliament's limited human resources and lack of political autonomy. According to a current member of the National Assembly's Finance Commission, the lack of human resources "is the biggest problem. The ideal would be for deputies to be supported by parliamentary staff, but this is not the case. The budget must be presented in a more simple fashion and [thus] be more accessible. There must be parliamentary staff and experts who can read the [economic and budgetary] framework and analyze the budget."

Although support staff for Parliament has increased recently, they are still few in number and characteristically without sufficient background in public finance or fiscal policy.[13] This lack of technical support, according to the president of a federation of Senegalese CSOs, prevents most MPs from intervening in the budget debate. In response to this need, international donors are working to provide MPs with training in public finance.

Even if a readable budget summary were provided and MPs were adequately trained to analyze it, the capacity of Parliament "to become a critical interlocutor with the executive branch at every stage of the budget cycle," as envisioned by the IMF residential representative, is likely to continue to be constrained by the current predominance of the ruling PDS in both legislative chambers. MEF officials as well as members of Senegal's opposition are critical of the lack of debate on the budget, which is largely attributed to MPs looking to defend rather than debate the policy preferences of the president.

In addition, the role of Parliament in the budget approval process is constrained by the limited time it has to review the executive's budget proposal. The sixty days guaranteed by the constitution reflects only two-thirds of the three-month minimum recommended under the Organization for Economic Cooperation and Development's best practices for budget transparency.[14] This time period is insufficient, particularly in light of the fact that it must be shared by the two chambers of Parliament. Initially, the 2001 constitution eliminated the Senate and allotted the National Assembly sixty days for budget deliberation; this was reduced to thirty days in 2007, when the newly recreated Senate was allocated fifteen days, with the remaining fifteen days presumably set aside for harmonizing any differences between the versions of the Finance Law approved by the two chambers.

The reduction in time allotted to the National Assembly is highly significant to Parliament's capacity for autonomous deliberation on the executive's proposed budget given the structure of the Senate. While the majority of the Senate under the Diouf regime was elected indirectly by a college of locally elected officials, indirect election in the new Senate is limited to only thirty-five of the 100 seats, with the president naming the remaining sixty-five senators. It is not surprising, therefore, that the Senate unanimously passed the 2011 budget; it also received a clear majority in the Assembly, which is overwhelmingly dominated by the ruling party, since most opposition parties boycotted the 2007 legislative elections.

Finally, none of the legal reforms designed to enhance the legislative role in the budget approval process addresses public access to budget information or

13. With the support of donors such as the European Union, the United Nations Development Programme, and the African Capacity Building Foundation, since 2006 technical assistance has been provided to MPs by retired civil servants with significant budgetary knowledge.
14. OECD (2002, pp. 7–14).

participation in budget debates. Justifying their absence, the IMF residential representative in Senegal asserted,

> In the majority of democratic governments in the world, it is the government that prepares the budget proposal and then Parliament, as the representatives of the people par excellence, who approves it with or without amendments. By contrast, the budget is supported by the country's economic development strategy, which ideally is prepared in a participatory manner.

A clear reference to the participatory nature of Senegal's PRSP, which has been criticized as insufficient to assure popular participation in the budget, this comparative analysis also fails to recognize the critical roles that CSOs play in countries with more transparent and participatory budget processes. While public officials (and it would seem IMF officials) may see such citizen participation as "redundant" to legislative involvement, CSOs can provide independent budget analyses and monitoring as well as help to educate and thus involve citizens in the budget process.[15]

In Senegal, however, most budget documents, including the executive's proposed budget, are not publicly disseminated, although budget information is typically "leaked" to the public via the Senegalese media. Consequently, Mouhamet Fall of Forum Civil, Senegal's Transparency International affiliate, who conducted the 2008 OBI survey, argued for significantly higher scores than Senegal was ultimately assigned.[16] The decision by the International Budget Partnership (IBP) to assign lower scores to Senegal is justified at least in part by the fact that, even with this informal dissemination, access to detailed budget information still requires "connections within the MEF, where [individual staff members] could provide information on particular points concerning certain sectors, though not the whole document," as one CSO leader pointed out. However, since 2008 information related to budget implementation is now available online.

Access to detailed budget documents, however, would be of limited use to most Senegalese. Just as MPs who are not schooled in public finance are in need of a budget summary, the lack of a citizen's budget is an even greater obstacle to popular participation in the budget process. Even with a literacy rate of less than 50 percent, a citizen's budget would permit CSOs working on budget transparency, anticorruption, and political advocacy in general to participate in the budget process. Nevertheless, a citizen's budget is currently "not a priority," due

---

15. Tanaka (2007, pp. 141–42, 144).
16. IBP (2008).

in part to a political climate perceived as unfavorable. Those seeking to enhance budget participation are instead focusing their energies on the introduction of public hearings, as "there is a lot of reticence" to the idea of a citizen's budget.

Budget Oversight: Increased Monitoring through Budget Oversight Laws

Judicial monitoring of public finances was initially under the jurisdiction of the Senegalese Supreme Court but was transferred to the Council of State (Conseil d'Etat) following Senegal's judicial reform in 1992, which divided the Supreme Court and its jurisdictions into three separate superior courts. In 1998 WAEMU established an Audit Court modeled after the French Audit Court (Cour des Comptes). As other WAEMU members began to follow suit, Senegal revised its constitution to add a fourth Audit Court to its judicial system in 1999, which was retained in the 2001 constitution under Article 92.

The Audit Court has the power to impose sanctions for financial mismanagement by public officials, to issue directives to the president regarding budget practices and implementation, and to publish the results of its investigations in an annual report.[17] Dissemination of its annual report is seen as one of the most critical advancements for budget transparency in Senegal, although the most recent report on its website is from 2008. The lag may be explained by both internal factors, specifically the Audit Court's limited budget and consequent lack of personnel, and external factors, particularly delays in the submission of budget reports by the various public entities under its jurisdiction.

The Audit Court is also constrained by its inability to conduct in-depth audits given the magistrates' lack of skills in the various administrative and economic sectors covered by the 560 different public entities under its jurisdiction. However, the Audit Court's jurisdiction can also be seen as too restrictive, in that it does not cover extra-budgetary funds, which are not analyzed in its annual reports. These constraints on the functioning of the Audit Court are less of an issue for the executive branch, which has its own internal audit agencies, than for the legislative branch, which relies heavily on the Audit Court's investigations and analysis to fulfill its role of oversight in the budget process.

Under Senegal's Organic Finance Law, the Audit Court provides a "general declaration of budget conformity" to the executive branch for incorporation into its proposed Budget Oversight Law (*projet de loi de réglementation*) to be delivered to Parliament along with an administrative audit by the MEF. The law referring to the previous fiscal year is supposed to be submitted by the end of each fiscal year so that it can inform Parliament's deliberation on the budget for

17. The various ministerial inspection units and the overarching General State Inspection all report directly and exclusively to the president, along with the National Commission against Non-Transparency, Corruption, and Misappropriation, which was created in 2004.

the following year. First adopted in 1995, no Budget Oversight Law was presented to Parliament until 2008, when legislators voted on a series of laws covering 1999–2002. Currently backlogged to 2006, MPs have been adopting new budgets with little to no information for assessing the effectiveness of public spending in previous years. The parliamentarians' frustration with these delays was evident during the 2010 budget debate, when an MP questioned the ministers of communications and finance about allegations of unreported proceeds from the sale of licenses by Senegal's telecommunications agency. He complained, "This is why we deplore the fact that the Budget Oversight Law is not promptly submitted for consideration at the end of each fiscal year."[18]

As another fiscal year ended in December 2010 without a proposed Budget Oversight Law on the table, a journalist for the independent daily *Sud Quotidien* charged that this constituted "a flagrant violation" of the constitution, which requires citizen involvement in governance and thus the public's right to give consent to and oversee implementation of the budget in order to determine the appropriate use of public funds.[19] The government pledged to bring its record up to date by the end of 2011, but this was a seemingly impossible feat given the government's past track record and the fact that no additional resources had been allocated to the Audit Court or the MEF to fulfill this commitment. This pledge, therefore, appears to be more about the perpetual "dance" between international donors and aid recipients, a dance in which countries agree to conditions that are unrealistic. In this case, the government was concurrently negotiating a new agreement with the IMF to endorse its macroeconomic policy framework, a critical prerequisite for receipt of further economic assistance and investments. Under this agreement, the government agreed to enhance its "public financial management by improving budget credibility and implementation," including bringing its Budget Oversight Laws up to date.[20] Unfortunately, going into hyper-drive to meet these deadlines sacrifices the quality and thus the value of a Budget Oversight Law for budgetary oversight by Parliament.

Fortunately, in 2012 all Budget Oversight Laws up through 2010 were passed. But even if the government submits comprehensive Budget Oversight Law proposals in a timely fashion, Parliament is unlikely to employ its constitutional right to request that members of the government account for their implementation of the budget, as invoking this check on the executive branch is likely to cost them their seat. The dismissal of Macky Sall, president of the National Assembly, serves as a clear warning to other MPs of the political consequences of exercising their role in budgetary oversight. In 2008 Sall and other PDS

18. Dabo (2010).
19. Ndaw (2010).
20. IMF (2010).

deputies requested that Karim Wade, head of the National Agency for the Organization of the Islamic Conference (ANOCI) and son of the president, appear before the Assembly. A government agency created to oversee preparations for the Organization of Islamic Conference summit in Dakar, ANOCI's legal status was ambiguous, with its accounts kept separate from the official budget and thus not subject to oversight by the MEF's controller. Based on allegations of kickbacks and other forms of corruption, the MPs asked Wade to submit an audit to Parliament.

Infuriated by the "audacity" of the legislature, President Wade pushed for legislation that shortened the term of the National Assembly president to one year, effectively dismissing Sall. The justification for this revision of the National Assembly's leadership explicitly referred to "misunderstandings between the executive and legislative power . . . [and] a crisis of confidence between the president of the republic . . . and the president of the National Assembly."[21] Ultimately Karim Wade did appear before members of the Senate—though not an entire plenary and notably not the somewhat more independent National Assembly—in a session that was closed to journalists and the public. As one opposition leader noted, "When they left, they took their documents with them." The ANOCI affair clearly reflects a lack of parliamentary autonomy to hold the executive fiscally accountable despite constitutional provisions for its oversight of the state budget.

Capturing the Impact of Senegal's Budget Reforms in Its OBI Ratings

Despite significant problems with its budget process, Senegal's introduction of budget orientation debates, Budget Oversight Laws, and an Audit Court as well as revision of its budget format and the training of parliamentarians in public finance have enhanced its budget transparency and particularly the participation of the legislature in the budget process. Nearly all of these reforms, however, predate the 2008 OBI survey, the first one in which Senegal was included; therefore, one would not anticipate that they would have resulted in an improved rating in 2010. In fact, given the ANOCI scandal, one might have anticipated a lower score.

This illustrates the failure of the current OBI measurements to capture variation among countries at the bottom of the scale. For example, Senegal's scores do not reflect the important role that informal dissemination of information plays in budget transparency and participation. Beyond the OBI's current evaluation of whether budget documents are produced and publicly

21. Dione (2008).

disseminated, a more differentiated scale is needed to assess whether budget information is available to the public through at least informal dissemination by individual legislators, MEF staff members, or the media. This would help to differentiate low-scoring countries such as Senegal where informed public debates take place regarding the allocation and execution of government budgets, despite the lack of official dissemination.

The failure to acknowledge the important role that informal dissemination can play in budget debates may reflect a more general bias in the OBI criteria toward weighing budget transparency more heavily than participation. It is easier to assess objectively whether the budget process is transparent in terms of the official production and dissemination of budget documents than to measure effective participation in the budget process. Nevertheless, transparency is a means to the end of enhancing participation so that citizens and their representatives can hold governments accountable for their management of public money. Consequently, budget documents must be not only officially disseminated but also accessible to the public in order to promote broader participation in the budget process. In this respect, a comparison of the availability of budget documents in Senegal and Mali is instructive.

As summarized in table 9-1, Mali publishes four of the eight documents identified by the IBP as critical, while Senegal publishes only three. Moreover, the documents that Senegal does make accessible to the public contain incomplete and often delayed information, reflected in the letter grades given for each document. The content of Senegal's published audit report, for example, is so low that it received a grade identical to unpublished and even unproduced documents such as the citizen's budget.

The grades reflect the comprehensiveness of the information included in each document, with A corresponding to extensive information and E denoting scant information. However, the OBI survey does not incorporate other important factors that may influence budget openness, specifically differences in how budget documents are published in Senegal and Mali.

In Senegal, all three of its published budget documents are available online; in Mali the four published documents are only available at the source where they are produced. Although not all citizens have equal access to the Internet, Senegal's web-based publication clearly permits easier access and therefore greater budget transparency and participation than Mali's provision of budget documents on demand. Despite this, both countries meet the OBI criteria for accessibility, as any budget document that a government is *willing* to provide to the public is considered "published" regardless of the method of dissemination. However, this may have a significant impact on accessibility, especially for rural

Table 9-1. *Availability and Comprehensiveness of Key Budget Documents in Senegal and Mali*

Documents	Senegal		Mali	
	Status	Grade	Status	Grade
Pre-budget statement	Produced but not published	E	Produced but not published	E
Executive's budget proposal	Produced but not published	E	Published	C
Enacted budget	Published	D	Published	A
Citizen's budget	Not produced	E	Not produced	E
In-year reports	Published	D	Produced but not published	E
Midyear review	Produced but not published	E	Published	C
Year-end report	Produced but not published	E	Published	A
Audit report	Published	E	Produced but not published	E
Overall score		3		35

Sources: IBP (2010); for Senegal, www.internationalbudget.org/what-we-do/open-budget-survey/?fa=countryDetails&id=2425&countryID=SN: for Mali, www.internationalbudget.org/what-we-do/open-budget-survey/?fa=countryDetails&id=3926&countryID=ML; personal communication, January 16, 2011. For methodology, see http://internationalbudget.org/what-we-do/open-budget-survey/research-resources/?fa=methodology.

inhabitants who must identify where to obtain a budget document and then physically seek it from a government official in the capital.

Indeed, the lack of Internet access to Mali's budget and other legal documents hindered our comparative analysis, as we could not evaluate the level of details provided, even though this significantly affected Mali's relatively higher OBI rating. Nor could we ascertain whether statutory provisions exist to assure public access, which is critical to determine if the relative openness of Mali's budget process reflects an institutionalized legal framework or merely the policy of the current administration or a particular official, which could easily erode in the face of a regime change, such as the one Mali has just experienced.

Despite Senegal's more far-reaching method of document dissemination, Mali's public provision of more budget documents and presumably more detailed information, as well as stronger legislative oversight, nevertheless warrant a higher OBI rating, but perhaps not so high. The question is *why* does Mali have a more open budget process than Senegal?

As two former French colonies, undoubtedly the variance in their budget processes is not a question of colonial legacy. General similarities in the deficiencies of the French budget process and that of its former colonies—the lack of public budget hearings, comprehensive midyear reviews, channels of communication between the supreme audit institution and the public, and reports on follow-up steps taken by the executive—suggest a "family resemblance." Neverthe-less, the disparity between Senegal's and Mali's scores is even greater because France's provision of "extensive" information, earning it an OBI score of eighty-seven—identical to that of Great Britain—effectively dispels the use of a French budgetary model as a cause for the lack of budget transparency in its former colonies. Therefore, other socioeconomic and political factors may be influenc-ing their relative budget transparency and participation.

Assessment of Factors Constraining Senegal's Budget Transparency and Participation

To assess the constraints on Senegal's budget openness, we need to consider what reforms would be necessary to enhance its budget transparency and participation. According to the 2010 OBI survey, Senegal should undertake the following:

—Publish the executive's budget proposal, pre-budget statement, midyear review, and year-end report on its website,

—Improve the comprehensiveness of the enacted budget, in-year reports, and audit report,

—Produce and publish a citizen's budget,

—Provide opportunities for the public to attend and testify at legislative hearings on the budget, and

—Increase the powers of the legislature and Audit Court to provide more comprehensive oversight of budget execution.

The easiest reform that the government could undertake, at least in terms of cost and technical capacity, would be to provide public access to the four key budget documents that it already produces but fails to publish. All that is re-quired is to modify the legal codes governing these documents and then to post them on government websites, which already provide an archive of numerous other documents. In fact, given the current power structure, the president could decide to do this without legislative action. Their lack of dissemination, there-fore, seems to be merely a matter of political will. Similarly, improving the com-prehensiveness of the currently published documents appears to be more a ques-tion of political commitment than an issue of technical constraint, as the MEF has well-trained staff.[22]

The inadequacy of the Audit Court's annual report, however, more likely reflects the limited resources at its disposal, although this may be tied more to political than to economic constraints. The lack of a citizen's budget can also be

22. Every stakeholder interviewed concurred that the MEF has sufficient human and material resources.

explained at least in part by a lack of resources, both fiscal and human. Financial obstacles are undoubtedly compounded by government resistance and weak demand for a citizen's budget by either international donors or civil society, indicating a potential need to rally support for budget openness or to strengthen the capacity of CSOs to demand greater budget transparency and participation.

As for implementation of the two remaining OBI recommendations regarding the capacity of the legislature and Audit Court to provide budget oversight and public participation in legislative budget hearings, these are less likely to result from limited resources and more likely to reflect Senegal's political system as well as current donor priorities. Despite recent efforts to enhance Parliament's oversight capacity, donors have not prioritized support for budget monitoring by civil society actors, which the OBI survey also overlooks.

Many of the constraints operating in Senegal are also present in Mali. How, then, has Mali been able to achieve at least a moderate level of budget openness? Through a comparative analysis of the four sets of factors identified as having a negative impact on Senegal's budget openness—economic resources, international pressure, political will, and societal demand—we try to determine which of these can best explain the differential between Senegal and Mali.

Economic Constraints: Lack of State Resources to Promote Budget Openness

One of the simplest and most obvious explanations (and thus justifications) for inadequate production and dissemination of budget documents is a lack of adequate resources within government. This would explain the generally poor performance of countries in the world's poorest region, sub-Saharan Africa, where a disproportionate percentage of countries appear in the bottom of the OBI scale.[23] But while there is some correlation between the 2010 OBI scores of African countries and their levels of per capita income, this does not explain the differential between Senegal and Mali. Given Mali's lower gross national income (GNI) per capita ($1,190), two-thirds the size of Senegal's ($1,810), it is difficult to argue that the government of Mali has more resources at its disposal to produce and publish more comprehensive budget documents.[24]

Limitations in this correlation are also evident in other parts of the continent. In fact, the African country with the highest GNI per capita, Equatorial Guinea, has the lowest OBI score: zero.[25] Meanwhile, Liberia, with a GNI per capita of only $396, has a 2010 OBI score of forty, a thirty-seven-point increase over its 2008 score. The Collaborative Africa Budget Reform Initiative attributes

23. CABRI (2011).

24. Senegal also has a substantially higher ranking on the Human Development Index, at 144 out of 169 countries, while Mali is ranked near the bottom, at 160. See UNDP (2010).

25. A comparison based on the Human Development Index reveals a similar lack of correlation.

Liberia's rapid improvement in budget openness to the political will of its government, although factors such as the prioritizing of governance issues by international donors may also play a role.[26]

In Equatorial Guinea, one of Africa's wealthy oil producers, the complete lack of budget openness may reflect the "resource curse" in which unearned rents render governments opaque and unresponsive to their citizenry.[27] Yet Botswana's reliance on revenues from the diamond industry does not prevent it from reaching a relatively high level of budget openness, earning it a score of fifty on the 2010 OBI survey. In resource-poor countries such as Senegal and Mali, however, the "aid curse" may be more relevant.

International Constraints: Donor Dependence and the "Aid Curse"

Recently, political analysts have begun to consider a potential "aid curse" similar to a "resource curse." The hypothesis is that if states raise "a substantial proportion of their revenues from the international community, [they] are less accountable to their citizens and under less pressure to maintain popular legitimacy."[28] In a process inverse to the state building that occurred in Western Europe,[29] Moss, Pattersson, and van de Walle (2006) assert that aid-dependent states are disconnected from their population:

> Large aid flows can result in a reduction in governmental accountability because governing elites no longer need to ensure the support of their publics and the assent of their legislatures when they do not need to raise revenues from the local economy, as long as they keep the donors happy and willing to provide alternative sources of funding. Although governments typically complain about [donor] conditions, it is still easier to manage donor demands than the slow and politically difficult task of building or improving domestic revenue collection.[30]

This lack of government accountability could also explain a lack of budget transparency and, more significantly, participation, as budget negotiations for aid-dependent governments place international donors rather than citizens and their representatives in the driver's seat.

However, once again there is no consistent correlation between OBI scores and aid dependency when calculated based on official development assistance (ODA) as a percentage of GNI. The poor performance of Equatorial Guinea

26. CABRI (2011).
27. Ross (1999).
28. Moss, Pattersson, and van de Walle (2006, p. 1). See also Brautigam and Knack (2004).
29. Tilly (1990).
30. Moss, Pattersson, and van de Walle (2006, pp. 14–15).

and the moderately better ratings of Liberia once again illustrate the lack of correlation.

In Senegal, ODA as a percentage of GNI has been declining since its height of 17 percent in 1994, down to 8 percent in 2008, making the country only "moderately dependent" on aid. While that may be statistically true, donors, especially the international financial institutions (IFIs), clearly play a major role in the budget process, both in its structure (for example, the introduction of multiyear budgets) and its content, implementation, and evaluation (for example, the size of the budget deficit). During interviews with MEF officials, the high level of consultation with the donor community at each stage of the budget process was very apparent. One of the more ironic statements, made by an MEF official, was in response to an inquiry about who receives the midyear budget report produced by the MEF. This question was posed to ascertain if the legislature as well as the president receives a copy. Instead, the MEF official responded with blatant honesty that it is produced for the IMF! This undoubtedly reflects the fact that many of the documents produced during the budget process are the product of demands from the donor community. In this sense, donor dependency may be interpreted as enhancing budget transparency, but, given the lack of public dissemination, the question is, transparency for whom?

In fact, another MEF official indicated that donor promotion of budget transparency focuses on the donors' own access to budget information, not necessarily that of Parliament or Senegalese citizens. He explained that donors are motivated by their need to monitor "the utilization of their aid in national expenditures." Nevertheless, there is a positive by-product of donor demands for government transparency. When questioned about the impact of aid dependency, a representative of the donor community hastened to note, "Because there is foreign funding, there is a demand [by donors] for more readable [budget information], which can further implicate civil society and permit them to demand an account" of public finances. A CSO leader echoed this view, saying that donors play a critical role in promoting budget transparency "because transparency is a conditionality of the donors." However, participation—the other critical element of budget openness—has not yet received the same level of donor promotion.

Nevertheless, contradictory statements by various stakeholders about the impact of Senegal's aid dependency suggest the Janus-faced nature of ODA. After initially asserting that "the presence of the donors increases budget transparency," an IFI official conceded that aid "dependency plays a moderately negative role," noting the limited involvement and understanding of the budget process among citizens. He admitted that in the budget process "the importance is placed on international donors not on representatives of civil society." One CSO representative noted that aid dependency does not appear to have enhanced "citizen participation in the budget process," but it has forced the government to undertake reforms that have enhanced transparency, such as submitting a Budget Oversight Law in a more timely fashion. The implications of aid dependency, therefore, cut both ways.

In terms of the predictive value of aid dependency for Senegal's poor performance on the OBI, a comparison with Mali is again instructive. Since 2002, ODA to Mali has been on the rise, reaching 11 percent of GNI by 2008 in contrast with 8 percent in Senegal. Thus an aid curse does not seem to be at work. As for the positive role of international aid, there is no apparent difference in international pressure for budget openness or government accountability in the two countries. Indeed, there appears to be little variation in how donors operate in these countries and the types of programs they are currently funding. Thus, for good or for bad, international aid does not appear to explain their relative performance on the OBI surveys.

Political Constraints: Hyper-Presidentialism, Dominant Ruling Party, and Restrained Civic Demand for Budget Reforms

Given that budget transparency and participation are governance issues, it is easy to imagine why Senegal's political climate would generate a low OBI score. Throughout our discussion of Senegal's budget process, we have made frequent references to political constraints, including hyper-presidentialism and a dominant party system, that undermine the separation of powers and social accountability critical to a transparent and participatory budget process. Many of these governance issues predate the Wade administration but have been on the rise, resulting in domestic and international criticism of corruption, harassment of the opposition and independent journalists, and infringements on civil liberties. As a result, Senegal's score on various governance indexes has been sliding, including the Freedom in the World survey of Freedom House and the Democracy Index of the Economist Intelligence Unit.

The question is whether the political constraints witnessed in Senegal can explain its lack of budget openness compared with better-performing countries. To enhance our comparison of Senegal with Mali, we have added Burkina Faso, another Francophone West African country that only publishes "scant" budget information according to the 2010 OBI survey, although it achieved a score of eleven. The varying levels of political liberalization among these neighboring countries appear aptly differentiated on the Democracy Index, but less so on the Freedom in the World survey (table 9-2).

As Senegal's score on these political indexes slipped, Mali's score improved on the Democracy Index and thus raised its categorization; Senegal was categorized as a "hybrid democracy" in both 2008 and 2010, while Mali improved from the

Table 9-2. *Budget Transparency and Governance Ratings in Burkina Faso, Mali, and Senegal, 2008 and 2010*

Country and indicator	OBI survey		Democracy Index		Freedom in the World[a]	
	2008	2010	2008	2010	2008	2010
Senegal						
Transparency	3	3	5.37 (rank 93)	5.27 (rank 95)	2, 3	3, 3
Governance	Scant	Scant	Hybrid democracy	Hybrid democracy	Partly free	Partly free
Burkina Faso						
Transparency	…	11	3.60 (rank 122)	3.59 (rank 120)	5, 3	5, 3
Governance	…	Scant	Authoritarian	Authoritarian	Partly free	Partly free
Mali						
Transparency	…	35	5.87 (rank 83)	6.01 (79 rank)	2, 3	2, 3
Governance	…	Minimal	Hybrid democracy	Flawed democracy	Free	Free

Sources: IBP (2008, 2010), EIU (2008, 2010), and Freedom House (2008, 2010).

a. Scores on the Freedom in the World survey refer to the level of political rights and civil liberties based on a seven-point scale, with 1 reflecting full freedom and 7 reflecting an absence of freedom.

… = Not applicable.

status of a hybrid democracy in 2008 to that of a "flawed democracy" in 2010, joining the ranks of a handful of other African countries, including South Africa. The reasons noted for this improvement include political developments that are critical to budget reform, particularly a politically restrained president who embarked on constitutional reforms to strengthen civil liberties.

While the differential in their scores on the Freedom in the World survey is nominal, the Freedom House summaries of political and civil rights in Mali and Senegal reflect critical political factors that may have influenced their relative budget transparency and participation. First and foremost, both Mali and Senegal have a presidential system. However, in Mali there were no reports of presidential dominance or manipulation of political institutions and legal codes, and President Amadou Toure was committed to stepping down in 2012 prior to his ouster by a military coup. In Senegal, President Wade introduced constitutional amendments to ensure his reelection to a third term in 2012, despite a two-term limit.

In terms of oversight by the judiciary and legislature, the Malian judiciary was reportedly weak and lacked sufficient autonomy to provide an effective check on executive power; however, President Toure did not enjoy a legislative majority, let alone the dominance that President Wade's ruling party had over both chambers of Parliament. In addition, there were no reports of harassment or attacks on Malian opposition leaders or journalists, and the Malian government largely permitted political protests. In Senegal, political demonstrations were regularly banned, protestors were detained, and journalists like Abdou Latif Coulibaly who published articles critical of the government were harassed and criminally prosecuted for defamation.[31] In this sense, Senegal's scores on the Freedom in the World survey, if not on the Democracy Index, may be inflated and, if lowered, might more aptly reflect the general correlation with OBI scores, thereby reinforcing the predictive value of relative levels of political constraints on an open budget process.

Given Senegal's history of hyper-presidentialism, there is little likelihood that the government will enhance its budget transparency or participation in the absence of a commitment from the new president, Macky Sall. With an impotent legislature and an anemic opposition, no forces within Senegal's political institutions have the power or the ability to demand greater budget openness. The prospects of Senegal's upcoming legislative elections changing this pattern seem slim at best. Meanwhile, international pressure from the donor commu-

31. Committee to Protect Journalists (2011). Criminalization of defamation is common in Africa and still on the books in Mali, although no journalist has been prosecuted since 2007. Freedom House (2009).

nity has been focused on enhancing the legislative capacity to participate in the budget process, without consideration of the political constraints that will continue to limit their autonomy vis-à-vis the executive.[32]

This leaves the demand for a more open budget process to the Senegalese media and civil society, both of which are remarkably vibrant and politically engaged. Despite growing infringements on freedom of the press, the Senegalese media disseminate essential budget information and provide a critical forum for budget debates in the absence of public hearings. However, journalists have contented themselves with unofficial and thus incomplete budget information, while concentrating on passage of a Freedom of Information Act, which Parliament has agreed to adopt after years of lobbying and international pressure from Article XIX in particular.[33] Whether such an act would ensure public dissemination of budget documents remains to be seen, but it will inevitably require demand and most likely sustained insistence from journalists or civil society leaders who, to date, have not placed a great deal of emphasis on the need for official budget documents.

At least two Senegalese CSOs have been implicated in budget issues, the Transparency International affiliate Forum Civil and the NGO federation CONGAD. While generally advocating for greater government transparency, they have not been vocal in demanding public dissemination of budget documents and are reticent to advocate for a citizen's budget given the current political climate. This may reflect their satisfaction or at least acceptance of the current informal channels of dissemination or their prioritization of other governance issues such as corruption. In either case, the priorities set out by IBP to enhance budget openness have not received a great deal of traction among these or other Senegalese CSOs.

In contrast, the Malian NGO Coalition des Alternatives Africaines Dette et Développement (CAD-Mali) has been working on national budget issues since 2004, promoting greater equity in national budget allocations for heath programs. In Burkina Faso, the Center for Democratic Governance (CDG), established in 2000, has been educating other CSOs and citizens about participation in budget debates. Both CAD-Mali and CDG have clearly enhanced public participation in the national budget processes of their respective countries, while CDG's budget advocacy undoubtedly contributed to the recent decision by the Burkinabe government to publish six of the eight key budget documents identified by the IBP.

---

32. It is too early to know how the recently elected President Macky Sall will influence this trend, although because he was prime minister under Wade, dramatic improvement is unlikely.

33. The Wade administration has made similar promises over the years, but this is the first sign that a law might be adopted. International Freedom of Expression Exchange Clearinghouse (2011).

Consequently, despite Senegal's moderately strong performance on governance indexes, political constraints have played a critical role in its poor performance on the OBI survey. A more vibrant, albeit flawed, democracy in Mali and effective CSO advocacy and collaboration with international actors such as the IBP in Burkina Faso have permitted a higher level of budget openness. In Senegal stakeholders will need to forge their own method of advancing budget transparency and participation.

Conclusions

Despite the concentration of Francophone African countries at the bottom of the OBI scale and certain "family resemblances" among the deficiencies identified by the IBP in the French budget process and those of its former colonies, neither a colonial legacy nor contemporary modeling of the French system can explain the poor performance of Senegal on the OBI survey, especially given Mali's performance and France's provision of "extensive" budget information to the public.

The Malian counterexample also challenges an economic explanation for Senegal's lack of budget transparency. The lack of correlation between OBI scores and GNI per capita demonstrates that the difference between Mali and Senegal must be due to other factors that permit countries such as Mali to overcome economic constraints.

Although international donors have consistently supported greater budget transparency, if only to ensure their own access to budget information, an "aid curse" may be undercutting government accountability to its own citizenry and their legislative representatives. This is clearly an issue in Senegal, where various budget documents are produced largely to placate donors, particularly the international financial institutions, which are consulted more frequently than legislators during the budget process. Nevertheless, donors have been instrumental in promoting budget reforms, particularly in countries that otherwise lack the political will to open their budget process. In this sense, international aid has had a mixed impact on budget transparency and participation.

The remaining category of possible explanatory variables consists of political constraints associated with the absence or weakness of democratic institutions. Among these political constraints are several critical issues that are undoubtedly undermining an open budget process in both Senegal and Burkina Faso, especially when contrasted with Mali's political regime prior to the recent coup: (a) the relative weakness of the legislature, which lacks autonomy to provide budget oversight, and hyper-presidential systems; (b) the dominance of ruling parties controlled by the president; and (c) an anemic political opposition that lacks the power to demand a more open budget process. Where Senegal and Burkina Faso may differ is in the level of commitment by their CSOs to demand and participate in an open budget process. The critical role of CDG in the promotion of budget transparency and participation has undoubtedly contributed to Burkina Faso's higher OBI score as well as its recent decision to publish a majority of key budget documents. To date, Senegalese CSOs engaged in budget debates have not prioritized the official publication of budget documents or the production of a citizen's budget.

Mobilizing CSO support for the political reforms identified by the IBP as critical to an open budget process may require greater acknowledgment among Senegalese stakeholders of the insufficiencies of its informal dissemination of budget information. The IBP needs to reconsider both its measurement of the public availability of budget documents, which by using a more differentiated scale captures the role of informal dissemination in the absence of official publication, and its criteria for publishing budget documents. Given that stakeholders in Senegal are either unable or uninterested in demanding greater budget transparency and participation, the next step for Sall's new government, if it is committed to opening up the budget process, will be to provide access to documents currently produced but not published.

References

Berg, Elliot. 1990. "Ajustement ajourné: Réforme de la politique économique du Sénégal dans les années 80." Dakar: USAID.

Brautigam, Deborah, and Stephen Knack. 2004. "Foreign Aid, Institutions, and Governance in Sub-Saharan Africa." *Economic Development and Cultural Change* 52 (January): 255–85.

CABRI (Collaborative Africa Budget Reform Initiative). 2011. "Open Budget Survey 2010: How Did Africa Perform?" Pretoria, September 12 (www.cabri-sbo.org/en/e-networking/blog/11-general/163-open-budget-survey-2010-how-did-africa-perform).

Committee to Protect Journalists. 2011. "Senegalese Editor Coulibaly Convicted of Defamation." New York, April 14.

Dabo, Bacary. 2010. "Les deputes denouncent le silence 'bavard' de Guirassy." *Sud Quotidien,* July 1.

Dione, Babacar. 2008. "Un résolution écourté le mandate du président." *Le Soleil,* November 10.

EIU (Economist Intelligence Unit). 2008. "Democracy Index." London.

———. 2010. "Democracy Index." London.

Freedom House. 2008. "Freedom in the World." Washington.

———. 2009. "Freedom of the Press: Mali." Washington.

———. 2010. "Freedom in the World." Washington.

IBP (International Budget Partnership). 2007. "Open Budgets Transform Lives: OBI Survey 2006." Washington (http://internationalbudget.org/files/FinalFullReportEnglish_lores.pdf).

————. 2008. "Open Budget Questionnaire: Senegal." Washington (www.international budget.org/files/IBPQuestionnaire2008Senegal1.pdf).

————. 2010. "Open Budget Questionnaire: Senegal." Washington.

IMF (International Monetary Fund). 2010. "IMF Executive Board Completes Final Review under PSI with Senegal and Approves New Three-Year PSI." Washington, December 3 (www.imf.org/external/np/sec/pr/2010/pr10469.htm).

International Freedom of Expression Exchange Clearinghouse. 2011. "Senegal: Parliament Commits to Passing Information Law." Toronto, June 23.

Moss, Todd, Gunilla Pattersson, and Nicolas van de Walle. 2006. "An Aid-Institutions Paradox? A Review Essay on Aid Dependency and State Building in Sub-Saharan Africa." Working Paper 74. Washington: Center for Global Development, January (www.cgdev.org/content/publications/detail/5646).

Ndaw, Malick. 2010. "Transparence budgetaire: Ces lois en souffrance." *Sud Quotidien*, December 18.

Ndiaye, Biram. 2010. "Débats d'orientation budgétaire." Sununews.com, June 30.

Ndiaye, Mamadou Aissa. 2010. "Les lois organiques senegalais relatives au lois de finances: Reflexion su l'evolution des pouvoirs de controle des deputes en matiere budgetaire."

OBI. 2011. "Country Information: Senegal." Washington (http://internationalbudget.org/files/OBI2010-Senegal.pdf).

OECD (Organization for Economic Cooperation and Development). 2002. "OECD Best Practices for Budget Transparency." *OECD Journal on Budgeting* 1, no. 3: 7–14.

Republic of Senegal. 1963. "Rapport général sur les perspectives de développement du Sénégal, première partie." Dakar, January.

Ross, Michael. 1999. "The Political Economy of the Resource Curse." *World Politics* 51 (January): 297–322.

Tanaka, Susan. 2007. "Engaging the Public in National Budgeting: A Non-Governmental Perspective." *OECD Journal on Budgeting* 7, no. 2: 139–77.

Tilly, Charles. 1990. *Coercion, Capital, and European States: AD 990–1990.* New York: Wiley-Blackwell.

UNDP (United Nations Development Programme). 2010. *Human Development Report 2010.* New York (http://hdr.undp.org/en/).

Contributors

JOHN M. ACKERMAN
Professor, Institute for Legal Research, National Autonomous University of Mexico, and editor-in-chief, *Mexican Law Review*

JORGE ANTONIO ALVES
Assistant Professor of Political Science, Queens College, City University of New York

LINDA BECK
Associate Professor of Political Science, University of Maine–Farmington, and research affiliate of the Institute of African Studies at Columbia University

ANNABELLA ESPAÑA-NAJÉRA
Assistant Professor at California State University–Fresno

ALIOU FAYE
Ministry of the Economy and Finance, Senegal

STEVEN FRIEDMAN
Director, Centre for the Study of Democracy, Rhodes University/University of Johannesburg

ARCHON FUNG
Ford Foundation Professor of Democracy and Citizenship, Kennedy School, Harvard University

PATRICK HELLER
Professor of Sociology and International Studies, Brown University

BARAK D. HOFFMAN
Executive Director, Center for Democracy and Civil Society, Georgetown University

SANJEEV KHAGRAM
John Parke Young Professor of Global Political Economy, Diplomacy and World Affairs, Occidental College, and Young Global Leader, World Economic Forum

WONHEE LEE
Professor, Department of Public Administration, Hankyung National University

HUONG NGUYEN
Doctoral candidate, History, University of Washington

PAOLO DE RENZIO
Senior Research Fellow, International Budget Partnership, and Research Associate, Overseas Development Institute, and Research Associate, Oxford University

AARON SCHNEIDER
Leo Block Associate Professor,
  Korbel School of International Studies,
University of Denver

E. H. SEYDOU NOUROU TOURE
Institut Fondamental de l'Afrique Noire

JONATHAN WARREN
Associate Professor, International Studies,
  University of Washington

JONG-SUNG YOU
Assistant Professor, Graduate School of
  International Relations and Pacific
  Studies, University of California,
  San Diego

Index